Practical C Programming

Practical C Programming

Steve Oualline

O'Reilly & Associates, Inc.
103 Morris Street, Suite A
Sebastopol, CA 95472

Practical C Programming
by Steve Oualline
Illustrations by Teresa Ellis

Printed in the United States of America.

Editor: Dale Dougherty

Printing History:

July 1991:	First Edition.
August 1992:	Minor corrections.
January 1993:	Second Edition. Bugs fixed; programs all now conform to ANSI C.
June 1993:	Minor corrections.

This book is printed on acid-free paper with 50% recycled content, 10-15% post-consumer waste. O'Reilly & Associates is committed to using paper with the highest recycled content available consistent with high quality.

ISBN: 1-56592-035-X [1/94]

Table of Contents

Page

Figures

Tables

Preface

This book is devoted to practical C programming. It teaches you not only the mechanics of the language, but also style and debugging. The entire life cycle of a program is discussed including conception, design, writing, debugging, release, documenting, maintenance, and revision.

Style is emphasized. Creating a good program requires more than just typing in code. It is an art where writing and programming skills blend themselves together to form a masterpiece. A well-written program not only functions correctly, but is simple and easy to understand. Comments allow the programmer to include descriptive text inside the program. Clearly written, a commented program is highly prized.

A program should be as simple as possible. A programmer should avoid clever tricks. This book stresses simple, practical rules. For example, there are 15 operator precedence rules in C. These can be simplified down to two rules:

1. Multiply and divide come before add and subtract.

2. Put parentheses around everything else.

Consider two programs: one was written by a clever programmer using all the tricks. It contains no comments, but it works. The other is well-commented and nicely structured, but it doesn't work. Which is more useful? In the long run, the broken one. It can be fixed. Although the clever one works now, sooner or later all programs have to be modified. The worst thing you will ever have to do is modify a cleverly written program.

Scope of This Handbook

This handbook is written for people with no previous programming experience or programmers who already know C and want to improve their style and reliability. You should have access to a computer and know how to use the basic functions such as a text editor and the filesystem.

Two dialects of C are presented: UNIX C (the portable C compiler) and ANSI standard C. There are only minor differences between the two and they are clearly indicated.

Specific instructions are given for producing and running programs using the UNIX operating system and the Turbo C package under MS-DOS. The book also gives examples of using the programming utility `make` for automated program production.

Chapter 1, *The Basics of Program Writing*, explains the basic programming process and gives you enough information to write a very simple program.

Chapter 2, *Style*, discusses programming style. How to comment a program is covered, as well as writing clear and simple code.

Chapter 3, *Basic Declarations and Expressions*, introduces you to simple C statements. Basic variables and the assignment statement are covered in detail along with the arithmetic operators: `+`, `-`, `*`, `/`, and `%`.

Chapter 4, *Arrays, Qualifiers, and Reading Numbers*, covers arrays and more complex variables. The shorthand operators `++`, `--`, `*=`, `=`, `+=`, `-=`, and `%=` are also described.

Chapter 5, *Decision and Control Statements*, explains simple decision statements including **if**, **else**, and **for**. The problem of == versus = is discussed.

Chapter 6, *The Programming Process*, takes you through all the necessary steps to create a simple program from specification through release. Structured programming, fast prototyping, and debugging are also discussed.

Chapter 7, *More Control Statements*, describes additional control statements. Included are **while, break**, and **continue**. The **switch** statement is discussed in detail.

Chapter 8, *Variable Scope and Functions*, introduces local variables, functions, and parameters.

Chapter 9, *The C Preprocessor*, describes the C preprocessor which gives the programmer tremendous flexibility in writing code. It also provides the programmer with a tremendous number of ways to mess up. Simple rules that help keep the preprocessor from becoming a problem are described.

Chapter 10, *Bit Operations*, discusses the logical C operators that work on bits.

Chapter 11, *Advanced Types*, explains structures and other advanced types. The **sizeof** operator and the **enum** type are included.

Chapter 12, *Simple Pointers*, introduces C pointer variables and shows some of their uses.

Chapter 13, *File Input/Output*, describes both buffered and unbuffered input/output. ASCII versus binary files are discussed, and you are shown how to construct a simple file.

Chapter 14, *Debugging and Optimization*, describes how to debug a program, as well as how to use an interactive debugger. You are shown not only how to debug a program, but also how to write a program so that it is easy to debug. This chapter also describes many optimization techniques to make your program run faster and more efficiently.

Chapter 15, *Floating Point*, uses a simple decimal floating-point format to introduce you to the problems inherent in floating point such as roundoff error, precision loss, overflow, and underflow.

Chapter 16, *Advanced Pointers*, describes advanced uses of pointers to construct dynamic structures such as linked lists and trees.

Chapter 17, *Modular Programming*, shows how to split a program into several files and use modular programming techniques. The `make` utility is explained in more detail.

Chapter 18, *Portability Problems*, describes the problems that can occur when *porting* a program (moving it from one machine to another).

Chapter 19, *C's Dustier Corners*, describes the **do/while** statement, the comma operator, and the **? :** operators.

Chapter 20, *Putting It All Together*, details the steps necessary to take a complex program from conception to completion. Information hiding and modular programming techniques are emphasized.

Chapter 21, *Programming Adages*, lists some programming adages that will help you construct good C programs.

Appendix A, *ASCII Chart*.

Appendix B, *Numeric Limits*.

Appendix C, *Operator Precedence Rules*.

Appendix D, *Program to Compute sine Using a Power Series*.

Appendix E, *Automatic Type Conversion Used When Passing Parameters*.

The *Glossary* defines many of the technical terms used throughout the book.

Computer languages are best learned by writing and debugging programs. Sweating over a broken program at 2:00 in the morning only to find you typed "=" where you should have typed "==" is a very effective teaching tool. There are many programming examples used throughout this book. Some examples don't work as expected and are posed as questions for the reader to solve. You are encouraged to enter them into your computer, run the program, and debug them. This introduces you to common errors using short programs so that you will know how to spot and correct them in larger programs of your own. You will find the answer to these questions at the end of the chapter. Also, at the end of many chapters, you will find a section called "Programming Problems." This section contains exercises that might be used in a programming class to test your knowledge of C programming.

Conventions Used in This Handbook

The following conventions are used in this book:

Italic — is used for directories and filenames and to emphasize new terms and concepts when they are introduced. Italic is also used to highlight comments in examples.

Bold — is used for C keywords.

`Constant Width` — is used in text for programs and the elements of a program and in examples to show the contents of files or the output from commands. A reference in text to a word or item used in an example or code fragment is also shown in constant width font.

`Constant Bold` is used in examples to show commands or other text that should be typed literally by the user. (For example, **`rm foo`** means to type "rm foo" exactly as it appears in the text or example.)

`Constant Italic` is used in examples to show variables for which a context-specific substitution should be made. (The variable *`filename`*, for example, would be replaced by some actual filename.)

Quotes are used to identify system messages or code fragments in explanatory text.

`%` is the UNIX C shell prompt.

$ is the UNIX Bourne shell or Korn shell prompt.

is the UNIX superuser prompt (either Bourne or C shell). We usually use this for examples that should be executed only by root.

[ ] surround optional values in a description of program syntax. (The brackets themselves should never be typed.)

. . . stands for text (usually computer output) that's been omitted for clarity or to save space.

The notation CTRL-X or ^X indicates use of *control* characters. It means hold down the "control" key while typing the character "x". We denote other keys similarly (e.g., RETURN indicates a carriage return).

All examples of command lines are followed by a RETURN unless otherwise indicated.

Acknowledgments

I wish to thank my father for his help in editing and Arthur Marquez for his aid in formatting this book.

I am grateful to all the gang at the Writers' Haven and Bookstore, Pearl, Alex, and Clyde, for their continued support. Thanks to Peg Kovar for help in editing. Special thanks to Dale Dougherty for ripping apart my book and forcing me to put it together right. My thanks also go to the production group of O'Reilly and Associates—especially Rosanne Wagger and Mike Sierra—for putting the finishing touches on this book. Finally, Jean Graham deserves a special credit for putting up with my writing all these years.

1

The Basics of Program Writing

A Simple Example
Getting Help

Profanity is the one language that all programmers understand.
—Anon.

A sufficiently high level of technology is indistinguishable from magic.
—Arthur C. Clarke

Computers run on magic. It's true—ask typical users about what goes on in their systems and you'll find out they don't know. To a user, it's a magic word processor, or a magic accounting machine that spews forth correct answers at the touch of a button.

To be a programmer, you must become a magician. It is the magic application, such as a word processing program, that transforms a dull, difficult-to-use, general-purpose computer into a machine that turns raw text into useful printouts.

To create a program, you must take the raw ingredients—like eye of newt, toe of frog, and a few bat wings—mix them together in a big pot and let it simmer for half an hour. Actually, you have to take data structures and instructions, mix them together, and produce a program.

A magician needs his magic wand and other equipment to cast his spells. Programmers need their own special set of tools. These include:

- Text editor
- Compiler
- Library
- Linker
- `make` utility
- Debugger

Let's see how these tools are used to create a program.

Text Editor

A programmer uses a text editor to write code. You should already be familiar with *vi*, *emacs*, or another editor on your system.

All C programs start as a text file. This file serves two functions: the code tells the machine what to do, and the comments tell the programmer about the code. A program should be written as a technical paper—clear, concise, and easy to understand. The last point must be emphasized. Computers are extremely confusing and anything that *can* be done to make them easier to understand *should* be done. This book tries to teach not only programming mechanics, but style as well. Chapter 2, *Style*, is devoted entirely to using good programming style to create high-quality code.

The program file created by the text editor is called the *source* or *source code*. The names of C source files must end with the extension *.c*.

Program 1-1 shows a very simple program in source form.

Program 1-1.

```
#include <stdio.h>
main()
{
    (void) printf("Hello World\n");
    return (0);
}
```

Compiler

The compiler takes a source file (which contains human-readable instructions) and translates it into an *object file* (which contains machine-readable instructions). This is the equivalent of the magician translating his instructions from English into the ancient language used by the fairy folk.

The source code is *machine independent*. You can take your source code from one machine to another without changes. Almost. (See Chapter 18, *Portability Problems*.)

Object files are *machine dependent*. They are custom-made for each machine and are nonportable.

The compiler's job is to translate C code (high-level code) into instructions that can be executed by the CPU (low-level code).

On UNIX, object filenames end with the extension *.o*, while on MS-DOS, they end with *.OBJ*.

The Library

A good magician keeps around a spell book containing all the standard spells. (After all, you don't want to have to invent a new spell every time you need to turn someone into a frog.) Similarly the programmer uses a set of *standard functions* called a *library*. It contains commonly used functions such as **printf**, **exit**, and **fgets**. (A short description of commonly used standard functions can be found in the glossary. For a complete description of all standard functions, see your C reference manual.)

The Linker

The magician has a giant cauldron in which to mix his ingredients. The programmer uses the *linker* to do his mixing. He takes the object file and combines it with the standard functions from the library to produce the final result, an executable program.

The linker does this by scanning the standard library, selecting the needed functions, and linking them into the object file. The final output is a program file that can be run by the user. On UNIX these files have no extension; on DOS they end with *.EXE*.

The utilities used to create a program can be seen in Figure 1-1.

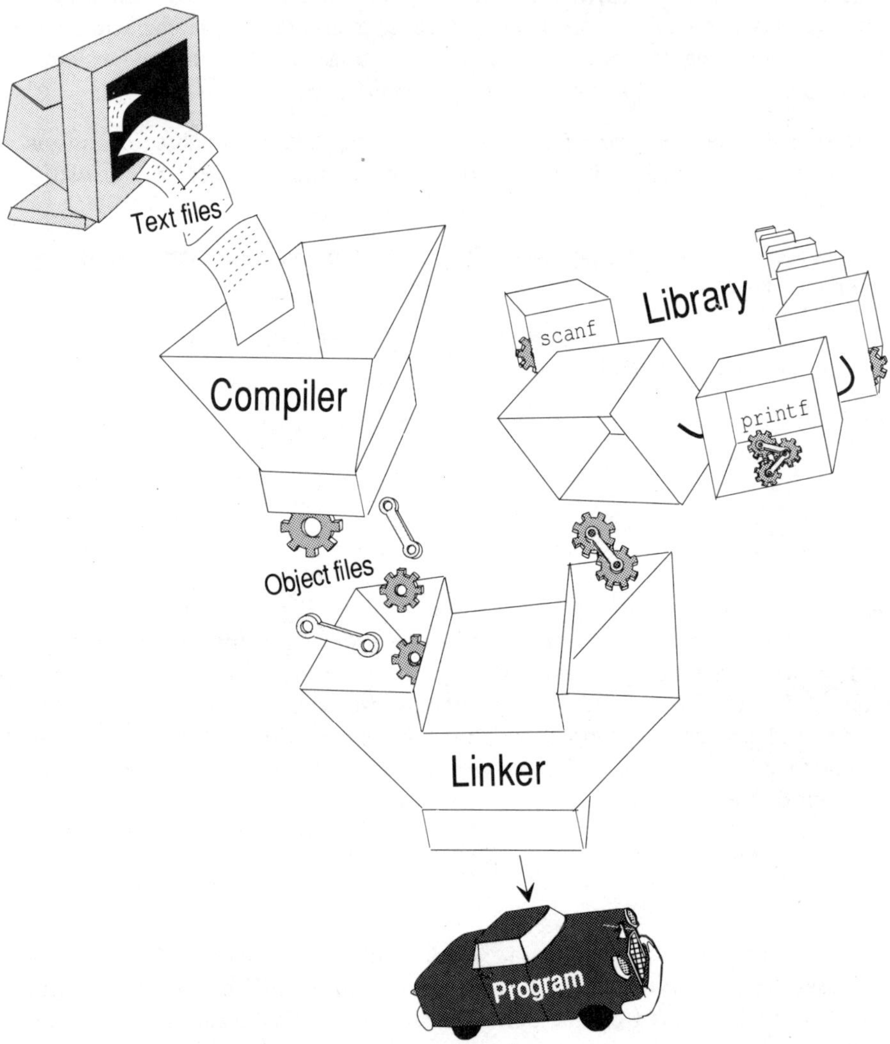

Figure 1-1. How a Program is Created

make Utility

In most cases the magician doesn't perform all the hard work—his apprentice does. The magician prepares a list of instructions and gives them to his assistant.

The **make** utility is designed to be the programmer's assistant; it helps automate the process of compiling and linking a program. The file *Makefile* contains information on how the program is constructed. **make** uses this to build a program. It checks the creation dates of the source and object files and rebuilds any objects which are out of date with their source. This utility will be discussed later in Chapter 6, *The Programming Process*, and Chapter 17, *Modular Programming*.

Debugger

Any nontrivial program will contain errors. Some of these errors will be caught at compile time; however, many will make it into the program.

A programmer can easily spend more than half of the time finding these errors, or *bugs*. The *debugger* can help in locating problems. It allows the programmer to open up a program while it is running.

A good debugger will have the following features:

- **Breakpoints**. They allow the programmer to stop the program on any line.
- **Single step**. The program can be executed a line at a time.
- **Display**. The programmer can print the value of variables and expressions at any time.
- **Browser**. This allows the programmer to display relevant portions of the source file.

Debugging and debuggers are discussed in Chapter 14, *Debugging and Optimization*.

Wrappers and Integrated Development Environments

The lines between the various utilities are being blurred by *wrapper* programs. A wrapper is a high-level executive that decides which utilities need to be run. For example, on UNIX the wrapper program **cc** will run the C compiler */lib/ccom* and the linker **ld**.

Turbo C provides the user with even more, the *Integrated Development Environment*. This combines an editor, compiler, linker, and debugger into a single-development environment. One of the advantages of this system is that all the pieces are designed to work together. For example, if the compiler detects an error, you are switched to the editor with the file positioned at the problem line.

Some UNIX systems have similar environments. For example, Saber-C, which runs on Sun Microsystems and Hewlett-Packard machines, contains its own compiler and debugger. It interfaces with the system's editor (`vi`, `emacs`, or other editors) and makes it possible to develop and test programs more rapidly.

A Simple Example

Suppose you are asked to write a program to print the message "Hello World". You would use a text editor to create a source file called *hello.c*. Program 1-2 shows the source.

Program 1-2.

```
#include <stdio.h>
main()
{
    (void) printf("Hello World\n");
    return (0);
}
```

This is one of the simplest programs and traditionally begins every C book. When compiled and executed, it prints `Hello World` on your terminal screen.

Functions are the basic building blocks of C. (This program consists of a single function called `main`.) `main` calls another function: `printf`. The `printf` function is not defined in our program; it is a standard function defined in the standard C library. The line `#include <stdio.h>` is required to use this routine. (See Chapter 13, *File Input/Output*.) In Chapter 3, *Basic Declarations and Expressions*, we'll go through this program in more detail to understand exactly how it works.

Once the program has been written, it must be translated into something the computer can understand. This job falls to the C compiler.

On UNIX, we run the compiler with the **cc** command as follows:

```
% cc -g -ohello hello.c
```

The **–g** option enables debugging. The **–ohello** option tells the compiler that the program is to be called **hello** and **hello.c** is the name of the source file. See your compiler manual for details on all the possible options.

On MS-DOS, using Turbo C, the command would be:

```
C:> tcc -w -A -ehello hello.c
```

The **–w** switch turns on all warnings. **–A** enables ANSI C mode. **–ehello** tells Turbo C to create a program named **HELLO** and **hello.c** is the name of the source file. See your Turbo C reference manual for a complete list of options.

The compiler first will create an *object file*. Our program uses **printf**, which must be brought in from the standard C library and linked with our object file. In most cases we don't have to do separate compile and link steps; the C compiler will automatically run the linker for us, leaving an executable program named *hello* on UNIX and *HELLO.EXE* on MS-DOS.

To run this program (on UNIX or DOS) type:

```
% hello
```

and the message:

```
Hello World
```

will appear on the screen.

Getting Help

Both UNIX and Turbo C provide a way of getting some help from the computer. Most UNIX systems have "man pages" online. These can be accessed with the **man** command. To get information about a particular subject, use the command:

```
% man subject
```

For example, to find out about the **printf** standard function, you would type:

```
% man printf
```

The command also has a keyword search mode:

```
% man keyword
```

To determine the name of every man page with the word "print" in their title, use the command:

```
% man -k print
```

Turbo C provides a different type of online help. The command **THELP** starts a terminate-and-stay resident program (a program that is always there lurking in the background). When you press "5" on the keypad, it will appear and present you with a set of menus designed to lead you to the information you want.

Exercise 1: On your computer, type in the *hello* program and execute it.

Exercise 2: Take several programming examples from any source, enter them into the computer, and run them.

2

Style

Summary

There is no programming language, no matter how structured, that will prevent programmers from writing bad programs.

—L. Flon

It is the nobility of their style which will make our writers of 1840 unreadable forty years from now.

—Stendhal

This chapter discusses how to use good programming style to create a simple, easy-to-read program. It may seem backward to discuss style before we know how to program, but style is the most important part of programming. Style is what separates the gems from the junk. It is what separates the programming artist from the butcher. You must learn good programming style first, before typing in your first line of code, so that everything you write will be of the highest quality.

Contrary to popular belief, programmers do not spend most of their time writing programs. Far more time is spent maintaining, upgrading, and debugging existing code than is ever spent on creating new works. According to Datamation, the amount of time spent on maintenance is sky-rocketing. From 1980 to 1990 the average number of lines in a typical application has gone from 23,000 to 1,200,000. The average system age has gone from 4.75 to 9.4 years.

What's worse, 74% of the managers surveyed at the 1990 Annual Meeting and Conference of the Software Maintenance Association reported that they "have systems in their department that have to be maintained by specific individuals because no one else understands them."

Most software is built on existing software. I recently completed coding for 12 new programs. Only one of these was created from scratch, the other 11 are adaptations of existing programs.

Programmers believe that the purpose of a program is only to present the computer with a compact set of instructions. This is not true. Programs written only for the machine have two problems:

- They are difficult to correct because sometimes even the author does not understand them.
- Modifications and upgrades are difficult to make because the maintenance programmer must spend a considerable amount of time figuring out what the program does from its code.

Ideally, a program serves two purposes: first, it presents the computer with a set of instructions, and second, it provides the programmer with a clear, easy-to-read description of what the program does.

Program 1-1 contains a glaring error. It is an error that many programmers still make, and one that causes more trouble than any other problem. *The program contains no comments.*

A working, but uncommented program is a time bomb waiting to explode. Sooner or later someone will have to modify or upgrade it, and the lack of comments will make the job ten times more difficult. A well-commented, simple program is a work of art. Learning how to comment is as important as learning how to code properly.

Comments in C start with a slash asterisk (`/*`) and end with an asterisk slash (`*/`). Program 2-1 is an improved version of Program 1-1.

Program 2-1.

```
/********************************************************
 * hello -- program to print out "Hello World".         *
 *      Not an especially earth-shattering program.     *
 *                                                      *
 * Author:  Steve Oualline                              *
 *                                                      *
 * Purpose:  Demonstration of a simple program          *
 *                                                      *
 * Usage:                                               *
 *      Run the program and the message appears        *
 ********************************************************/
#include <stdio.h>
main()
{
    /* Tell the world hello */
    (void) printf("Hello World\n");
    return (0);
}
```

In this example, we put the beginning comments in a box of asterisks (*) called a *comment box*. This is done to emphasize the more important comments, much like we use bold characters for the headings in this book. Less important comments are not boxed. For example:

```
/* Tell the world hello */
(void)printf("Hello World\n");
```

In order to write a program, you must have a clear idea of what you are going to do. One of the best ways to organize your thoughts is to write them down in a language that is clear and easy to understand. Once the process has been clearly stated, it can be translated into a computer program.

Understanding what you are doing is the most important part of programming. I once wrote two pages of comments describing a complex graphics algorithm. The comments were revised twice before I even started coding. The actual instructions took only half a page. Because I had organized my thoughts well (and was lucky), the program worked the first time.

Your program should read like an essay. It should be as clear and easy to understand as possible. Good programming style comes from experience and practice. The style described in the following pages is the result of many years of programming experience. It can be used as a starting point for developing your own style. These are not rules, only suggestions. The only rule is: make your program as *clear*, *concise*, and *simple* as possible.

Poor Man's Typesetting

In typesetting, you can use letter size, **bold**, and *italic* to make different parts of your text stand out. In programming, you are limited to a single, mono-spaced font, however, people have come up with ingenious ways to get around the limitations of the typeface.

Some of the various commenting tricks are:

```
/************************************************************
 ************************************************************
 ******** WARNING:  This is an example of a       *******
 ********   warning message that grabs the        *******
 ********   attention of the programmer.          *******
 ************************************************************
 ************************************************************/


/*------------> Another, less important warning<---------*/


/*>>>>>>>>>>>>>  Major section header  <<<<<<<<<<<<<<<<< */


/************************************************************
 * We use boxed comments in this book to denote the        *
 * beginning of a section or program                       *
 ************************************************************/


/*----------------------------------------------------------*\
 * This is another way of drawing boxes                     *
\*----------------------------------------------------------*/


/*
 * This is the beginning of a section
 * ^^^^ ^^ ^^^ ^^^^^^^^^ ^^ ^ ^^^^^^^
 *
 * In the paragraph that follows we explain what
 * the section does and how it works.
 */


/*
 * A medium-level comment explaining the next
 * dozen or so lines of code.  Even though we don't have
 * the bold typeface we can **emphasize** words.
 */


/* A simple comment explaining the next line */
```

At the beginning of the program is a comment block that contains information about the program. Boxing the comments makes them stand out. The list that follows contains some of the sections that should be included at the beginning of your program. Not all programs will need all sections, so use only those that apply:

- **Heading**. The first comment should contain the name of the program. Also include a short description of what it does. You may have the most amazing program, one that slices, dices, and solves all the world's problems, but it is useless if no one knows what it is.
- **Author**. You've gone to a lot of trouble to create this program. Take credit for it. Also, anyone who has to modify the program can come to you for information and help.
- **Purpose**. Why did you write this program? What does it do?
- **Usage**. In this section give a short explanation of how to run the program. In an ideal world, every program comes with a set of documents describing how to use it. The world is not ideal. Oualline's law of documentation states: 90% of the time the documentation is lost. Out of the remaining 10%, 9% of the time the revision of the documentation is different from the revision of the program and therefore completely useless. The 1% of the time you actually have documentation and the correct revision of the documentation, it will be written in Japanese.

  To avoid Oualline's law of documentation, put the documentation in the program.
- **References**. Creative copying is a legitimate form of programming (if you don't break the copyright laws in the process). In the real world, it doesn't matter how you get a working program, as long as you get it, but give credit where credit is due. In this section you should reference the original author of any work you copied.
- **File formats**. List the files that your program reads or writes and a short description of their format.
- **Restrictions**. List any limits or restrictions that apply to the program, such as "the data file must be correctly formatted" or "the program does not check for input errors."
- **Revision history**. This section contains a list indicating who modified the program and when and what changes were made. Many computers have a source control system (UNIX: RCS and SCCS; DOS: MKS-RCS) that will keep track of this information for you.
- **Error handling**. If the program detects an error, describe what it does with it.

- **Notes**. Include special comments or other information that has not already been covered.

The format of your beginning comments will depend on what is needed for the environment in which you are programming. For example, if you are a student, the instructor may ask you to include in the program heading the assignment number, your name, student identification number, and other information. In industry, a project number or part number might be included.

Comments should explain everything the programmer needs to know about the program, but no more. It is possible to over-comment a program. (It is rare, but it does happen.) When deciding on the format for your heading comments, make sure there is a reason for everything you include.

Inserting Comments—The Easy Way

If you are using the UNIX editor **vi**, put the following in your *.exrc* file to make it easier to construct boxes:

```
:abbr #b /***********************************************
:abbr #e ***********************************************/
```

These two lines define **vi** abbreviations **#b** and **#e**, so that typing:

#b RETURN

at the beginning of a block will cause the string:

```
/***********************************************
```

to appear (for beginning a comment box). Typing:

#e RETURN

will end a box. The number of stars was carefully selected so that the end of the box is aligned on a tab stop.

The actual code for your program consists of two parts: variables and executable instructions. Variables are used to hold the data used by your program. Executable instructions tell the computer what to do with the data.

Common Coding Practices

A *variable* is a place in the computer's memory for storing a value. C identifies that place by the variable-name. Names can be any length and should be chosen so their meaning is clear. (Actually, there is a limit, but it is so large that you probably will never encounter it.) Every variable in C must be declared.

Variable declarations will be discussed in Chapter 8, *Variable Scope and Functions*. The following declaration tells C that we are going to use three integer (**int**) variables named `p`, `q`, and `r`:

```
int p,q,r;
```

But what are these variables for? The reader has no idea. They could represent the number of angels on the head of a pin or the location and acceleration of a plasma bolt in a game of space invaders. Avoid abbreviations. Exs. abb. are diff. to rd. and hd. to ustnd. (Excess abbreviations are difficult to read and hard to understand.)

Now consider another declaration:

```
int account_number;
int balance_owed;
```

Now we know that we are dealing with an accounting program, but we could still use some more information. For example, is the `balance_owed` in dollars or cents? It would be much better if we added a comment after each declaration explaining what we are doing. For example:

```
int account_number;         /* Index for account table */
int balance_owed;           /* Total owed us (in pennies)*/
```

By putting a comment after each declaration, we, in effect, create a mini-dictionary where we define the meaning of each variable-name. Since the definition of each variable is in a known place, it's easy to look up the meaning of a name. (Programming tools like editors, cross-referencers, and `grep` can also help you quickly find a variable's definition.)

Units are very important. I was once asked to modify a program that converted plot data files from one format to another. Many different units of length were used throughout the program, and none of the variable declarations were commented. I tried very hard to figure out what was going on, but it was impossible to determine what units were being used in the program. Finally, I gave up and put the following comment in the program:

```
/********************************************************
 * Note: I have no idea what the input units are, nor  *
 *       do I have any idea what the output units are, *
 *       but I have discovered that if I divide by 3   *
 *       the plots look about the right size.          *
 ********************************************************/
```

You should take every opportunity to make sure your program is clear and easy to understand. Do not be clever. Clever kills. Clever makes for unreadable and unmaintainable programs. Programs, by their nature, are extremely complex.

Anything you can to do to cut down on this complexity will make your programs better. Consider the following code, written by a very clever programmer:

```
while ('\n' != *p++ = *q++);
```

It is almost impossible for the reader to tell at a glance what this mess does. Properly written this would be:

```
while (1) {
    *destination_ptr = *source_ptr;
    if (*destination_ptr == '\n')
        break;    /* Exit the loop if done */
    destination_ptr++;
    source_ptr++;
}
```

Although the second version is longer, it is much clearer and easier to understand. Even a novice programmer who does not know C well can tell that this program has something to do with moving data from a source to a destination.

The computer doesn't care which version is used. A good compiler will generate the same machine code for both versions. It is the programmer who benefits from the verbose code.

Coding Religion

Computer scientists have devised many programming styles. These include structured programming, top-down programming, and goto-less programming. Each of these styles has its own following or cult. I use the term "religion" because people are taught to follow the rules blindly without knowing the reasons behind them. For example, followers of the goto-less cult will never use a **goto** statement, even when it is natural to do so.

The rules presented in this book are the result of years of programming experience. I have discovered that by following these rules, I can create better programs. You do not have to follow them blindly. If you find a better system, by all means use it. (If it really works, drop me a line. I'd like to use it too.)

Indentation and Code Format

In order to make programs easier to understand, most programmers indent their programs. The general rule for a C program is to indent one level for each new block or conditional. In our previous example, there are three levels of logic, each with its own indentation level. The **while** statement is outermost. The statements inside the **while** are at the next level. Finally, the statement inside the **if** (**break**) is at the innermost level.

There are two styles of indentation, and a vast religious war is being raged in the programming community as to which is better. The first is the short form:

```
while (! done) {
    (void)printf("Processing\n");
    next_entry();
}
if (total <= 0) {
    (void)printf("You owe nothing\n");
    total = 0;
} else {
    (void)printf("You owe %d dollars\n", total);
    all_totals = all_totals + total;
}
```

In this case, curly braces ({}) are put on the same line as the statements. The other style puts the {} on lines by themselves:

```
while (! done)
{
    (void)printf("Processing\n");
    next_entry();
}
if (total <= 0)
{
   (void)printf("You owe nothing\n");
   total = 0;
}
else
{
   (void)printf("You owe %d dollars\n", total);
   all_totals = all_totals + total;
}
```

Both formats are commonly used. You should use the format you feel most comfortable with. This book uses the short form.

The amount of indentation is left to the programmer. Two, four, and eight spaces are common. Studies have shown that a four-space indent makes the most readable code. It does not matter which indent size you use as long as you are consistent.

Clarity

A program should read like a technical paper. It should be organized into sections and paragraphs. Procedures form a natural section boundary. You must organize your code into paragraphs. It is a good idea to begin a paragraph with a topic sentence comment and separate it from other paragraphs by a blank line. For example:

```
/* poor programming practice */
temp = box_x1;
box_x1 = box_x2;
box_x2 = temp;
temp = box_y1;
box_y1 = box_y2;
box_y2 = temp;
```

A better version would be:

```
/*
 * Swap the two corners
 */

/* Swap X coordinate */
temp = box_x1;
box_x1 = box_x2;
box_x2 = temp;

/* Swap Y coordinate */
temp = box_y1;
box_y1 = box_y2;
box_y2 = temp;
```

Simplicity

Your program should be simple. Some general rules of thumb are:

- A single function should not be longer than two or three pages. (See Chapter 8, *Variable Scope and Functions*.) If it gets longer, it can probably be split into two simpler functions. This rule comes about because the human mind can only hold so much in short-term memory. Three pages is about the most that the human mind can wrap itself around in one sitting.
- Avoid complex logic like multiply-nested **if**s. The more complex your code, the more indentation levels you will need. About the time you start running into the right margin you should think about splitting your code into multiple procedures, thus decreasing the level of complexity.
- Did you ever read a sentence, like this one, where the author went on and on, stringing together sentence after sentence with the word "and" and didn't seem to understand the fact that several shorter sentences would do the job much better, and didn't it bother you? C statements should not go on forever. Long statements should be avoided. If an equation or formula looks like it is

going to be longer than one or two lines, you should split it into two shorter equations.

- Finally, the most important rule: make your program as simple and easy to understand as possible, even if it means breaking some of the rules. The goal is clarity, and the rules given in this chapter are designed to help you accomplish that goal. If they get in the way, get rid of them. I have seen one program with a single statement that spanned over 20 pages; however, because of the specialized nature of the program, this statement was simple and easy to understand.

Summary

A program should be concise and easy to read. It must serve as a set of computer instructions, but also as a reference work describing the algorithms and data used inside it. Everything should be documented with comments. Comments serve two purposes. First, they tell the programmer to follow the code, and second, they help you remember what you did.

Class discussion: Create a style sheet for class assignments. Discuss what comments should go into the programs and why.

3

Basic Declarations and Expressions

Elements of a Program
Basic Program Structure
Simple Expressions
Variables and Storage
Variable Declarations
Integers
Assignment Statements
printf Function
Floating Point
Characters

A journey of a thousand miles must begin with a single step.
—Lao-zi

If carpenters made buildings the way programmers make programs, the first woodpecker to come along would destroy all of civilization.
—Anon.

Elements of a Program

If you are going to construct a building, you need two things: the bricks and a blueprint that tells you how to put them together. In computer programming you need two things: data (variables) and instructions (code or functions). Variables are the basic building blocks of a program. Instructions tell the computer what to do with the variables.

Comments are used to describe the variables and instructions. They are notes by the author documenting the program so that it is clear and easy to read. Comments are ignored by the computer.

In construction, before we can start we must order our materials: "We need 500 large bricks, 80 half-size bricks, and four flagstones." Similarly, in C we must declare all our variables before we can use them. We must name each one of our "bricks" and tell C what type of brick to use.

Once our variables are defined, we can begin to use them. In construction the basic structure is a room. By combining many rooms we form a building. In C the basic structure is a function. Functions can be combined to form a program.

An apprentice builder does not start out building the Empire State Building, but rather starts on a one-room house. In this chapter we will concentrate on constructing simple one-function programs.

Basic Program Structure

The basic elements of a program are the data declarations, functions, and comments. Let's see how these can be organized into a simple C program.

The basic structure of a one-function program is:

```
/*****************************************************
 * ...Heading comments...                            *
 *****************************************************/
...Data declarations...
main()
{
    ...Executable statements...
    return (0);
}
```

where the *heading comments* tell the programmer all about the program and the *data declarations* describe the data that the program is going to use.

Our single function is named **main**. The name **main** is special, because it is the first function called. Any other functions are called directly or indirectly from **main**. The function **main** begins with:

```
main()
{
```

and ends with:

```
    return (0);
}
```

The line **return(0);** is used to tell the operating system (UNIX or MS-DOS) that the program exited normally (Status=0). A nonzero status indicates an error—the bigger the return value, the more severe the error. Typically, 1 is used for most simple errors like a missing file or bad command-line syntax.

Now let's take a look at our "Hello World" program (Program 2-1).

At the beginning of the program is a comment box enclosed in /* and */. Following this is the line:

```
#include <stdio.h>
```

This statement signals C that we are going to use the standard I/O package. It is a type of data declaration.* Later we use the function **printf** from this package.

Our main routine contains the instruction:

```
(void)printf("Hello World\n");
```

which is an executable statement instructing C to print the message "Hello World" on the screen. C uses a semicolon (;) to end a statement much the same way we use a period to end a sentence. Unlike line-oriented languages such as BASIC, an end-of-line does not end a statement. The sentences in this book can span several lines—the end of a line is treated as space separating words. C works the same way. A single statement can span several lines. Similarly, you can put several sentences on the same line, just as you can put several C statements on the same line. However, most of the time your program is more readable if each statement starts on a separate line.

The standard function **printf** is used to output our message. A library routine is a C procedure or function that has been written and put into a library or collection of useful functions. Such routines perform sorting, input, output, mathematical functions, and file manipulation. See your C reference manual for a complete list of library functions.

*Technically, it causes a set of data declarations to be taken from an include file. Chapter 9, *The C Preprocessor*, discusses include files.

The function **printf** returns a value indicating whether or not the output was done successfully. Our program discards this value. To let C know that "Yes, we do know that **printf** returns a value, but we don't care what it is," we use the cast **(void)**. Casting and function return values are discussed further in Chapter 8, *Variable Scope and Functions*, and Chapter 11, *Advanced Types*.

"Hello World" is one of the simplest C programs; it contains no computations, it merely sends a single message to the screen. It is a starting point. Once you have mastered this simple program, you have done a number of things right. The program is not as simple as it looks. But once you get it working, you can then move on to create more complex code.

Simple Expressions

Computers can do more than just print strings—they can also perform calculations. Expressions are used to specify simple computations. The five simple operators in C are listed in Table 3-1.

Table 3-1. Simple Operators

Operator	Meaning
*	Multiply
/	Divide
+	Add
–	Subtract
%	Modulus (return the remainder after division)

Multiply (*), divide (/), and modulus (%) have precedence over addition (+) and subtraction (–). Parentheses, (), may be used to group terms. Thus:

```
(1 + 2) * 4
```

yields 12, while:

```
1 + 2 * 4
```

yields 9.

Program 3-1 computes the value of the expression `(1 + 2) * 4`.

Program 3-1.

```
main()
{
    (1 + 2) * 4;
    return (0);
}
```

Although we calculate the answer, we don't do anything with it. (This program will generate a "null effect" warning to indicate that there is a correctly written, but useless, statement in the program.)

If we were constructing a building, think about how confused a workman would be if we said, "Take your wheelbarrow and go back and forth between the truck and the building site."

"Do you want me to carry bricks in it?"

"No. Just go back and forth."

We need to store the results of our calculations.

Variables and Storage

C allows us to store values in *variables*. Each variable is identified by a *variable-name*.

Additionally, each variable has a *variable type*. The type tells C how the variable is going to be used and what kind of numbers (real, integer) it can hold. Names start with a letter or underscore (_) followed by any number of letters, digits, or underscores. Uppercase is different from lowercase, so the names sam, Sam, and SAM specify three different variables. However, to avoid confusion, it is better to use different names for variables and not depend on case differences.

Most C programmers use all lowercase variable-names. Some names like **int**, **while**, **for**, and **float** have a special meaning to C and are considered *reserved words*. They cannot be used for variable-names.

The following is an example of some variable-names:

```
average            /* average of all grades */
pi                 /* pi to 6 decimal places */
number_of_students /* number students in this class */
```

The following are *not* variable-names:

```
3rd_entry    /* Begins with a number */
all$done     /* Contains a "$" */
the end      /* Contains a space */
int          /* Reserved word */
```

Avoid variable-names that are similar. For example, the following illustrates a poor choice of variable-names:

```
total        /* total number of items in current entry */
totals       /* total of all entries */
```

A much better set of names is:

```
entry_total /* total number of items in current entry */
all_total   /* total of all entries */
```

Variable Declarations

Before you can use a variable in C, it must be defined in a *declaration statement.*

A variable declaration serves three purposes:

1. It defines the name of the variable.
2. It defines the type of the variable (integer, real, character, etc.).
3. It gives the programmer a description of the variable.

The declaration of a variable `answer` can be:

```
int answer;       /* the result of our expression */
```

The keyword **int** tells C that this variable contains an integer value. (Integers are defined below.) The variable-name is `answer`. The semicolon (`;`) is used for end of statement, and the comment is used to define this variable for the programmer.

The general form of a variable declaration is:

type name; /* *comment* */

where *type* is one of the C variable types (**int**, **float**, etc.) and *name* is any valid variable-name. This explains what the variable is and what it will be used for. (In Chapter 8, *Variable Scope and Functions*, we will see how local variables may be declared elsewhere.)

Variable declarations come just before the **main()** line at the top of a program.

Integers

One variable type is integer. Integer numbers (also known as whole numbers) have no fractional part or decimal point. Numbers such as 1, 87, –222 are integers. The number 8.3 is not an integer because it contains a decimal point. The general form of an integer declaration is:

int *name*;   /* *comment* */

A calculator with an 8-digit display can only handle numbers between 99999999 and –99999999. If you try to add 1 to 99999999, you will get an overflow error. Computers have similar limits. The limits on integers are implementation-dependent, meaning they change from computer to computer.

Calculators use decimal digits (0-9). Computers use binary digits (0-1) called bits. Eight bits make a byte. The number of bits used to hold an integer varies from machine to machine. Numbers are converted from binary to decimal for printing.

On most UNIX machines integers are 32 bits (4 bytes), providing a range of 2147483647 ($2^{31}-1$) to –2147483648. On the PC under Turbo C only 16 bits (2 bytes) are used, so the range is 32767 ($2^{15}-1$) to –32768.

Question 3–1: The following will work on a UNIX machine, but will fail on a PC:

```
int zip;       /* zip code for current address */
.........
zip = 92126;
```

Why does this fail? What will be the result when run on a PC?

Assignment Statements

Declarations create space for variables. Figure 3-1 illustrates a variable declaration for the variable **answer**. We have not yet assigned it a value so it is known as an *uninitialized variable*. The question mark indicates that the value of this variable is unknown.

```
int answer;
```

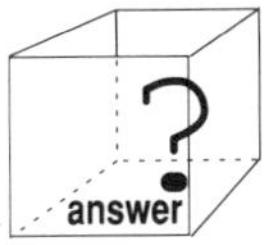

The variable `answer` has not been assigned a value. (So we put a "?" in it to indicate that it's in an unknown state.)

```
answer = (1+2) * 4;
```

The variable `answer` is assigned the value of the expression `(1+2)*4`. The box is shown containing the value 12.

Figure 3-1. Declaration of answer

Assignment statements are used to give a variable a value. For example:

```
answer = (1 + 2) * 4;
```

is an assignment. The variable **`answer`** on the left side of the equals operator (=) is assigned the value of the expression **`(1 + 2) * 4`**. So the variable **`answer`** gets the value **`12`** as illustrated in Figure 3-2.

The general form of the assignment statement is:

variable = *expression* **;**

The = is used for assignment, not equality.

In Program 3-2 we use the variable **`term`** to store an integer value which is used in two later expressions.

Program 3-2.

```
#include <stdio.h>

int term;       /* term used in two expressions */
int term_2;     /* twice term */
int term_3;     /* three times term */
main()
```

```
{
    term = 3 * 5;
    term_2 = 2 * term;
    term_3 = 3 * term;
    return (0);
}
```

There is a problem with this program. How can we tell if it is working or not? We need some way of printing the answers.

printf Function

The library function **printf** can be used to print the results. If we put in the statement:

```
(void)printf("Twice %d is %d\n", term, 2 * term);
```

the program will print:

```
Twice 15 is 30
```

The special characters **%d** are called the *integer conversion specification*. When **printf** encounters a **%d**, it will print the value of the next expression in the list following the format string. This is called the *parameter list*.

The general form of the **printf** statement is:

(void)printf(*format*, *expression-1*, *expression-2*, ...);

where *format* is the string describing what to print. Everything inside this string is printed as is except for the **%d** conversions. The value of *expression-1* is printed in place of the first **%d**, *expression-2* the second, and so on.

Figure 3-3 shows how the elements of the **printf** statement work together to generate the final result.

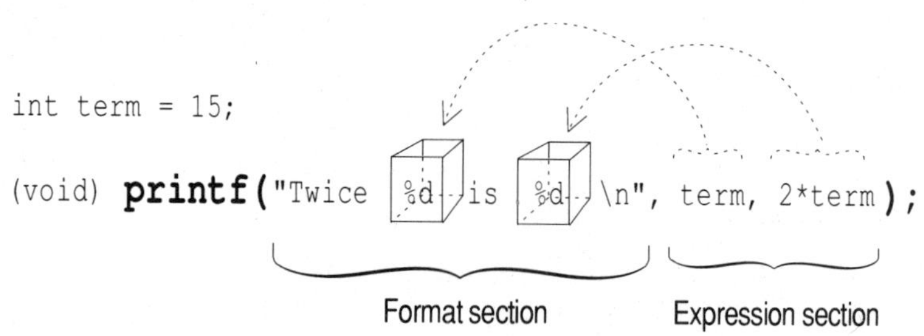

Figure 3-2. printf Structure

The format string **"Twice %d is %d\n"** tells **printf** to print out **Twice** followed by a space, the value of the first expression, then a space followed by **is** and a space, followed by the second expression, finishing with an end-of-line (indicated by **\n**).

Program 3-3 shows a program that computes **term** and prints it in two **printf** functions.

Program 3-3.

```
#include <stdio.h>

int term;        /* term used in two expressions */
main()
{

    term = 3 * 5;
    (void)printf("Twice %d is %d\n", term, 2*term);
    (void)printf("Three time %d is %d\n", term, 3*term);
    return (0);
}
```

The number of **%d** conversions in the format should exactly match the number of expressions in the **printf**. C will not check for this. If too many expressions are supplied, the extra ones will be ignored. If there are not enough expressions, C will generate strange numbers for the missing expressions.

Floating Point

Real numbers are numbers that have a fractional part. Because of the way they are stored internally, real numbers are also known as floating-point numbers. The numbers 5.5, 8.3, and –12.6 are all floating-point numbers. C uses the decimal point to distinguish between floating-point numbers and integers. So 5.0 is a floating-point number, while 5 is an integer. Floating-point numbers must contain a decimal point. Floating-point numbers include: 3.14159, 0.5, 1.0, and 8.88.

Although it is possible to omit digits before the decimal point and specify a number as .5 instead of 0.5, the extra 0 makes it clear that you are using a floating-point number. A similar rule applies to 12. versus 12.0. A floating-point zero should be written as 0.0.

Additionally, the number may include an exponent specification of the form:

e±*exp*

For example, 1.2e34, is shorthand for 1.2×10^{34}.

The form of a floating-point declaration is:

float *variable* ;   /* *comment* */

Again, there is a limit on the range of floating-point numbers that the computer can handle. These vary widely from computer to computer. Floating-point accuracy will be discussed further in Chapter 15, *Floating Point.*

When writing a floating-point number using **printf**, the **%f** conversion is used. To print the expression **1.0/3.0**, we use this statement:

```
(void)printf("The answer is %f\n", 1.0/3.0);
```

Floating Point Versus Integer Divide

The division operator is special. There is a vast difference between an integer divide and a floating-point divide. In an integer divide, the result is truncated (any fractional part is discarded). So the value of 19/10 is 1.

If either the divisor or the dividend is a floating-point number, a floating-point divide is executed. So 19.0/10.0 is 1.9. (19/10.0 and 19.0/10 are also floating-point divides; however, 19.0/10.0 is preferred for clarity.) There are several examples in Table 3-2.

Table 3-2. Expression Examples

Expression	Result	Result Type
1+2	3	Integer
1.0+2.0	3.0	Floating point
1.0+2	3.0	Floating point
19/10	1	Integer
19.0/10.0	1.9	Floating point

C allows the assignment of an integer expression to a floating-point variable. C will automatically perform the integer to floating-point conversion. A similar conversion is performed when assigning a floating-point number to an integer. For example:

```
int   integer;  /* an integer */
float floating; /* a floating-point number */

main()
{
```

```
        floating = 1.0 / 2.0;          /* assign "floating" 0.5 */
        integer = 1 / 3;               /* assign integer 0 */
        floating = (1 / 2) + (1 / 2); /* assign floating 0.0 */
        floating = 3.0 / 2.0;          /* assign floating 1.5 */
        integer = floating;            /* assign integer 1 */
        return (0);
}
```

Notice that the expression `1 / 2` is an integer expression resulting in an integer divide and an integer result of 0.

Question 3–2: Why is the result of the following program "0"? What must be done to this program to fix it?

```
#include <stdio.h>

float answer;  /* the result of the divide */

main()
{
    answer = 1/3;
    (void)printf("The value of 1/3 is %f\n",
                 answer);
    return (0);
}
```

Question 3–3: Why does 2 + 2 = 5928? (Your results may vary.)

```
#include <stdio.h>

/* variable for computation results */
int answer;

main()
{
      answer = 2 + 2;

      (void)printf("The answer is %d\n");
      return (0);
}
```

Question 3–4: Why is an incorrect result printed?

```
#include <stdio.h>

float result;
main()
{
    result = 7.0 / 22.0;
    (void)printf("The result is %d\n", result);
    return (0);
}
```

Characters

The type **char** represents single characters. The form of a character declaration is:

```
char variable;      /* comment */
```

Characters are enclosed in single quotes ('). 'A', 'a', and '!' are character constants. The backslash character (\) is called the *escape character*. It is used to signal that a special character follows. For example the characters \" can be used to put a double quote inside a string. A single quote is represented by \'. \n is the newline character. It causes the output device to go to the beginning of the next line (similar to a return key on a typewriter). The characters \\ are the backslash itself. Finally, characters can be specified by *nnn*, where *nnn* is the octal code for the character. Table 3-3 summarizes these special characters. Appendix A, *ASCII Chart*, contains a table of ASCII character codes.

Table 3-3. Special Characters

Character	Name	Meaning
\b	Backspace	Move the cursor to the left one character.
\f	Form feed	Go to the top of a new page.
\n	Newline	Go to the next line.
\r	Return	Go to the beginning of the current line.
\t	Tab	Advance to the next tab stop (eight-column boundary).
\'	Apostrophe	The character '.
\"	Double quote	The character ".
\\	Backslash	The character \.
nnn		The character number *nnn*.

NOTE

While characters are enclosed in single quotes ('), a different data type, the string, is enclosed in double quotes ("). A good way to remember the difference between these two types of quotes is that single characters are enclosed in single quotes. Strings can have any number of characters (including double characters), and they are enclosed in double quotes.

Characters use the **printf** conversion **%c**. Program 3-4 reverses three characters.

Program 3-4.

```
#include <stdio.h>

char char1;      /* first character */
char char2;      /* second character */
char char3;      /* third character */

main()
{
    char1 = 'A';
    char2 = 'B';
    char3 = 'C';
    (void)printf("%c%c%c reversed is %c%c%c\n",
        char1, char2, char3,
        char3, char2, char1);
    return (0);
}
```

When executed, this program prints:

```
ABC reversed is CBA
```

Answers

Answer 3–1: The largest number that can be stored in an **int** on a UNIX machine is 2147483647. When using Turbo C the limit is 32767. The zip code 92126 is larger than 32767, so it is mangled, and the result is 26590.

This problem can be fixed by using a **long int** instead of just an **int**. The various types of integers will be discussed in Chapter 4, *Arrays, Qualifiers, and Reading Numbers.*

Answer 3–2: The problem concerns the division: `1/3`. The number 1 and the number 3 are both integers, so this is an integer divide. Fractions are truncated in an integer divide. The expression should be written as:

```
answer = 1.0 / 3.0
```

Answer 3–3: The **printf** statement:

```
(void)printf("The answer is %d\n");
```

tells the program to print a decimal number, but there is no variable specified. C does not check to make sure **printf** is given the right number of parameters.

Since no value was specified, C makes one up. The proper `printf` statement should be:

```
(void)printf("The answer is %d\n", answer);
```

Answer 3–4: The problem is that in the `printf` statement we used a `%d` to specify that an integer was to be printed, but the parameter for this conversion was a floating-point number. The `printf` function has no way of checking its parameters for type. So if you give it a floating-point number, but the format specifies an integer, the function will treat it as an integer and print unexpected results.

Programming Exercises

Exercise 1: Write a program to print your name, social security number, and date of birth.

Exercise 2: Write a program to print a block E using asterisks (`*`), where the E is seven characters high and five characters wide.

Exercise 3: Write a program to compute the area and circumference of a rectangle 3 inches wide by 5 inches long. What changes must be made to program so it works for a square 6.8 inches wide by 2.3 inches long?

Exercise 4: Write a program to print "HELLO" in big block letters where each letter is seven characters high and five characters wide.

Exercise 5: Write a program that deliberately makes the following mistakes:

- Prints a floating-point number using the `%d` conversion.
- Prints an integer using the `%f` conversion.
- Prints a character using the `%d` conversion.

4

Arrays, Qualifiers, and Reading Numbers

That mysterious independent variable of political calculations, Public Opinion.
—Thomas Henry Huxley

Arrays

In constructing our building, we have identified each brick (variable) by name. That is fine for a small number of bricks, but what happens when we want to construct something larger? We would like to point to a stack of bricks and say, "That's for the left wall. That's brick 1, brick 2, brick 3 . . . "

Arrays allow us to do something similar with variables. An array is a set of consecutive memory locations used to store data. Each item in the array is called an element. The number of elements in an array is called the dimension of the array. A typical array declaration is:

```
/* List of data to be sorted and averaged */
int    data_list[3];
```

This declares **data_list** to be an array of three elements. **data_list[0]**, **data_list[1]**, and **data_list[2]** are separate variables. To reference an element of an array, you use a number called the index—the number inside the square brackets ([ ]). C is a funny language that likes to start counting at 0. So our three elements are numbered 0-2.

NOTE

> Common sense tells you that when you declare **data_list** to be three elements long, **data_list[3]** would be valid. Common sense is wrong and **data_list[3]** is illegal.

Program 4-1 computes the total and average of five numbers.

Program 4-1.

```
#include <stdio.h>

float data[5];   /* data to average and total */
float total;     /* the total of the data items */
float average;   /* average of the items */

main()
{
    data[0] = 34.0;
    data[1] = 27.0;
    data[2] = 45.0;
    data[3] = 82.0;
    data[4] = 22.0;

    total = data[0] + data[1] + data[2] + data[3] + data[4];
    average =  total / 5.0;
    (void)printf("Total %f Average %f\n", total, average);
    return (0);
}
```

This program outputs:

```
Total 210.000000 Average 42.000000
```

Strings

Strings are arrays of characters. The special character `'\0'` (NUL) is used to indicate the end of a string.

For example:

```
char    name[4];
main()
{
    name[0] = 'S';
    name[1] = 'a';
    name[2] = 'm';
    name[3] = '\0';
    return (0);
}
```

This creates a character array four elements long. Note that we had to allocate one character for the end-of-string marker.

String constants consist of text enclosed in double quotes ("). You may have noticed that the first parameter to `printf` is a string constant. C does not allow one array to be assigned to another, so we can't write an assignment of the form:

```
name = "Sam";     /* Illegal */
```

Instead we must use the standard library function `strcpy` to copy the string constant into the variable. (`strcpy` copies the whole string including the end-of-string character.) To initialize the variable `name` to `Sam`, we would write:

```
#include <string.h>
char    name[4];
main()
{
    (void)strcpy(name, "Sam");    /* Legal */
    return (0);
}
```

NOTE

The line `#include <string.h>` is needed to inform C that we are using the string function library. The construct `(void)` indicates we are not using the return value of `strcpy`.

C uses variable-length strings. For example, the declaration:

```
#include <string.h>
char string[50];
main()
{
    (void)strcpy(string,"Sam");
```

creates an array (`string`) that can contain up to 50 characters. The size of the array is 50, but the length of the string is 3. Any string up to 49 characters long can be stored in `string`. (One character is reserved for the NUL that indicates end-of-string.)

NOTE

String and character constants are very different. Strings are surrounded by double quotes (") and characters by single quotes ('). So `"X"` is a one-character string, while `'Y'` is just a single character.

There are several standard routines that work on string variables, as shown in Table 4-1.

Table 4-1. String Functions

Function	Description
`strcpy(string1, string2)`	Copy `string2` into `string1`.
`strcat(string1, string2)`	Concatenate `string2` onto the end of `string1`.
`length = strlen(string)`	Get the length of a string.
`strcmp(string1, string2)`	0 if `string1` equals `string2`, otherwise nonzero.

`printf` uses the conversion `%s` for printing string variables. Program 4-2 gives an example.

Program 4-2.

```
#include <string.h>
#include <stdio.h>
char name[30];     /* First name of someone */
main()
```

```
{
    (void)strcpy(name, "Sam");    /* Initialize the name */
    (void)printf("The name is %s\n", name);
    return (0);
}
```

Program 4-3 takes a first name and a last name and combines the two strings.

The program works by initializing the variable **first** to the first name (Steve). The last name (Oualline) is put in the variable **last**. To construct the full name, the first name is copied into **full_name**. Then **strcat** is used to add a space. We call **strcat** again to tack on the last name.

The dimension of the string variable is 100 because we know that no one we are going to encounter has a name more than 99 characters long. (If we get a name more than 99 characters long, our program will mess up.)

Program 4-3.

```
#include <string.h>
#include <stdio.h>

char first[100];        /* first name */
char last[100];         /* last name */
char full_name[200];    /* full version of first and last name */

main()
{
    (void)strcpy(first, "Steve");       /* Initialize first name */
    (void)strcpy(last, "Oualline");     /* Initialize last name */

    (void)strcpy(full_name, first);     /* full = "Steve" */
    /* Note: strcat not strcpy */
    (void)strcat(full_name, " ");       /* full = "Steve " */
    (void)strcat(full_name, last);      /* full = "Steve Oualline" */

    (void)printf("The full name is %s\n", full_name);
    return (0);
}
```

The output of this program is:

```
The full name is Steve Oualline
```

Question 4–1: The following program prints `John'=(3` instead of `John Doe`. Why? (Your results may vary.)

```
#include <stdio.h>
#include <string.h>

char first[100];        /* first name of person */
```

```
char last[100];         /* His last name */

/* First and last name of the person (computed) */
char full[200];
main() {
    (void)strcpy(first, "John");
    (void)strcpy(last, "Doe");

    (void)strcpy(full, first);
    (void)strcat(full, ' ');
    (void)strcat(full, last);

    (void)printf("The name is %s\n", full);
    return (0);
}
```

Reading Strings

The standard function **fgets** can be used to read a string from the keyboard. The general form of an **fgets** call is:

(void)fgets(*name*, sizeof(*name*), stdin);

where *name* identifies a string variable. (**fgets** will be explained in detail in Chapter 13, *File Input/Output*.)

where:

name — is the name of a character array. The line (including the end-of-line character) is read into this array.

sizeof(*name*) — is used to indicate the maximum characters to read minus one for the end-of-string character. The **sizeof** function provides a convenient way of limiting the number of characters read to the maximum the variable can hold. This function will be discussed in more detail in Chapter 13.

stdin — is the file to read. In this case it is the standard input or keyboard. Other files are discussed in Chapter 13.

Program 4-4 reads a line from the keyboard and reports its length.

Program 4-4.

```
#include <string.h>
#include <stdio.h>

char line[100];

main()
{
    (void)printf("Enter a line: ");
    (void)fgets(line, sizeof(line), stdin);

    (void)printf("The length of the line is: %d\n", strlen(line));
    return (0);
}
```

When we run this program, we get:

```
Enter a line: test
The length of the line is: 5
```

But since the string `test` is only four characters, where's the extra character coming from? It turns out that `fgets` includes the end-of-line in the string. So the fifth character is newline (`\n`).

Suppose we wanted to change our name program to ask the user for his first and last name. Program 4-5 shows how we could write the program.

Program 4-5.

```
#include <stdio.h>
#include <string.h>

char first[100];        /* first name of person we are working with */
char last[100];         /* His last name */

/* First and last name of the person (computed) */
char full[200];
main() {
    (void)printf("Enter first name: ");
    (void)fgets(first, sizeof(first), stdin);

    (void)printf("Enter last name: ");
    (void)fgets(last, sizeof(last), stdin);

    (void)strcpy(full, first);
    (void)strcat(full, " ");
    (void)strcat(full, last);

    (void)printf("The name is %s\n", full);
    return (0);
}
```

However, when we run this program we get the results:

```
% name2
Enter first name: John
Enter last name: Doe
The name is John
 Doe
%
```

What we wanted was "John Doe" all on the same line. What happened? The `fgets` function gets the entire line, *including the end-of-line*. We must get rid of this character before printing.

For example, the name "John" would be stored as:

```
first[0] = 'J'
first[1] = 'o'
first[2] = 'h'
first[3] = 'n'
first[4] = '\n'
first[5] = '\0'     /* end of string */
```

By setting `first[4]` to NUL (`'\0'`), we can shorten the string by one character and get rid of the unwanted newline. This can be done with the statement:

```
first[4] = '\0';
```

The problem is that this will only work for four-character names. We need a general algorithm to solve this problem. The length of this string is the index of the end-of-string null character. The character before it is the one we want to get rid of, so to trim the string we use the statement:

```
first[strlen(first)-1] = '\0';
```

Our new program is shown as Program 4-6.

Program 4-6.

```
#include <stdio.h>
#include <string.h>

char first[100];        /* first name of person we are working with */
char last[100];         /* His last name */

/* First and last name of the person (computed) */
char full[100];
main() {
    (void)printf("Enter first name: ");
    (void)fgets(first, sizeof(first), stdin);
    /* trim off last character */
    first[strlen(first)-1] = '\0';

    (void)printf("Enter last name: ");
```

```
    (void)fgets(last, sizeof(last), stdin);
    /* trim off last character */
    last[strlen(last)-1] = '\0';

    (void)strcpy(full, first);
    (void)strcat(full, " ");
    (void)strcat(full, last);

    (void)printf("The name is %s\n", full);
    return (0);
}
```

Running this program gives us the following results:

```
Enter first name:  John
Enter last name:  Smith
The name is John Smith
```

Multiple Dimensional Arrays

Arrays can have more than one dimension. The declaration for a two-dimensional array is:

> /* *...Comment...* */
> *type variable*[*size1*][*size2*];

For example:

```
/* a typical matrix */
int matrix[2][4];
```

Notice that C does *not* follow the notation used in other languages of `matrix[10,12]`.

To access an element of the `matrix`, we use the notation:

```
matrix[1][2] = 10;
```

C allows the programmer to use as many dimensions as needed (only limited by the amount of memory available). Additional dimensions can be tacked on:

```
four_dimensions[10][12][9][5];
```

Initializing multi-dimensional arrays is similar to initializing single-dimension arrays. A set of curly braces ({}) encloses each element. The declaration:

```
/* a typical matrix */
int matrix[2][4];
```

can be thought of as a declaration of an array of dimension 2 whose elements are arrays of dimension 4. This array is initialized as follows:

```
/* a typical matrix */
int matrix[2][4] =
    {
        {1, 2, 3, 4},
        {10, 20, 30, 40}
    };
```

Question 4–2: Why does the following program print the wrong answer?

```
#include <stdio.h>

int array[3][5]  = {
    { 0,  1,  2,  3,  4 },
    {10, 11, 12, 13, 14 },
    {20, 21, 22, 23, 24 }
};

main()
{
    int x,y;

    x = 2;
    y = 3;

    printf("Element is %d\n",  array[x,y]);
    return (0);
}
```

Reading Numbers

So far we have only read simple strings, but we want more. We want to read numbers as well. The function `scanf` works like `printf` except that it reads numbers instead of writing them. It provides a simple and easy way of reading numbers *that almost never works.* The function `scanf` is notorious for its poor end-of-line handling, which makes it almost impossible for anyone except an expert to use.

However, we've found a simple way to get around the deficiencies of **scanf**—we don't use it. Instead we use **fgets** to read a line of input and **sscanf** to convert the text into numbers.

Normally, we use the variable **line** for lines read from the keyboard:

```
char line[100];     /* Line of keyboard input */
```

When we want to process input, we use the statements:

```
(void)fgets(line, sizeof(line), stdin);
(void)sscanf(line, format, &variable1, &variable2 . . .);
```

Here **fgets** reads a line and **sscanf** processes it. *format* is a string similar to the **printf** format string. Note the ampersand (**&**) in front of the variable-names. This is used to indicate that **sscanf** will change the value of these variables. (For information on why we need the ampersand, see Chapter 12, *Simple Pointers*.)

WARNING

> If you forget to put **&** in front of each variable for **sscanf**, the result could be a "Segmentation violation core dumped" or "Illegal memory access" error. In some cases a random variable or instruction will be changed. This is not too common on UNIX machines, but DOS, with its lack of memory protection, cannot easily detect this problem. On DOS, omitting **&** can cause a program or system crash.

In Program 4-7, we use **sscanf** to get a number from the user and double it.

Program 4-7.

```
#include <stdio.h>
char  line[100];    /* input line from console */
int   value;        /* a value to double */

main()
{
    (void) printf("Enter a value: ");
    (void) fgets(line, sizeof(line), stdin);
    (void) sscanf(line, "%d", &value);
    (void) printf("Twice %d is %d\n",
                  value, value * 2);
    return (0);
}
```

This program reads in a single number and doubles it. Notice that there is no **\n** at the end of **Enter a value:**. This is because we do not want the computer to print a newline after the prompt. For example, a sample run of the program might look like:

```
Enter a value: 12
Twice 12 is 24
```

If we replaced **Enter a value:** with **Enter a value:\n**, the result would be:

```
Enter a value:
12
Twice 12 is 24
```

Question 4–3: The program that follows computes the area of a triangle, given its width and height. For some strange reason, the compiler refuses to believe that we declared the variable **width**. The declaration is right there on line 2, just after the definition of height. Why isn't the compiler seeing it?

```
#include <stdio.h>
char line[100];/* line of input data */
int  height;    /* the height of the triangle
int  width;     /* the width of the triangle */
int  area;      /* area of the triangle (computed) */

main()
{
    (void) printf("Enter width height? ");
    (void) fgets(line, sizeof(line), stdin);
    (void) sscanf(line, "%d %d", &width, &height);
    area = (width * height) / 2;
    (void) printf("The area is %d\n", area);
    return (0);
}
```

Initializing Variables

C allows variables to be initialized in the declaration statement. For example, the following statement declares the integer **counter** and initializes it to **0**:

```
int counter = 0;     /* number cases counted so far */
```

Arrays can also be initialized this way. The element list must be enclosed in curly braces ({}). For example:

```
/* Product numbers for the parts we are making */
int product_codes[3] = {10, 972, 45};
```

This is equivalent to:

```
product_codes[0] = 10;
product_codes[1] = 972;
product_codes[2] = 45;
```

The number of elements in {} does not have to match the array size. If too many numbers are present, a warning will be issued. If there are not enough, not all the elements are initialized.

If no dimension is given, C will determine the dimension from the number of elements in the initialization list. For example, we could have initialized our variable `product_codes` with the statement:

```
/* Product numbers for the parts we are making */
int product_codes[] = {10, 972, 45};
```

Strings can be initialized in a similar manner. For example, to initialize the variable `name` to the string "Sam", we use the statement:

```
char    name[] = {'S', 'a', 'm', '\0'};
```

C has a special shorthand for initializing strings; surround the string with double quotes (") to simplify initialization. The previous example could have been written:

```
char name[] = "Sam";
```

The dimension of `name` is four, because C allocates a place for the `'\0'` character that ends the string.

The following declaration:

```
char string[50] = "Sam";
```

is equivalent to:

```
char string[50];
.
.
.
(void) strcpy(string,"SAM");
```

An array of 50 characters is allocated but the length of the string is 3.

Types of Integers

C is considered a medium-level language because it allows you to get very close to the actual hardware of the machine. Some languages, like BASIC, go to great lengths to completely isolate the user from the details of how the processor works. This consistency comes at a great loss of efficiency. C lets you give detailed information about how the hardware is to be used.

For example, most machines let you use different length numbers. BASIC provides the programmer with only one number type. This simplifies the programming, but BASIC programs are extremely inefficient. C allows the programmer to specify many different flavors of integers, so the programmer can make best use of hardware.

The type specifier **int** tells C to use the most efficient size (for the machine you are using) for the integer. This can be 2 to 4 bytes depending on the machine. Sometimes you need extra digits to store numbers larger than are allowed in a normal **int**. The declaration:

```
long int answer;    /* the answer of our calculations */
```

is used to allocate a long integer. The **long** qualifier informs C that we wish to allocate extra storage for the integer. If we are going to use small numbers and wish to reduce storage, we use the qualifier **short**. For example:

```
short int year;             /* Year including the 19xx part */
```

C guarantees that the storage for **short <= int <= long**. In actual practice, **short** almost always allocates 2 bytes, **long** 4 bytes, and **int** 2 or 4 bytes. (See Appendix B, *Numeric Limits*, for numeric ranges.)

The type **short int** uses 2 bytes, or 16 bits. Fifteen bits are used normally for the number and 1 bit for the sign. This gives it a range of –32768 (-2^{15}) to 32767 ($2^{15}-1$). An **unsigned short int** uses all 16 bits for the number, giving it the range of 0 to 65535 (2^{16}). All **int** declarations default to **signed**, so that the declaration:

```
signed long int answer;     /* final result */
```

is the same as:

```
long int answer;            /* final result */
```

Finally, there is the very short integer. It is the type **char**. Character variables take up 1 byte. They can also be used for numbers in the range of –128 to 127 or 0 to 255. Unlike integers, they do not default to **signed**; the default is compiler dependent.* Very short integers may be printed using the integer conversion (`%d`). There is no way to read a very short integer directly. You must read the number into an integer and then use an assignment statement.

Table 4-2 contains the `printf` and `sscanf` conversions for integers.

Table 4-2. Integer printf/sscanf Conversions

%Conversions	Uses
`%h`	**(signed) short int**
`%d`	**(signed) int**
`%ld`	**(signed) long int**
`%H`	**unsigned short int**
`%u`	**unsigned int**
`%lu`	**unsigned long int**

The range of the various flavors of integers is listed in Appendix B, *Numeric Limits*.

long int declarations allow the program to explicitly specify extra precision where it is needed (at the expense of memory). **short int** numbers save space but have a more limited range. The most compact integers have type **char**. They also have the most limited range.

unsigned numbers provide a way of doubling the range at the expense of eliminating negative numbers.

The flavor of number you use will depend on your program and storage requirements.

Types of Floats

The **float** type also comes in various flavors. **float** denotes normal precision (usually 4 bytes). **double** indicates double precision (usually 8 bytes). Double precision gives the programmer twice the range and precision of single-precision (**float**) variables.

*Turbo C even has a command-line switch to make the default for type **char** either **signed** or **unsigned**.

The qualifier **long double** denotes extended precision. On some systems, this is the same as **double**; on others, it offers additional precision. All types of floating-point numbers are always signed.

Table 4-3 contains the `printf` and `sscanf` conversions for floating-point numbers.

Table 4-3. Float printf/sscanf Conversions

%Conversions	Uses
`%f`	**float**
`%lf`	**double**
`%L`	**long double**

On most machines single-precision, floating-point instructions execute faster (but less accurately) than double precision. Double precision gains accuracy at the expense of time and storage. In most cases **float** is adequate; however, if accuracy is a problem, switch to **double**. (See Chapter 15, *Floating Point.*)

Hexadecimal and Octal Constants

Integer numbers are specified as a string of digits, such as 1234, 88, –123, etc. These are decimal (base 10) numbers: 174 or 174_{10}. Computers deal with binary (base 2) numbers: 10101110_2. The octal (base 8) system easily converts to and from binary. Each group of three digits (2^3=8) can be transformed into a single octal digit. Thus 10101110_2 can be written as 10 101 110_2 and changed to the octal 256_8. Hexadecimal (base 16) numbers have a similar conversion, only 4 bits at a time are used.

The C language has conventions for representing octal and hexadecimal values. Leading zeros are used to signal an octal constant. For example, 0123 is 123 (octal) or 83 (decimal). Starting a number with "0x" indicates a hexadecimal (base 16) constant. So 0x15 is 21 (decimal). Table 4-4 shows several numbers in all three bases.

Table 4-4. Integer Examples

Base 10	Base 8	Base 16
6	06	0x6
9	011	0x9
15	017	0xF

Operators for Performing Shortcuts

C not only provides you with a rich set of declarations, but also gives you a large number of special purpose operators.

Frequently, the programmer wants to increment (add 1 to) a variable. Using a normal assignment statement, this would look like:

```
total_entries = total_entries + 1;
```

C provides us with a shorthand for performing this common task. The ++ operator is used for incrementing:

```
total_entries++;
```

A similar operator, --, can be used for decrementing (subtracting 1 from) a variable:

```
number_left--;
/* is the same as */
number_left = number_left - 1;
```

But suppose that we want to add 2 instead of 1. Then we can use the following notation:

```
total_entries += 2;
```

This is equivalent to:

```
total_entries = total_entries + 2;
```

Each of the simple operators, as shown in Table 4-5, can be used in this manner.

Table 4-5. Shorthand Operators

Operator	Shorthand	Equivalent Statement
+=	x += 2;	x = x + 2;
-=	x -= 2;	x = x - 2;
*=	x *= 2;	x = x * 2;
/=	x /= 2;	x = x / 2;
%=	x %= 2;	x = x % 2;

Side Effects

Unfortunately, C allows the programmer to use *side effects*. A side effect is an operation that is performed in addition to the main operation executed by the statement. For example, the following is legal C code:

```
size = 5;
result = size++;
```

The first statement assigns to **size** the value of 5. The second statement assigns to **result** the value of **size** (main operation) and increments **size** (side effect).

But in what order? There are four possible answers:

1. **result** is assigned the value of **size** (5), then **size** is incremented. **result** is 5 and **size** is 6.

2. **size** is incremented, then **result** is assigned the value of **size** (6). **result** is 6 and **size** is 6.

3. The answer is compiler dependent and varies from computer to computer.

4. If we don't write code like this, we don't have to worry about these sorts of questions.

The correct answer is number 1; the assignment occurs before the increment. However, 4 is a much better answer. The main effects of C are confusing enough without having to worry about side effects.

NOTE

Some programmers value compact code highly. This is a holdover from the early days of computing when storage cost a significant amount of money. It is my view that the art of programming has evolved to the point where clarity is much more valuable than compactness. (Great novels, which a lot of people enjoy reading, are not written in shorthand.)

C actually provides two flavors of the ++ operator. One is *variable*++ and the other is ++*variable*. The first:

```
number = 5;
result = number++;
```

evaluates the expressions, then increments the number, so `result` is 5. The second:

```
number = 5;
result = ++number;
```

increments first, then evaluates the expression. In this case, `result` is 6. However, using ++ or -- in this way can lead to some surprising code:

```
o = --o - o--;
```

The problem with this is that it looks like someone is writing Morse code. The programmer doesn't read this statement, but rather decodes it. If we never use ++ or -- as part of any other statement, but always put them on a line by themselves, the difference between the two flavors of these operators is not noticeable.

More complex side effects can confuse even the C compiler. Consider the following code fragment:

```
value = 1;
result = (value++ * 5) + (value++ * 3);
```

This expression tells C to perform the following steps:

1. Multiply `value` by 5, add 1 to `value`.
2. Multiply `value` by 3, add 1 to `value`.
3. Add the results of the two multiplications together.

Steps 1 and 2 are of equal priority, unlike the previous example, so the compiler can execute them in any order it wants to. Suppose it decides to execute step 1 first, as shown in Figure 4-1.

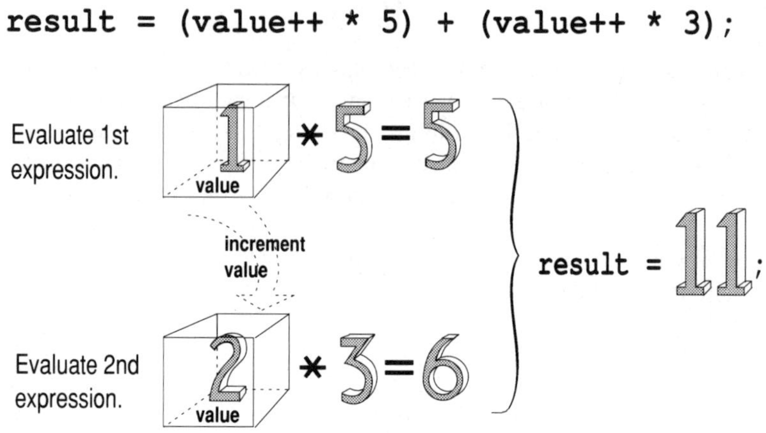

Figure 4-1. Expression Evaluation Method 1

Or suppose it executes step 2 first, as shown in Figure 4-2.

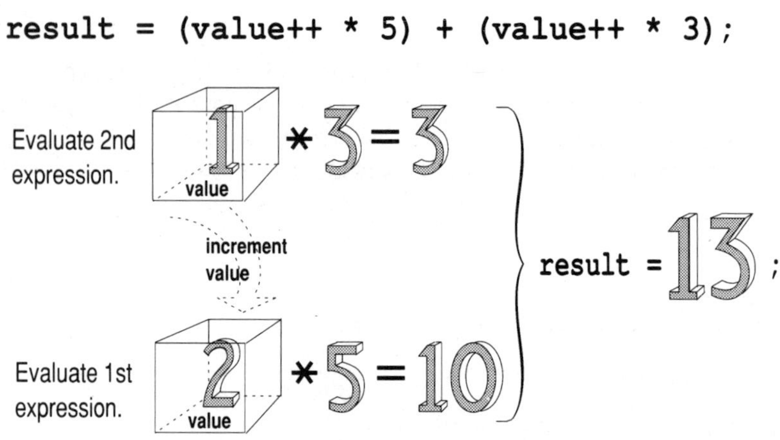

Figure 4-2. Expression Evaluation Method 2

By using the first method, we get a result of 11, and by using the second method, we get a result of 13. The result of this expression is ambiguous. By using the operator ++ in the middle of a larger expression, we created a problem. (This is not the only problem that ++ and -- can cause. We will get into more trouble in Chapter 9, *The C Preprocessor*.)

In order to avoid trouble and keep the program simple, always put ++ and -- on a line by themselves.

Answers

Answer 4–1: The function **strcat** takes two strings as its arguments. In the statement **strcat(full, ' ')**, the first argument, **full**, is a string; the second, **' '**, is a character. Using a character instead of a string is illegal. C does not type check parameters, so this error gets by the compiler. The character **' '** should be replaced by the string " ".

Answer 4–2: The problem is the use of the expression **array[x,y]** in the **printf** statement:

```
(void)printf("%d ", array[x,y]);
```

Each index to a multi-dimension array must be placed inside its own set of square brackets ([]). The statement should read:

```
(void)printf("%d ", array[x][y]);
```

For those of you who want to read ahead a little, the comma operator can be used to string multiple expressions together, the value of this operator is the value of the last expressions. So **x,y** is equivalent to **y** and **array[y]** is actually a pointer to row y of the array. Since pointers have strange values, the **printf** outputs strange results. (See Chapter 16, *Advanced Pointers*, and Chapter 19, *C's Dustier Corners*.)

Answer 4–3: The programmer accidentally omitted the end comment (*/) after the comment for height. The comment continues onto the next line and engulfs the declaration, as shown in Figure 4-3.

```
int height;          /* the height of the triangle
int width;           /*the width of the triangle*/
int area;            /*area of the triangle (computed) */

main()  {
    (void)printf("Enter width height? ");
    (void)scanf("%d %d", &width, &height);
    area = (width * height) / 2;
    (void)printf("The area is %d\n", area);
}
```

Figure 4-3. Comment Answer

Programming Exercises

Exercise 1: Write a program that converts Centigrade to Fahrenheit.

$$F = \frac{9}{5}C + 32$$

Exercise 2: Write a program to calculate the volume of a sphere.

$$\frac{4}{3}r^3$$

Exercise 3: Write a program to print out the perimeter of a rectangle given its height and width.

$$perimeter = 2 \times (width + height)$$

Exercise 4: Write a program that converts miles per hour to kilometers per hour.

$$miles = kilometers \times 0.6213712$$

Exercise 5: Write a program that takes hours and minutes as input and outputs the total number of minutes. (1 hour 30 minutes = 90 minutes).

Exercise 6: Write a program that takes an integer as the number of minutes and outputs the total hours and minutes (90 minutes = 1 hour 30 minutes).

5

Decision and Control Statements

Once a decision was made, I did not worry about it afterward.

—Harry Truman

Calculations and expressions are only a small part of computer programming. Decision and control statements are needed. They specify the order in which statements are to be executed.

So far, we have constructed *linear programs*, that is, programs that execute in a straight line, one statement after another. In this chapter we will see how to change the *control flow* of a program with *branching statements* and *looping statements*. Branching statements cause one section of code to be executed or not depending on a *conditional clause*. Looping statements are used to repeat a section of code a number of times or until some condition occurs.

if Statement

The **if** statement allows us to put some decision-making into our programs. The general form of the **if** statement is:

> if **(** *condition* **)**
>   *statement* **;**

If the expression is true (nonzero), the statement will be executed. If the expression is false (0), the statement will not be executed. For example, suppose we are writing a billing program. At the end if the customer owes us nothing or has a credit (owes us a negative amount), we want to print a message. In C this is written:

```
if (total_owed <= 0)
    (void)printf("You owe nothing.\n);
```

The operator <= is a relational operator that represents *less than or equal to.* This statement reads "if the `total_owed` is less than or equal to zero, print the message." The complete list of relational operators is found in Table 5-1.

Table 5-1. Relational Operators

Operator	Meaning
<=	Less than or equal to
<	Less than
>	Greater than
>=	Greater than or equal to
==	Equal
!=	Not equal

Multiple statements may be grouped by putting them inside curly braces ({}). For example:

```
if (total_owed <= 0) {
    zero_count++;
    (void)printf("You owe nothing.\n");
}
```

For readability, the statements enclosed in {} are usually indented. This allows the programmer to quickly tell which statements are to be conditionally executed. As we will see later, mistakes in indentation can result in programs that are misleading and hard to read.

else Statement

An alternate form of the **if** statement is:

```
if (condition)
    statement;
else
    statement;
```

If the condition is true (nonzero), the first statement is executed. If it is false (0), the second statement is executed. In our accounting example, we only wrote out a message if nothing was owed. In real life we probably would want to tell the customer how much is owed if there is a balance due.

```
if (total_owed <= 0)
    (void)printf("You owe nothing.\n");
else
    (void)printf("You owe %d dollars\n", total_owed);
```

Note to PASCAL programmers: unlike PASCAL, C requires you to put a semicolon at the end of the statement preceding **else**.

Now consider this program fragment:

```
if (count < 10)       /* if #1 */
if ((count % 4) == 2)    /* if #2 */
    (void)printf("Condition:White\n");
else
    (void)printf("Condition:Tan\n");
```

There are two **if** statements and one **else**. Which **if** does the **else** belong to?

a) It belongs to **if** #1.

b) It belongs to **if** #2.

c) Don't worry about this situation if you never write code like this.

The correct answer is "c." According to the C syntax rules, the **else** goes with the nearest **if**, so "b" is syntactically correct. But writing code like this violates the KISS principle (Keep It Simple, Stupid). It is best to write our code as clearly and simply as possible. This code fragment should be written as:

```
if (count < 10) {          /* if #1 */
    if ((count % 4) == 2)    /* if #2 */
        (void)printf("Condition:White\n");
    else
        (void)printf("Condition:Tan\n");
}
```

From our original example, it was not clear which **if** statement had the **else** clause; however, by adding an extra set of braces, we improve readability, understanding, and clarity.

How Not to Use strcmp

The function **strcmp** compares two strings and returns zero if they are equal and nonzero if they are different. To check if two strings are equal, we use the code:

```
/* Check for Equal */
if (strcmp(string1, string2) == 0)
    (void)printf("Strings equal\n");
else
    (void)printf("Strings not equal\n");
```

Some programmers omit the comment and the `== 0` clause, leading to the following, confusing code:

```
if (strcmp(string1, string2))
    (void)printf("......");
```

At first glance, this program obviously compares two strings and executes the **printf** statement if they are equal. Unfortunately, the obvious is wrong. If the strings are equal, **strcmp** returns 0, and the **printf** is not executed. Because of this backward behavior of **strcmp**, you should be very careful in your use of **strcmp** and always comment its use.

Looping Statements

Looping statements allow the program to repeat a section of code any number of times or until some condition occurs. For example, loops are used to count the number of words in a document or to count the number of accounts that have past-due balances.

while Statement

The **while** statement is used when the program needs to perform repetitive tasks. The general form of a **while** statement is:

```
while (condition)
    statement;
```

The program will repeatedly execute the statement inside the **while** until the condition becomes false (0). (If the condition is initially false, the statement will not be executed.)

For example, Program 5-1 will compute all the Fibonacci numbers that are less than 100. The Fibonacci sequence is:

```
1 1 2 3 5 8
```

The terms are computed from the equations:

```
1
1
2 = 1 + 1
3 = 1 + 2
5 = 2 + 3
etc.
```

In general terms this is:

$$f_n = f_{n-1} + f_{n-2}$$

This is a mathematical equation using mathematical variable names (f_n). Mathematicians use this very terse style of naming variables. In programming, terse is dangerous so we translate these names into something verbose for C:

f_n	=>	`next_number`
f_{n-1}	=>	`current_number`
f_{n-2}	=>	`old_number`

In C code, the equation is expressed as:

```
next_number = current_number + old_number;
```

We want to loop until our current term is 100 or larger. The **while** loop:

```
while (current_number < 100)
```

will repeat our computation and printing until we reach this limit.

In our **while** loop, we compute the value of `current_number` and print it. Next we need to advance one term, as shown in Figure 5-1. Then we go through the loop again and advance another term as shown in Figure 5-2. We continue going through the loop until `current_number` is greater than or equal to 100.

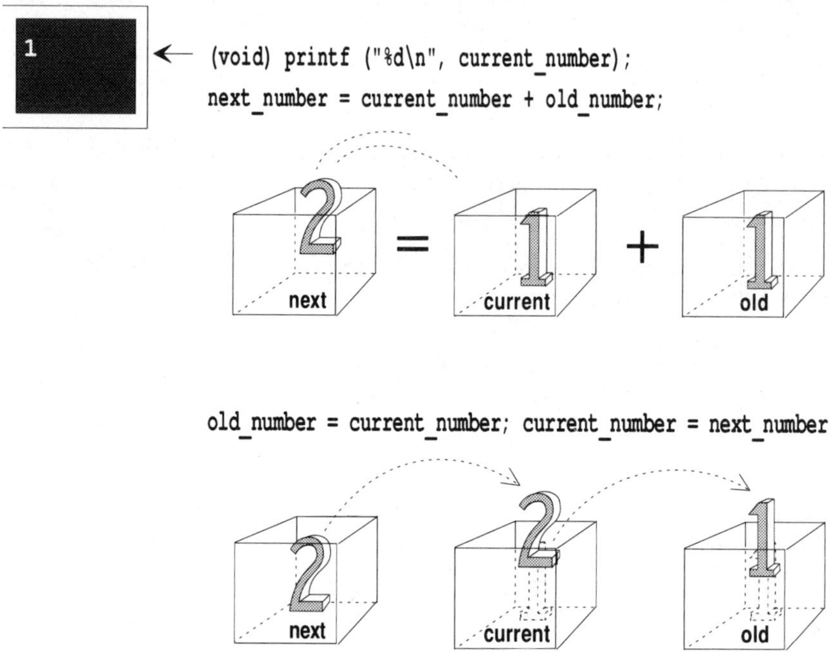

Figure 5-1. Advancing One Term

This completes the body of the loop. The first two terms of the Fibonacci sequence are 1 and 1. We initialize our first two terms to these values. Putting it all together, we get the code in Program 5-1.

Program 5-1.

```
#include <stdio.h>
int   old_number;     /* previous Fibonacci number */

int   current_number; /* current Fibonacci number */

int   next_number;    /* next number in the series */

main()
{
    /* start things out */
    old_number = 1;
    current_number = 1;
```

```
    (void)printf("1\n");     /* Print first number */

    while (current_number < 100) {

        (void) printf("%d\n", current_number);
        next_number = current_number + old_number;

        old_number = current_number;
        current_number = next_number;
    }
    return (0);
}
```

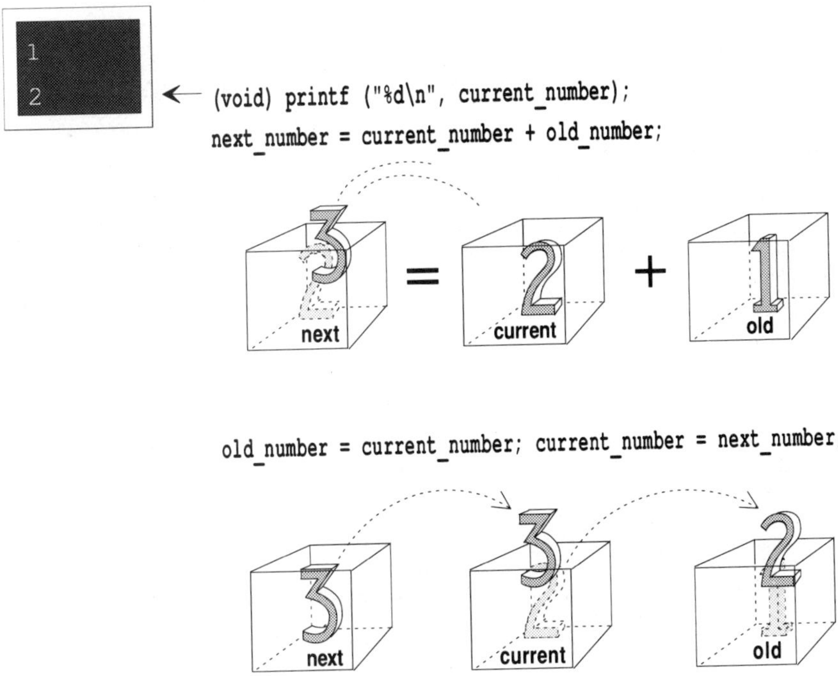

Figure 5-2. Advancing Another Term

break Statement

We have used a **while** statement to compute the Fibonacci numbers less than 100. The loop exits when the condition at the beginning becomes false (0). Loops can be exited at any point through the use of a **break** statement.

Suppose we want to add a series of numbers, but we don't know how many numbers are to be added together. We need some way of letting the program know we have reached the end of our list. In Program 5-2 we use the number zero (0) to signal the end of list.

Note that the **while** statement begins with:

```
while (1) {
```

The program will loop forever because the **while** will exit only when the expression 1 is 0. The only way to exit this loop is through a **break** statement.

When we see the end of the list indicator (0), we use the statement:

```
if (item == 0)
        break;
```

to exit the loop.

Program 5-2.

```
#include <stdio.h>
char  line[100];/* line of data for input */

/* Running total of all numbers so far */
int   total;

/* next item to add to the list */
int   item;

main()
{
    total = 0;
    while (1) {
        (void) printf("Enter # to add \n");
        (void) printf("  or 0 to stop:");
        (void) fgets(line, sizeof(line), stdin);
        (void) sscanf(line, "%d", &item);
        if (item == 0)
            break;
        total += item;
        (void) printf("Total: %d\n", total);
    }
    (void) printf("Final total %d\n", total);
    return (0);
}
```

continue Statement

The **continue** statement is very similar to the **break** statement, except that instead of terminating the loop, it starts executing the body of the loop over from the top. For example, if we want to modify the previous program to total only numbers larger than 0, we could write a program such as Program 5-3.

Program 5-3.

```
#include <stdio.h>
char  line[100];    /* line from input */

/* Running total of all numbers so far */
int   total;

/* next item to add to the list */
int   item;

/* number of negative items */
int   minus_items;

main()
{
    total = 0;
    minus_items = 0;
    while (1) {
        (void) printf("Enter # to add\n");
        (void) printf("  or 0 to stop:");
        (void) fgets(line, sizeof(line), stdin);
        (void) sscanf(line, "%d", &item);

        if (item == 0)
            break;

        if (item < 0) {
            minus_items++;
            continue;
        }
        total += item;
        (void) printf("Total: %d\n", total);
    }

    (void) printf("Final total %d\n", total);
    (void) printf("with %d negative items omitted\n",
                  minus_items);
    return (0);
}
```

The Assignment Anywhere Side Effect

C allows the use of assignment statements almost any place. For example, you can put assignment statements inside another assignment statement:

```
/* don't program like this */
average = total_value / (number_of_entries = last - first);
```

This is the equivalent of saying:

```
/* program like this */
number_of_entries = last - first;
average = total_value / number_of_entries;
```

The first version buries the assignment of `number_of_entries` inside the expression. Programs should be clear and simple and should not hide anything. The most important rule of programming is *keep it simple.*

C also allows the programmer to put assignment statements in the **while** conditional. For example:

```
/* do not program like this */
while ((current_number = last_number + old_number) < 100)
    (void)printf("Term %d\n", current_number);
```

Avoid this type of programming. Notice how much clearer the logic is in the following version:

```
/* program like this */
while (1) {
    current_number = last_number + old_number;
    if (current_number >= 100)
        break;
    (void)printf("Term %d\n", current_number);
}
```

Question 5–1: For some strange reason, this program thinks that everyone owes a balance of 0 dollars. Why?

```
#include <stdio.h>
char  line[80];          /* input line */
int   balance_owed;      /* amount owed */

main()
{
    (void) printf("Enter number of dollars owed:");
    (void) fgets(line, sizeof(line), stdin);
    (void) sscanf(line, "%d", &balance_owed);

    if (balance_owed = 0)
        (void) printf("You owe nothing.\n");
    else
```

```
        (void) printf("You owe %d dollars.\n",
                      balance_owed);

    return (0);
}
```

Sample output:

```
Enter number of dollars owed: 12
You owe 0 dollars.
```

(Your results may vary.)

Answers

Answer 5–1: This program illustrates one of the most common and frustrating of C errors. The problem is that C allows assignment statements inside **if** conditionals. The statement:

```
if (balance_owed = 0)
```

uses a single equal sign (=) instead of the double equal sign (==). C will assign `balance_owed` the value 0 and test the result (which is 0). If it were nonzero (true), the **if** clause would be executed. Since it is 0 (false), the **else** clause is executed and the program prints the wrong answer.

The statement:

```
if (balance_owed = 0)
```

is equivalent to:

```
balance_owed = 0;
if (balanced_owed != 0)
```

The statement should be written:

```
if (balance_owed == 0)
```

This is the most common error beginning programmers make.

Programming Problems

Exercise 1: Write a program to find the distance between two points.

Exercise 2: A professor generates letter grades using the following table:

% Right	Grade
0-60	F
61-70	D
71-80	C
81-90	B
91-100	A

Given a numeric grade, print the letter.

Exercise 3: Modify the previous program to print out a + or – after the letter grade based on the last digit of the score.

Last Digit	Modifier
1-3	–
4-7	<blank>
8-0	+

For example 81=B–, 94=A, 68=D+. An F is only an F; there is no F+ or F–.

NOTE

Programmers frequently have to modify code that someone else wrote. A good exercise is to take someone else's, such as the program someone wrote for Exercise 2, and modify it.

Exercise 4: Given an amount (less than $1.00), compute the number of quarters, dimes, nickels, and pennies needed.

Exercise 5: A leap year is any year divisible by 4 unless it is divisible by 100, but not 400. Write a program to tell if a year is a leap year.

Exercise 6: Write a program that, given the number of hours an employee worked and the hourly wage, computes the employee's weekly pay. Count any hours over 40 as overtime at time and a half.

6

The Programming Process

It's just a simple matter of programming.

—Any boss who has never written a program

Programming is more than just writing code. Software has a life cycle. It is born, grows up, becomes mature, and finally dies, only to be replaced by a newer, younger product. Figure 6-1 illustrates the life cycle of a program. Understanding this cycle is important because as a programmer you will spend only a small amount of time writing new code. Most programming time is spent modifying and debugging existing code. Software does not exist in a vacuum; it must be documented, maintained, enhanced, and sold. In this section we will take a look at a small programming project using one programmer. Larger projects that involve many people will be discussed in Chapter 17, *Modular Programming*. Although our final code is less than a hundred lines, the principles used in its construction can be applied to programs with thousands of lines of code.

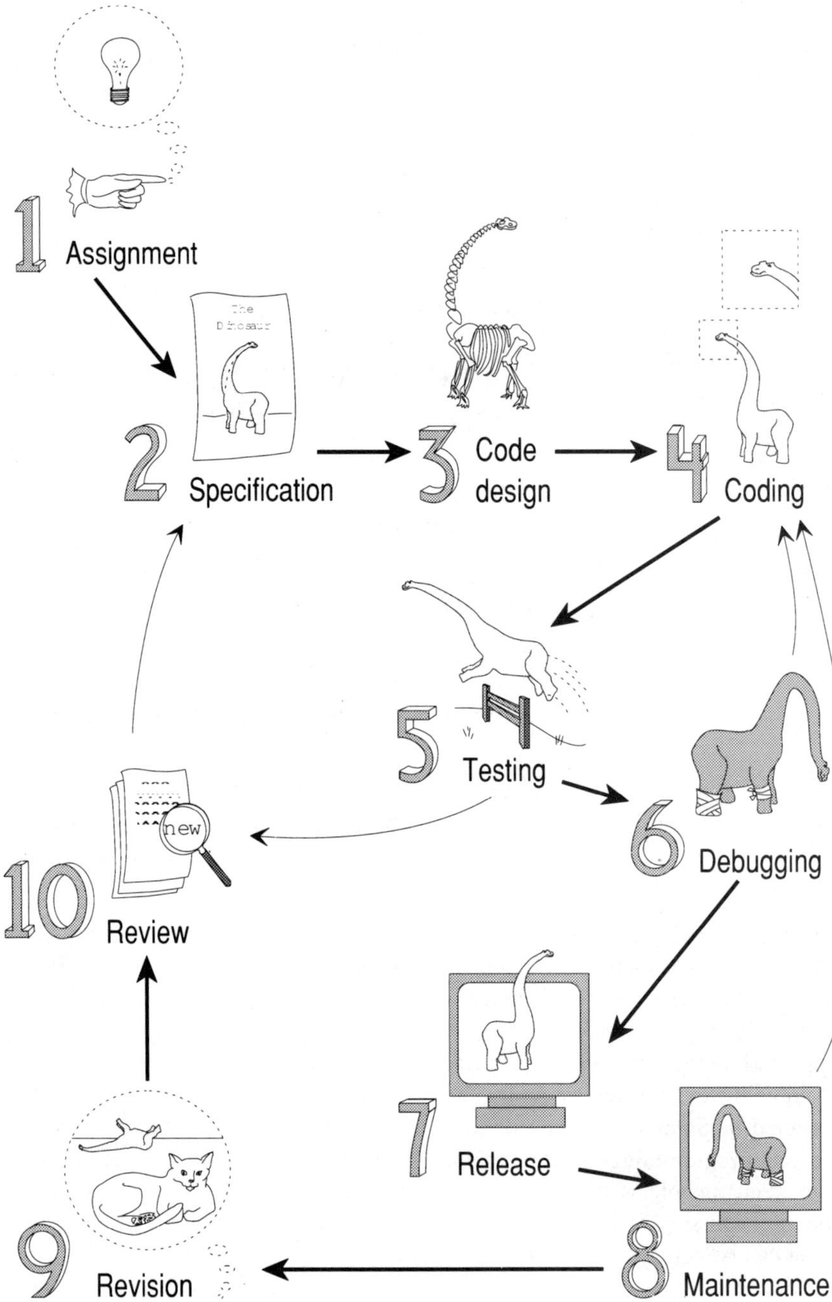

Figure 6-1. Software Life Cycle

The major steps in making a program are:

- **Requirements.** Programs start when someone gets an idea and starts to implement it. The requirement document describes, in very general terms, what is wanted.
- **Specification program.** A description of what the program does. In the beginning, a *preliminary specification* is used to describe what the program is going to do. Later as the program becomes more refined, so does the specification. Finally, when the program is finished, the specification serves as complete description of what the program does.
- **Code design.** The programmer does an overall design of the program. The design should include major algorithms, module definitions, file formats, and data structures.
- **Coding.** The next step is writing the program. This involves first writing a prototype and then filling it in to create the full program.
- **Testing.** The programmer should design a test plan and use it to test his program. It is a good idea, when possible, to have someone else test the program.
- **Debugging.** Unfortunately, very few programs work the first time. They must be corrected and tested again.
- **Release.** The program is packaged, documented, and sent out into the world to be used.
- **Maintenance.** Programs are never perfect. Bugs will be found and will need correction. This is the maintenance phase of programming.
- **Revision and updating.** After a program has been working for a while, the users will want changes, such as more features or more intelligent algorithms. At this point a new specification is created and the process starts again.

Setting Up

The operating system allows you to group files in directories. Just as file folders serve as a way of keeping papers together in a filing cabinet, directories serve as a way of keeping files together. In this chapter we will be creating a simple calculator program. All the files for this program will be stored in a directory named *calc*. In UNIX, we create a new directory off of our home directory and then move to it, as shown in the following example:

```
% cd ~
% mkdir calc
% cd ~/calc
```

On MS-DOS type:

```
C:\> cd \
C:\> mkdir calc
C:\> cd \calc
C:\CALC>
```

More information on how to organize directories can be found in your operating system manual.

The Specification

For this chapter we assume that we have an assignment to "write a program that acts like a four-function calculator." Typically, the specification that you are given is vague and incomplete. It is up to the programmer to refine it into something that exactly defines the program that he is going to produce. So the first step is to write a preliminary users' specification document which describes what your program is going to do and how to use it. It does not describe the internal structure of the program or the algorithm you plan on using. A sample specification for our four-function calculator appears in the inset entitled "Calc" on the following page.

The preliminary specification serves two purposes. First, you should give it to your boss (or customer) to make sure that you agree on what each of you said. Second, you can circulate it among your colleagues and see if they have any suggestions or corrections.

This preliminary specification was circulated and received the comments:

1. How are you going to get out of the program?

2. What happens when you try to divide by 0?

Calc
A Four-function Calculator
Preliminary Specification
Dec 10, 1989
Steve Oualline

Warning: This is a preliminary specification. Any resemblance to any software living or dead is purely coincidental.

Calc is a program that allows the user to turn a $10,000 computer into a $1.98 four-function calculator. The program will add, subtract, multiply, and divide simple integers.

When the program is run, it will zero the result register and display its contents. The user can then type in an operator and number. The result will be updated and displayed. The following operators are valid:

Operator	Meaning
+	Addition
–	Subtraction
*	Multiplication
/	Division

For example: (user input is in bold face)

```
calc
Result:  0
Enter operator and number:  + 123
Result:  123
Enter operator and number:  - 23
Result:  100
Enter operator and number:  / 25
Result:  4
Enter operator and number:  * 4
Result:  16
```

So, we add a new operator, **q** for quit, and we add the statement:

> "Dividing by 0 results in an error message and the result register is left unchanged."

IV + IX = XIII?

A college instructor once gave his students an assignment to "write a four-function calculator." One of his students noticed that this was a pretty loose specification and decided to have a little fun. The professor didn't say what sort of numbers had to be used, so the student created a program that worked only with Roman numerals (IV + III = VII). The program came with a complete user manual—written in Latin.

Code Design

After the preliminary specification has been approved, we can start designing code. In the code design phase, the programmer plans his work. In large programming projects involving many people, the code would be broken up into modules for each programmer. At this stage, file formats are planned, data structures are designed, and major algorithms decided upon.

Our simple calculator uses no files and requires no fancy data structures. What's left for this phase is to design the major algorithm. Outlined in pseudo-code, a shorthand halfway between English and real code, is:

```
Loop
  Read an operator and number
  Do the calculation
  Display the result
End-Loop
```

The Prototype

Once the code design is completed, we can begin writing the program. But rather than try to write the entire program at once and then debug it, we will use a method called *fast prototyping*. We implement the smallest portion of the specification that will still do something. In our case, we will cut our four functions down to a one-function calculator. Once we get this small part working, we can build the rest of the functions onto this stable foundation. Also, the prototype gives the boss something to look at and play with, giving him a good idea of the project's direction. Good communication is the key to good programming and the more you can show someone the better. The code for the first version of our four-function calculator is found in Program 6-1.

Program 6-1.

```
#include <stdio.h>
char  line[100];/* line of data from the input */

int   result;   /* the result of the calculations */
char  operator; /* operator the user specified */
int   value;    /* value specified after the operator */
main()
{
    result = 0; /* initialize the result */

    /* Loop forever (or till we hit the break statement) */
    while (1) {
        (void) printf("Result: %d\n", result);

        (void) printf("Enter operator and number: ");
        (void) fgets(line, sizeof(line), stdin);
        (void) sscanf(line, "%c %d", &operator, &value);

        if (operator = '+') {
            result += value;
        } else {
            (void) printf("Unknown operator %c\n", operator);
        }
    }
}
```

The program begins by initializing the variable `result` to 0. The main body of the program is a loop starting with:

```
while (1) {
```

This will loop until a **break** statement is reached. The code:

```
(void) printf("Enter operator and number: ");
(void) fgets(line, sizeof(line), stdin);
(void) sscanf(line,"%c %d", &operator, &value);
```

asks the user for an operator and number. These are scanned and stored in the variables `operator` and `value`. Finally, we start checking the operators. If the operator is a plus sign (+), we perform an addition using the line:

```
if (operator = '+') {
    result += value;
```

So far we only recognize the plus (+) operator. As soon as this works, we will add more operators by adding more **if** statements.

Finally, if an illegal operator is entered, the line:

```
} else {
     (void) printf("Unknown operator %c\n", operator);
}
```

will write an error message telling the user he made a mistake.

The Makefile

Once the source has been entered, it needs to be compiled and linked. Up until now we have been running the compiler manually. This is somewhat tedious and prone to error. Also, larger programs consist of many modules and are extremely difficult to compile by hand. Fortunately, both UNIX and Turbo C have a utility called **make** that will handle the details of compilation. For now, use this example as a template and substitute the name of your program in place of "**calc**." **make** will be discussed in detail in Chapter 17, *Modular Programming*. The program looks at the file called *Makefile* for a description of how to compile your program and runs the compiler for you. For a UNIX system the *Makefile* should be:

```
#
# Makefile for the program calc
#
# Turn on debugging
CFLAGS=-g
calc:calc.o
    $(CC) $(CFLAGS) -o calc calc.o
lint:
    lint -hx calc.c
    $(CC) $(CFLAGS) -c $@
```

NOTE

Programmers using SYSTEM V UNIX should use the **lint** line:

```
lint -x calc.c
```

because on SYSTEM V UNIX the meaning of **–h** is the exact opposite of that of BSD UNIX.

For Turbo C, the *Makefile* should be:

```
#
# Turn on debugging, all warnings, ANSI mode
#       and set model to large
#
CFLAGS=-g -w -A -ml
```

```
CC=tcc
calc1.exe: calc1.obj
        $(CC) $(CFLAGS) -ocalc1.exe calc1.obj

calc1.obj: calc1.c
        $(CC) $(CFLAGS) -c calc1.c
```

To compile the program, just execute the **make** command. **make** will determine what compilation commands are needed and execute them.

make uses the modification dates of the files to determine whether or not a compile is necessary. Compilation creates an object file. The modification date of the object file is later than the modification date of its source. If the source is edited, its modification date is updated, making the object file out of date. **make** checks these dates, and if the source was modified after the object, it recompiles the object. (Note to MS-DOS users: if your system does not have an automatic clock, you must set the date for **make** to work properly.)

C will let you "get away" with an awful lot of strange programming practices such as not initializing variables, mixing up data types, and other strange things. Turbo C has lot of internal checks that are designed to catch common programming mistakes. On UNIX there is a separate program called `lint` that performs a similar function. To run `lint` on your program, enter the command:

```
% make lint
```

Your programs should be free of warnings and errors. `lint` should generate no error messages. Whenever possible, you should use all available tools to check your program for errors.

Testing

Once the program is compiled without errors, we can move on to the testing phase. Now is the time to start writing a test plan. This document is simply a list of the steps we perform to make sure the program works. It is written for two reasons:

- If a bug is found, we want to be able to reproduce it.
- If we ever change the program, we will want to retest it to make sure new code did not break any of the sections of the program that were previously working.

Our test plan starts out as:

```
Try the following operations:

+ 123  Result should be 123
+ 52   Result should be 175
x 37   Error message should be output
```

Running the program we get:

```
Result: 0
Enter operator and number: + 123
Result: 123
Enter operator and number: + 52
Result: 175
Enter operator and number: x 37
Result: 212
```

Something is clearly wrong. The entry **x 37** should have generated an error message, but it didn't. There is a bug in the program. So we begin the debugging phase. One of the advantages to making a small working prototype is that we can isolate errors early.

Debugging

First we inspect the program to see if we can detect the error. In such a small program it is not difficult to spot the mistake. However, let's assume that instead of a 21-line program, we have a much larger one containing 5,000 lines. Such a program would make inspection more difficult, so we need to proceed to the next step.

Most systems have C debugging programs; however, each system is different. Some systems have no debugger. In that case we must resort to a diagnostic print statement. The technique is simple: put a **printf** where you're sure the data is good (just to make sure it is *really* good). Then put a **printf** where the data is bad. Run the program and keep putting in **printf**s until you isolate the area in the program that contains the mistake. Our program, with diagnostic **printf**s added, looks like:

```
(void)printf("Enter operator and number: ");
(void)fgets(line, sizeof(line), stdin);
(void)sscanf("%d %c", &value, &operator);
(void)printf("## after scanf %c\n", operator);
if (operator = '+') {
    (void)printf("## after if %c\n", operator);
    result += value;
```

NOTE

The ## at the beginning of each `printf` is used to indicate a temporary debugging `printf`. When the debugging is complete, the ## makes the statements easy to identify and remove.

Running our program again results in:

```
Result: 0
Enter operator and number: + 123
Result: 123
Enter operator and number: + 52
## after scanf +
## after if +
Result: 175
Enter operator and number: x 37
## after scanf x
## after if +
Result: 212
```

From this we see that something is going wrong with the **if** statement. Somehow the variable operator is an "x" going in and a "+" coming out. Closer inspection reveals that we have the old mistake of using = instead of ==. After fixing this bug, the program runs correctly. Building on this working foundation, we add in the code for the other operators: dash (–), asterisk (*), and slash (/) to create Program 6-2.

Program 6-2.

```
#include <stdio.h>
char  line[100];/* line of text from input */

int   result;   /* the result of the calculations */
char  operator; /* operator the user specified */
int   value;    /* value specified after the operator */
main()
{
    result = 0; /* initialize the result */

    /* loop forever (or until break reached) */
    while (1) {
        (void) printf("Result: %d\n", result);
        (void) printf("Enter operator and number: ");

        (void) fgets(line, sizeof(line), stdin);
        (void) sscanf(line, "%c %d", &operator, &value);

        if ((operator == 'q') || (operator == 'Q'))
            break;
```

```
        if (operator == '+') {
            result += value;
        } else if (operator == '-') {
            result -= value;
        } else if (operator == '*') {
            result *= value;
        } else if (operator == '/') {
            if (value == 0) {
                (void)printf("Error:Divide by zero\n");
                (void)printf("    operation ignored\n");
            } else
                result /= value;
        } else {
            (void) printf("Unknown operator %c\n", operator);
        }
    }
    return (0);
}
```

We expand our test plan to include the new operators and try it again.

```
+ 123     Result should be 123
+ 52      Result should be 175
x 37      Error message should be output
- 175     Result should be zero
+ 10      Result should be 10
/ 5       Result should be 2
/ 0       Divide by zero error
* 8       Result should be 16
q         Program should exit
```

Testing the program, we find much to our surprise that it works. The word "Preliminary" is removed from the specification, and the program, test plan, and specification are released.

Maintenance

Good programmers put their programs through a long and rigorous testing process before releasing it to the outside world. Then the first user tries the program and almost immediately finds a bug. This is the maintenance phase. Bugs are fixed, the program is tested (to make sure that the fixes didn't break anything), and the program is released again.

Revisions

Although the program is officially finished, we are not done with it. After it is in use for a few months, someone will come to us and ask, "Can you add a modulus operator?" So we revise the specifications, add the change to the program, update the test plan, test the program, and release it again.

As time passes, more people will come to us with additional requests for changes. Soon our program has trig functions, linear regressions, statistics, binary arithmetic, and financial calculations. Our design is based on the idea of one-character operators. Soon we find ourselves running out of characters to use. At this point our program is doing work far in excess of what it was initially designed to do. Sooner or later we reach the point where the program needs to be scrapped and a new one written from scratch. At this point we write a preliminary specification and start the process over again.

Electronic Archaeology

Electronic archeology is the art of digging through old code to discover amazing things (like how and why the code works).

Unfortunately, most programmers don't start a project at the design step. Instead, they are immediately thrust into the maintenance or revision stage. This means that the programmer is now faced with the worst possible job: understanding and modifying someone else's code.

Your computer can aid greatly in your search to discover the true meaning of someone else's code. There are many tools available for examining and formatting code. Some of these include:

- **Cross references.** These programs have names like `xref`, `cxref`, and `cross`. SYSTEM V UNIX has the utility `cscope`. They print out a list of variables and where they are used.
- **Program indenters.** Programs like `cb` and `indent` will take a program and indent it *correctly* (correct indentation is something defined by the tool maker).
- **Pretty printers.** A pretty printer such as `vgrind` or `cprint` will take the source and typeset it for printing on a laser printer.

- **Call graphs.** On SYSTEM V UNIX the program **cflow** can be used to analyze the program. On other systems there is a public-domain utility, **calls**, which produces call graphs, showing who calls whom and who is called by whom.

Which tools should you use? Whichever work for you. Different programmers work in different ways. Some of the techniques for examining code are listed in the sections that follow. Choose the ones that work for you and use them.

Marking Up the Program

Take a printout of the program and make notes all over it. Use red or blue ink so that you can tell the difference between the printout and the notes. Use a highlighter to emphasize important sections. These notes are useful; put them in the program as comments, then make a new printout and start the process over again.

Using the Debugger

The debugger is a great tool for understanding how something works. Most debuggers allow the user to step through the program one line at a time, examining variables and discovering how things really work. Once you find out what the code does, make notes and put them in as comments.

Text Editor as a Browser

One of the best tools for going through someone else's code is your text editor. Suppose you want to find out what the variable **sc** is used for. Use the search command to find the first place **sc** is used. Search again and find the second time it is used. Continue searching until you know what the variable does.

Suppose you find out that **sc** is used as a sequence counter. Since you're already in the editor, you can easily do a global search and replace to change **sc** to **sequence_counter**. (Disaster warning: *Before* you make the change, make sure that **sequence_counter** is not already defined as a variable. Also watch out for unwanted replacements, such as changing the *sc* in "escape.") Comment the declaration and you're on your way to creating an understandable program.

Add Comments

Don't be afraid of putting any information you have, no matter how little, into the comments. Some of the comments I've used include:

```
int state;   /* Controls some sort of state machine */
int rmxy;    /* Something to do with color correction ? */
```

Finally, there is a catch-all comment:

```
int idn;     /* ??? */
```

which means "I have no idea what this variable does." Even though the purpose is unknown, it is now marked as something that needs more work.

As you go through someone else's code adding comments and improving style, the structure will become clearer to you. By inserting notes (comments), you make the code better and easier to understand for future programmers.

For example, suppose we are confronted with the following program written by someone from "The-Terser-the-Better" school of programming. Our assignment is to figure out what this code does. First we pencil in some comments, as shown in Figure 6-2.

NOTE

> We use ANSI C throughout this book. The line `#include <stdlib.h>` may not work on older UNIX compilers and may need to be omitted.

Our mystery program requires some work. After going through it and applying the principles described in this section, we get a well-commented, easy-to-understand program, such as Program 6-3.

```
#include <stdio.h>
#include <stdlib.h>
int   g, l, h, c, n;
char  line[80];
main()
{
    while (1) {
        /*Not Really*/
        g = rand() % 100 + 1;
        l = 0;
        h = 100;
        c = 0;
        while (1) {
            (void) printf("Bounds %d - %d\n", l, h);
            (void) printf("Value[%d]? ", c);
            c++;
            (void) fgets(line, sizeof(line), stdin);
            (void) sscanf(line, "%d", &n);
            if (n == g)
                break;
            if (n < g)
                l = n;
            else
                h = n;
        }
        (void) printf("Bingo\n");
    }
    return (0);
}
```


Figure 6-2. A Terse Program

Program 6-3.

```
/********************************************************
 * guess -- a simple guessing game                      *
 *                                                      *
 * Usage:                                               *
 *      guess                                           *
 *                                                      *
 *      A random number is chosen between 1 and 100.    *
 *      The player is given a set of bounds and         *
 *      must choose a number between them.              *
 *      If the player chooses the correct number he wins*
 *      Otherwise the bounds are adjusted to reflect    *
 *      the player's guess and the game continues.      *
 *                                                      *
```

```
 *                                                      *
 * Restrictions:                                        *
 *      The random number is generated by the statement *
 *      rand() % 100.  Because rand() returns a number  *
 *      0 <= rand() <= maxint  this slightly favors     *
 *      the lower numbers.                              *
 ********************************************************/
#include <stdio.h>
#include <stdlib.h>     /* ANSI Standard only */
int   number_to_guess;  /* random number to be guessed */
int   low_limit;        /* current lower limit of player's range */
int   high_limit;       /* current upper limit of player's range */
int   guess_count;      /* number of times player guessed */
int   player_number;    /* number gotten from the player */
char  line[80];         /* input buffer for a single line */
main()
{
    while (1) {
        /*
         * Not a pure random number, see restrictions
         */
        number_to_guess = rand() % 100 + 1;

        /* Initialize variables for loop */
        low_limit = 0;
        high_limit = 100;
        guess_count = 0;

        while (1) {
            /* tell user what the bounds are and get his guess */
            (void) printf("Bounds %d - %d\n", low_limit, high_limit);
            (void) printf("Value[%d]? ", guess_count);

            guess_count++;

            (void) fgets(line, sizeof(line), stdin);
            (void) sscanf(line, "%d", &player_number);

            /* did he guess right? */
            if (player_number == number_to_guess)
                break;

            /* adjust bounds for next guess */
            if (player_number < number_to_guess)
                low_limit = player_number;
            else
                high_limit = player_number;

        }
        (void) printf("Bingo\n");
    }
    return (0);
}
```

Programming Exercises

For each of these assignments, follow the software life cycle from specification through release.

Exercise 1: Write a program to convert English units to metric (i.e., miles to kilometers, gallons to liters, etc.). Include a specification and a code design.

Exercise 2: Write a program to perform date arithmetic such as how many days there are between 6/1/90 and 8/3/92. Include a specification and a code design.

Exercise 3: A serial transmission line can transmit 960 characters a second. Write a program that will calculate how long it will take to send a file, given its size. Try it on a 400MB (419,430,400-byte) file. Use appropriate units. (A 400MB file takes days.)

Exercise 4: Write a program to add an 8% sales tax to a given amount and round the result to the nearest penny.

Exercise 5: Write a program to tell if a number is prime.

Exercise 6: Write a program that takes a series of numbers and counts the number of positive and negative values.

7

More Control Statements

for Statement
switch Statement
switch, break, and continue

Grammar, which knows how to control even kings . . .
—Molière

for Statement

The **for** statement allows the programmer to execute a block of code for a specified number of times. The general form of the **for** statement is:

for **(** *initial-statement* **;** *condition* **;** *iteration-statement* **)**
    body-statement **;**

This is equivalent to:

> *initial-statement* **;**
> while **(** *condition* **)** **{**
>   *body-statement* **;**
>   *iteration-statement* **;**
> **}**

For example, Program 7-1 uses a **while** loop to add five numbers.

Program 7-1.

```
#include <stdio.h>

int total;      /* total of all the numbers */
int current;    /* current value from the user */
int counter;    /* while loop counter */

char line[80];  /* Line from keyboard */

main() {
    total = 0;

    counter = 0;
    while (counter < 5) {
        (void)printf("Number? ");

        (void)fgets(line, sizeof(line), stdin);
        (void)sscanf(line, "%d", &current);
        total += current;

        counter++;
    }
    (void)printf("The grand total is %d\n", total);
    return (0);
}
```

The same program can be rewritten using a **for** statement as shown in Program 7-2.

Program 7-2.

```
#include <stdio.h>

int total;      /* total of all the numbers */
int current;    /* current value from the user */
int counter;    /* for loop counter */

char line[80];  /* Input from keyboard */

main() {
    total = 0;
```

```
    for (counter = 0; counter < 5; counter++) {
        (void)printf("Number? ");

        (void)fgets(line, sizeof(line), stdin);
        (void)sscanf(line, "%d", &current);
        total += current;
    }
    (void)printf("The grand total is %d\n", total);
    return (0);
}
```

Note that **counter** goes from 0 to 4. Ordinarily you count five items as 1, 2, 3, 4, 5, but you will get along much better in C if you change your thinking to zero-based counting and count five items as 0, 1, 2, 3, 4. (One-based counting is one of the main causes of array overflow errors. See Chapter 4, *Arrays, Qualifiers, and Reading Numbers*.)

Many older programming languages do not allow you to change the control variable (in this case, **counter**) inside the loop. C is not so picky. You can change the control variable any time you wish—you can jump into and out of the loop and generally do things that would make a PASCAL or FORTRAN programmer cringe. (Even though C gives you the freedom to do such insane things, that doesn't mean you should do them.)

Question 7–1: When the following program is run, it prints out:

```
Celsius:101 Fahrenheit:213
```

and nothing more. Why?

```
#include <stdio.h>
/*
 * This program produces a Celsius to Fahrenheit conversion
 *    chart for the numbers 0 to 100.
 */

/* the current Celsius temperature we are working with */
int celsius;
main() {
    for (celsius = 0; celsius <= 100; celsius++);
        (void)printf("celsius:%d Fahrenheit:%d\n",
            celsius, (celsius * 9) / 5 + 32);
    return (0);
}
```

Question 7-2: The following program reads a list of five numbers and counts the number of 3's and 7's in the data. Why does it give us the wrong answers?

```
#include <stdio.h>
char line[100];         /* line of input */
int seven_count;        /* number of sevens in the data */
int data[5];            /* the data to count 3 and 7 in */
int three_count;        /* the number of threes in the data */
int index;              /* index into the data */

main() {

    seven_count = 0;
    three_count = 0;
    (void)printf("Enter 5 numbers\n");
    (void)fgets(line, sizeof(line), stdin);
    (void)sscanf(line, "%d %d %d %d %d",
        &data[1], &data[2], &data[3],
        &data[4], &data[5]);

    for (index = 1; index <= 5; index++) {

        if (data[index] == 3)
            three_count++;

        if (data[index] == 7)
            seven_count++;
    }
    (void)printf("Threes %d Sevens %d\n",
            three_count, seven_count);
    return (0);
}
```

When we run this program with the data 3 7 3 0 2, the results are:

```
Threes 4 Sevens 1
```

(Your results may vary.)

switch Statement

The **switch** statement is similar to a chain of **if/else** statements. The general form of a **switch** statement is:

```
switch ( expression ) {
      case constant1 :
            statement
   . . . .
            break
   case constant2 :
            statement
   . . . .
            /* Fall through */
      default :
            statement
   . . . .
            break
   case constant3 :
            statement
   . . . .
            /* Fall through */
}
```

The **switch** statement evaluates the value of an expression and branches to one of the case labels. Duplicate labels are not allowed, so only one case will be selected. The expression must evaluate an integer, character, or enumeration.

The **case** labels can be in any order and must be constants. The **default** label can be put anywhere in the **switch**. No two **case** labels can have the same value.

When C sees a **switch** statement, it evaluates the expression and then looks for a matching **case** label. If none is found, the **default** label is used. If no **default** is found, the statement does nothing.

NOTE

The **switch** statement is very similar to the PASCAL **case** statement. The main differences are that while PASCAL allows only one statement after the label, C allows many. C will keep executing until it hits a **break** statement. In PASCAL you can't fall through from one **case** to another, but in C you can.

Program 6-2 contains a series of **if/then/else** statements:

```
if (operator == '+') {
    result += value;
} else if (operator == '-') {
    result -= value;
} else if (operator == '*') {
    result *= value;
} else if (operator == '/') {
    if (value == 0) {
        (void) printf("Error:Divide by zero\n");
        (void) printf("   operation ignored\n");
    } else
        result /= value;
    } else {
        (void) printf("Unknown operator %c\n", operator);
    }
```

This section of code can easily be rewritten as a **switch** statement. In this **switch**, we use a different **case** for each operation. The **default** clause takes care of all the illegal operators.

Rewriting our program using a **switch** statement makes it not only simpler, but easier to read. Our revised `calc` program is shown as Program 7-3.

Program 7-3.

```
#include <stdio.h>
char  line[100];    /* line of text from input */

int   result;       /* the result of the calculations */
char  operator;     /* operator the user specified */
int   value;        /* value specified after the operator */
main()
{
    result = 0;     /* initialize the result */

    /* loop forever (or until break reached) */
    while (1) {
        (void) printf("Result: %d\n", result);
        (void) printf("Enter operator and number: ");

        (void) fgets(line, sizeof(line), stdin);
        (void) sscanf(line, "%c %d", &operator, &value);

        if ((operator == 'q') || (operator == 'Q'))
            break;
```

```
        switch (operator) {
        case '+':
            result += value;
            break;
        case '-':
            result -= value;
            break;
        case '*':
            result *= value;
            break;
        case '/':
            if (value == 0) {
                (void)printf("Error:Divide by zero\n");
                (void)printf("   operation ignored\n");
            } else
                result /= value;
            break;
        default:
            (void) printf("Unknown operator %c\n", operator);
            break;
        }
    }
    return (0);
}
```

A **break** statement inside a **switch** tells the computer to continue execution after the **switch**. If it is not there, execution will continue with the next statement.

For example:

```
control = 0;
/* a not so good example of programming */
switch (control) {
        case 0:
                (void) printf("Reset\n");
        case 1:
                (void) printf("Initializing\n");
                break;
        case 2:
                (void) printf("Working\n");
}
```

In this case, when `control == 0`, the program will print:

```
Reset
Initializing
```

case 0 does not end with a **break** statement. After printing **Reset**, the program falls through to the next statement (**case 1**) and prints **Initializing**.

But there is a problem with this syntax. It is not clear whether the program is supposed to fall through from **case 0** to **case 1** or if the programmer forgot to put in a **break** statement. In order to clear up this confusion, a **case** section should always end with a **break** statement or the comment **/* Fall through */**, as shown in the following example:

```
/* a better example of programming */
switch (control) {
        case 0:
                (void) printf("Reset\n");
                /* Fall through */
        case 1:
                (void) printf("Initializing\n");
                break;
        case 2:
                (void) printf("Working\n");
}
```

Because **case 2** is last, it doesn't need a **break** statement. A **break** would cause the program to skip to the end of the **switch**, and we're already there.

But suppose we modify the program slightly and add another **case** to the **switch**:

```
/* We have a little problem */
switch (control) {
        case 0:
                (void) printf("Reset\n");
                /* Fall through */
        case 1:
                (void) printf("Initializing\n");
                break;
        case 2:
                (void) printf("Working\n");
        case 3:
                (void) printf("Closing down\n");
}
```

Now when **control == 2**, the program prints:

```
Working
Closing down
```

This is an unpleasant surprise. The problem is caused by the fact that `case 2` is no longer the last **case**. We fall through. (Unintentionally or otherwise, we would have included a `/* Fall through */` comment.) A **break** is now necessary. If we always put in a **break** statement, we don't have to worry about whether or not it is really needed.

```
/* Almost there */
switch (control) {
        case 0:
                (void) printf("Reset\n");
                /* Fall through */
        case 1:
                (void) printf("Initializing\n");
                break;
        case 2:
                (void) printf("Working\n");
                break;
}
```

Finally, we ask the question: what happens when `control == 5`? In this case, since there is no matching **case** or a default clause, the entire **switch** statement is skipped.

In this example, the programmer did not include a **default** statement because `control` will never be anything but 0, 1, or 2. However, variables can get assigned strange values, so we need a little more defensive programming, as shown in the following example:

```
/* The final version */
switch (control) {
    case 0:
        (void) printf("Reset\n");
        /* Fall through */
    case 1:
        (void) printf("Initializing\n");
        break;
    case 2:
        (void) printf("Working\n");
        break;
    default:
        (void) printf(
            "Internal error, control value (%d) impossible\n",
                control);
        break;
}
```

Although a **default** is not required, it should be put in every **switch**. Even though the **default** may be:

```
default:
        /* Do nothing */
        break;
```

it should be included. This at least indicates that you want to ignore out-of-range data.

switch, break, and continue

The **break** statement has two uses. Used inside a **switch**, it causes the program to go to the end of the **switch**. Inside a **for** or **while** loop, it will cause a loop exit. The **continue** statement is only valid inside a loop. It will cause the program to go to the top of the loop. Figure 7-1 illustrates both **continue** and **break** inside a **switch** statement.

The program in Figure 7-1 is designed to convert an integer with a number of different formats into different bases. For example, if you want to know the value of an octal number, you would enter `o` for octal and the number. The command `q` is used to quit the program. For example:

```
Enter conversion and number: o 55
Result is 45
Enter conversion and number: q
```

The `help` command is special because we don't want to print a number after the command. After all, the result of `help` is a few lines of text, not a number. So a **continue** is used inside the **switch** to start the loop over from the beginning. Inside the **switch**, the **continue** statement works on the loop, while the **break** statement works on the **switch**.

There is one **break** outside the **switch** designed to let the user exit the program. The control flow for this program can be seen in Figure 7-1.

```
#include <stdio.h>

int    number;      /* Number we are converting */
char  type;      /* Type of conversion to do */
char  line[80];      /* input line */

main()
{
    while (1) {

        (void) printf("Enter conversion and number: ");

        (void) fgets(line, sizeof(line), stdin);
        (void) sscanf(line, "%c", &type);

        if ((type == 'q') || (type == 'Q'))
            break;

        switch (type) {
            case 'o':
            case 'O':  /* Octal conversion */
                (void) sscanf(line, "%c %o", &type, &number);
                break;

            case 'x':
            case 'X':  /* Hexidecimal conversion */
                (void) sscanf(line, "%c %x", &type, &number);
                break;

            case 'd':
            case 'D':  /* Decimal (For completeness) */
                (void) sscanf(line, "%c %d", &type, &number);
                break;

            case '?':
            case 'h':  /* Help */
                (void) printf("Letter  Conversion\n");
                (void) printf("  o      Octal\n");
                (void) printf("  x      Hexidecimal\n");
                (void) printf("  d      Decimal\n");
                (void) printf("  q      Quit program\n");
                 /* Don't print the number */
                continue;

             default:
                (void) printf("Type ? for help\n");
                 /* Don't print the nubmer */
                continue;
        }
        (void) printf("Result is %d\n", number);
    }
    return (0);
}
```

Break Inside Switch

Continue (inside switch)

Break Outside Switch

Figure 7-1. switch/continue

Answers

Answer 7–1: The problem lies with the semicolon (`;`) at the end of the **for** statement. The body of the **for** statement is between the closing parentheses and the semicolon. In this case, it is nothing. Even though the `printf` statement is indented, it is not part of the **for** statement. The indentation is misleading. The C compiler does not look at indentation. The program does nothing until the expression:

```
centigrade <= 100
```

becomes false `(centigrade == 101)`. Then the `printf` is executed.

Answer 7–2: The problem is that we read the number into `data[1]` through `data[5]`. In C the range of legal array indices is 0 to *array-size*–1, or in this case, 0 to 4. `data[5]` is illegal. When we use it, strange things happen; in this case, the variable `three_count` is changed. The solution is to only use `data[0]` to `data[4]`.

Programming Exercises

Exercise 1: Print a checkerboard (8 × 8 grid). Each square should be five by three characters wide. A 2 × 2 example follows:

```
+-----+-----+
|     |     |
|     |     |
|     |     |
+-----+-----+
|     |     |
|     |     |
|     |     |
+-----+-----+
```

Exercise 2: The total resistance of *n* resistors in parallel is:

$$\frac{1}{R} = \frac{1}{R_1} + \frac{1}{R_2} \cdots + \frac{1}{R_n}$$

Suppose we have a network of two resistors with the values 400Ω and 200Ω. Then our equation would be:

$$\frac{1}{R} = \frac{1}{R_1} + \frac{1}{R_2}$$

Substituting in the value of the resistors, we get:

$$\frac{1}{R} = \frac{1}{400} + \frac{1}{200}$$

$$\frac{1}{R} = \frac{3}{400}$$

$$R = \frac{400}{3} = 133.3$$

So the total resistance of our two resistor network is 133.3Ω.

Exercise 3: Write a program to compute the total resistance for any number of parallel resistors.

Exercise 4: Write a program to average *n* numbers.

Exercise 5: Write a program to print out the multiplication table.

Exercise 6: Write a program that reads a character and prints out whether or not it is a vowel or a consonant.

Exercise 7: Write a program that converts numbers to words. For example, 895 results in "eight nine five."

Exercise 8: The number 85 is pronounced "eighty-five," not "eight five." Modify the previous program to handle the numbers 0 through 100 so that all numbers come out as we really say them. For example, 13 would be "thirteen" and 100 would be "one hundred."

8

Variable Scope and Functions

But in the gross and scope of my opinion
This bodes some strange eruption to our state.
—Shakespeare [*Hamlet*, Act I, Scene I]

So far we have been using only global variables. In this chapter we will learn about other kinds of variables and how to use them. This chapter also tells you how to divide your code into functions.

Scope and Class

All variables have two attributes, scope and class. The *scope* of a variable is the area of the program where the variable is valid. A *global variable* is valid everywhere (hence the name global), so its scope is the whole program. A *local variable*'s scope is limited to the block where it is declared and cannot be accessed outside that block. A *block* is a section of code enclosed in curly braces ({}). Figure 8-1 shows the difference between local and global variables.

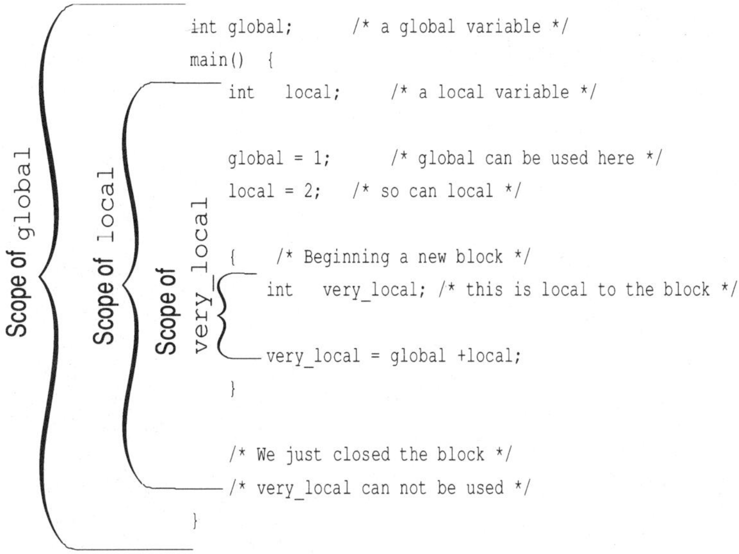

Figure 8-1. Local and Global Variables

It is possible to declare a local variable with the same name as a global variable. Normally, the scope of the variable **count** (first declaration) would be the whole program. The declaration of a second local **count** takes precedence over the global declaration inside the small block where the local **count** is declared. In this block, the global **count** is *hidden*. You can also nest local declarations and hide local variables. Figure 8-2 illustrates a hidden variable.

The variable **count** is declared as both a local variable and a global variable. Normally, the scope of **count** (global) is the entire program; however, when a variable is declared inside a block, that instance of the variable becomes the active one for the length of the block. The global **count** has been hidden by the local **count** for the scope of this block. The shaded block in the figure shows where the scope of **count** (global) is hidden.

Because hiding variables is considered poor programming practice, the program **lint** will warn you about them. The problem is that when you have the statement:

```
count = 1;
```

it is difficult to tell which **count** you are referring to. Is it the global count, the one declared at the top of main, or the one in the middle of the **while** loop? It is

Scope of global variable `count`

Local variable `count` hides global variable `count` in this area

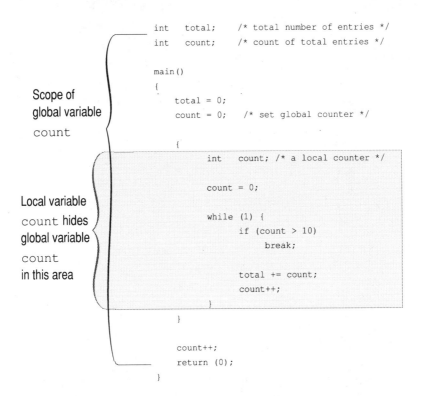

```
int   total;      /* total number of entries */
int   count;      /* count of total entries */

main()
{
    total = 0;
    count = 0;    /* set global counter */

    {
        int   count; /* a local counter */

        count = 0;

        while (1) {
            if (count > 10)
                break;

            total += count;
            count++;
        }
    }

    count++;
    return (0);
}
```

Figure 8-2. Hidden Variables

better to give these variables different names, like **`total_count`**, **`current_count`**, and **`item_count`**.

The *class* of a variable may be either *permanent* or *temporary*. Global variables are always permanent. They are created and initialized before the program starts and remain until it terminates. Temporary variables are allocated from a section of memory called the *stack* at the beginning of the block. If you try to allocate too many temporary variables, you will get a "Stack overflow" error. The space used by the temporary variables is returned to the stack at the end of the block. Each time the block is entered, the temporary variables are initialized.

The size of the stack depends on the system and compiler you are using. On many UNIX systems, the program is automatically allocated the largest possible stack. On other systems, a default stack size is allocated which can be changed by a compiler switch. In Turbo C the stack space must be less than 64,000 bytes. This may seem like a lot of space; however, several large arrays can eat it up quickly. You should consider making all large arrays permanent.

Local variables are temporary unless they are declared **static**.

NOTE

> **static** has an entirely different meaning when used with global variables. It indicates that a variable is local to the current file. See Chapter 17, *Modular Programming*.

Program 8-1 illustrates the difference between permanent and temporary variables. We have chosen obvious variables: `temporary` is a temporary variable, while `permanent` is permanent. The variable `temporary` is initialized each time it is created (at the beginning of the **for** statement block). The variable `permanent` is initialized only once, at startup time.

In the loop, both variables are incremented. However, at the top of the loop, `temporary` is initialized to one, as shown in Program 8-1.

Program 8-1.

```
#include <stdio.h>

main() {
    int counter;    /* loop counter */
    for (counter = 0; counter < 3; counter++) {
        int temporary = 1;
        static int permanent = 1;

        (void)printf("Temporary %d Permanent %d\n",
            temporary, permanent);
        temporary++;
        permanent++;
    }
    return (0);
}
```

The output of this program is:

```
Temporary 1 Permanent 1
Temporary 1 Permanent 2
Temporary 1 Permanent 3
```

NOTE

> Temporary variables are sometimes referred to as *automatic* variables because the space for them is allocated automatically. The qualifier **auto** can be used to denote a temporary variable; however, in practice it is almost never used.

Table 8-1 describes the different ways a variable can be declared.

Table 8-1. Declaration Modifiers

Declared	Scope	Class	Initialized
Outside all blocks	Global	Permanent	Once
static outside all blocks	Global*	Permanent	Once
Inside a block	Local	Temporary	Each time block is entered
static inside a block	Local	Permanent	Once

In UNIX C, only permanent arrays may be initialized. (Both permanent and temporary simple variables may be initialized.) Arrays must be global or **static** to be initialized. Local nonstatic arrays may not be initialized.

In ANSI standard C, all arrays may be initialized.

For example:

```
int global[3] = {1, 2, 3};          /* Permanent -- legal initialization */
main() {
    int data[3] = {1, 2, 3};        /* Temporary -- illegal in UNIX - C */
                                    /*              but legal in ANSI C" */
    static int stuff[3]= {1, 2, 3}; /* Permanent -- legal initialization */
    ...
```

Functions

Functions allow us to group commonly used code into a compact unit that can be used repeatedly. We have already encountered one function, `main`. It is a special function called at the beginning of the program. All other functions are directly or indirectly called from `main`.

Suppose we want to write a program to compute the area of three triangles. We could write out the formula three times, or we could create a function to do the

*A **static** declaration made outside blocks indicates the variable is local to the file where it's declared. (See Chapter 17, *Modular Programming*, for more information on programming with multiple files.)

work. Each function should begin with a comment block containing the following:

Name Name of the function.

Description Description of what the function does.

Parameters Description of each of the parameters to the function.

Returns Description of the return value of the function.

Additional sections may be added such as file formats, references, or notes. Refer to Chapter 2, *Style*, for other suggestions.

Our function to compute the area of a triangle begins with:

```
/********************************************
 * triangle -- compute area of a triangle    *
 *                                           *
 * Parameters                                *
 *   width -- width of the triangle          *
 *   height -- height of the triangle        *
 *                                           *
 * Returns                                   *
 *   area of the triangle                    *
 ********************************************/
```

The function proper begins with the line:

```
float triangle(float width, float height)
```

float is the function type. The two parameters are `width` and `height`. They are of type **float** also. Parameters are variables local to the function used to pass information into the function.

NOTE

> The function type is not required by C. If no function type is declared, it defaults to **int**. However, if you omit the type it is not clear whether you want to have the function default to **int** or if you forgot to declare a type. To avoid this confusion, always declare the function type and do not use the default.

The function computes the area with the statement:

```
area = width * height / 2.0;
```

What's left is to give the result to the caller. This is done with the **return** statement:

```
return (area)
```

Here's our full triangle function:

```
/********************************************
 * triangle -- compute area of a triangle    *
 *                                           *
 * Parameters                                *
 *   width -- width of the triangle          *
 *   height -- height of the triangle        *
 *                                           *
 * Returns                                   *
 *   area of the triangle                    *
 ********************************************/
float triangle(float width, float height)
{
    float area:      /* Area of the triangle */

    area = width * height / 2.0;
    return (area):
}
```

The line:

```
size = triangle(1.3, 8.3)
```

is a call to the function `triangle`. C assigns `1.3` to the parameter `width` and `8.3` to `height`.

If functions are the rooms of our building, then parameters are the doors between the rooms. In this case, the value `1.3` is going through the door marked `width`. Parameters' doors are one way. Things can go in, but can't go out. The **return** statement is how we get data out of the function. In our `triangle` example, the function assigns the local variable `area` the value `5.4`, then executes the statement `return (area);`.

The return value of this function is `5.4`, so our statement:

```
size = triangle (1.3, 8.3)
```

assigns `size` the value `5.4`.

Program 8-2 computes the area of three triangles:

Program 8-2.

```
#include <cstdio.h>

main()
```

```
{
    /* Compute a triangle */
    float triangle(float width, float height);

    (void)printf("Triangle #1 %f\n", triangle(1.3, 8.3));
    (void)printf("Triangle #2 %f\n", triangle(4.8, 9.8));
    (void)printf("Triangle #3 %f\n", triangle(1.2, 2.0));
    return (0);
}

/********************************************
 * triangle -- compute area of a triangle    *
 *                                           *
 * Parameters                                *
 *   width -- width of the triangle          *
 *   height -- height of the triangle        *
 *                                           *
 * Returns                                   *
 *   area of the triangle                    *
 ********************************************/
float triangle(float width, float height)
{
    float area;     /* Area of the triangle */

    area = width * height / 2.0;
    return (area);
}
```

The function must be declared just like a variable to inform the compiler about the function. We've use the declaration:

```
/* Compute a triangle */
float triangle (float width, float height);
```

for the `triangle` function. This declaration is called the *function prototype*.

NOTE

The variable names are not required when declaring a function prototype. Our prototype could have just as easily been written as:

```
float triangle(float, float);
```

However, we use the longer version because it gives the programmer additional information, and it's easy to create variables using the editor's cut and paste functions.

Strictly speaking, the prototypes are optional for some functions. If no prototype is specified, the C compiler will assume the function returns an **int** and takes any number of parameters. Omitting a prototype robs the C compiler of valuable information it can use to check function calls. Most ANSI compilers have a compile time switch that warns the programmer if it detects a call to a function without a prototype.

Older-style K&R Function Declarations

The function prototype is a relatively new addition to the C language. Many older compilers only allow the older, K&R-style function declarations. For example, using a K&R-style declaration, our `triangle` function looks like:

```
float triangle(width, height)
float width;
float height;
{
    /* Function body */
```

Before using the function, it must be declared. The declaration looks much like a prototype, except there's nothing inside the parentheses `()`:

```
main()
{
    float triangle();
```

When using K&R-style functions, C does *not* check the parameter types. For example, if our program contained the line:

```
size = triangle(1, 3);
```

C would not warn you that you are sending integers to the function, but expecting **floats**. The result would be a very strange number. To avoid problems like this, prototypes were invented and should be used whenever possible.

Functions With No Parameters

A function can have any number of parameters, including none. But even when using a function with no parameters, you still need the parenthesis.

```
value = next_index();
```

Declaring a prototype for a zero parameter is a little tricky. You can't use the statement:

```
int next_index();
```

because the C compiler will see the empty parenthesis and assume that this is a K&R-style function declaration. The keyword **void** is used to indicate an empty parameter list. So the prototype for our `next_index` function is:

```
int next_index(void);
```

void is also used to indicate that a function does not return a value. (This is similar to the FORTRAN subroutine or PASCAL procedure.) For example, this function just prints a result; it does not return a value:

```
void print_answer(int answer)
{
    if (answer < 0) {
        (void) printf("Answer corrupt\n");
        return;
    }
    (void) printf("The answer is %d\n", answer);
}
```

Question 8–1: The following function should compute the length of a string.* Instead it insists that all strings are of length 0. Why?

```
/********************************************************
 * length -- compute the length of a string             *
 *                                                      *
 * Parameters                                           *
 *      string -- the string whose length we want       *
 *                                                      *
 * Returns                                              *
 *      the length of the string                        *
 ********************************************************/
int  length(char string[])
{
    int index;      /* index into the string */

    /*
     * Loop until we reach the end-of-string character
     */
    for (index = 0; string[index] != '\0'; index++)
        /* do nothing */
    return (index);
}
```

Question 8–2: Why does the following program always report the average as –31809? (Your answers may vary.)

*This function performs the same function as the library function `strlen`.

NOTE

The following program is written for an old UNIX C compiler. It will not compile using ANSI Standard C.

Hint: Run the program through `lint`.

```
#include <stdio.h>
char line[100];  /* input line */

main()
{
    int n1, n2, n3;  /* 3 numbers to average */

    int ave();  /* average 3 numbers */

    (void)printf("Enter 3 numbers ");

    (void)fgets(line, sizeof(line), stdin);
    (void)sscanf(line, "%d %d %d", &n1, &n2, &n3);

    (void)printf("Average %d\n", ave(n1, n2, n3));
    return (0);
}

int ave(n1, n2, n3)
{
    int n1, n2, n3;

    return ((n1 + n2 + n3) / 3);
}
```

NOTE

There are two ways of specifying a function: the old-style PCC (UNIX) and the newer ANSI standard. This book uses the ANSI standard. If you are using a nonstandard UNIX compiler, you should be aware that you will have to convert your function declarations before they will compile.

Structured Programming

Computer scientists spend a great deal of time and effort studying how to program. The result is that they come up with absolutely, positively, the best programming methodology—a new one each month. Some of these systems include flow charts, top-down programming, bottom-up programming, and structured programming.

Now that we have learned about functions, we can talk about using *structured programming techniques* to design programs. This is a way of dividing up or structuring a program into small, well-defined functions. It makes the program easy to write and easy to understand. I don't claim that this system is the absolute best way to program. It happens to be the system that works best for me. If another system works better for you, use it.

The first step in programming is to decide what you are going to do. This has already been described in Chapter 6, *The Programming Process*. Next, decide how you are going to structure your data.

Finally, the coding phase begins. When writing a paper, you start with an outline of each section in the paper described by a single sentence. The details will be filled in later. Writing a program is similar. You start with an outline, and this becomes your main function. The details can be hidden within other functions. For example, Program 8-3 solves all the world's problems.

Program 8-3.

```
main()
{

    init();
    solve_problems();
    finish_up();
}
```

Of course some of the details will have to be filled in later.

Start by writing the main function. It should be less than three pages long. If it grows longer, consider splitting it up into two smaller, simpler functions. Once the main function is complete, you can start in on the others.

This type of structured programming is called *top-down programming*. You start at the top (`main`) and work your way down.

Another type of coding is called *bottom-up programming*. This involves writing the lowest-level function first, testing it, and then building on that working set. I tend to use some bottom-up techniques when I'm working with a new standard function that I haven't used before. I write a small function to make sure I really know how the function works and continue from there. This is the approach used in Chapter 6, *The Programming Process*, to construct the calculator program.

So in actual practice, both techniques are useful. This results in a mostly top-down, partially bottom-up technique. Computer scientists have a term for this methodology: chaos. The one rule you should follow in programming is "use what works best."

Recursion

Recursion occurs when a function calls itself directly or indirectly. Some programming functions lend themselves naturally to recursive algorithms such as the factorial.

A recursive function must follow two basic rules:

1. It must have an ending point.
2. It must make the problem simpler.

A definition of factorial is:

```
fact(0) = 1

fact(n) = n * fact(n-1)
```

In C this is:

```
int fact(int number)
{
    if (number == 0)
        return (1);
    /* else */
    return (number * fact(number-1));
}
```

This satisfies our two rules. First, it has a definite ending point (when `number == 0`). Second, it simplifies the problem because the `fact(number-1)` is simpler than `fact(number)`.

Factorial is legal only for `number >= 0`. But what happens if we try to compute `fact(-3)`? The program will abort with a stack overflow or similar message. `fact(-3)` calls `fact(-4)` which calls `fact(-5)` etc. There is no ending point. This is referred to as an infinite recursion error.

Many things that we do iteratively can be done recursively—for example, summing up the elements of an array. We define a function to add elements *m-n* of an array as follows:

- If we have only one element, then the sum is simple.
- Otherwise, it is the sum of the first element and the sum of the rest.

In C this is:

```
int sum(int first, int last, int array[])
{
    if (first == last)
        return (array[first]);
    /* else */
        return (array[first] + sum(first+1, last, array));
}
```

For example:

```
Sum(1 8 3 2) =
    1 + Sum(8 3 2) =
        8 + Sum(3 2) =
            3 + Sum (2) =
                2
            3 + 2 = 5
        8 + 5 = 13
    1 + 13 = 14
Answer = 14
```

Answers

Answer 8–1: The programmer went to a lot of trouble to explain that the **for** loop did nothing (except increment the index). However, there is no semicolon (`;`) at the end of the **for**. C keeps on reading until it sees a statement (in this case `return(index)`) and puts that in the **for** loop. Properly done, this program should be:

```
int  length(char string[])
{
    int index;      /* index into the string */

    /*
     * Loop until we reach the end-of-string character
     */

    for (index = 0; string[index] != '\0'; index++)
        /* do nothing */ ;
    return (index);
}
```

Answer 8–2: If a parameter is not declared, C will assume that it is an **int**. So:

```
int total(count)
int count;
{
```

and:

```
int total(count)
{
```

are equivalent. Parameters must be declared outside the curly braces ({ }) or they default to **int**.

In the function `ave` the parameters `n1`, `n2`, and `n3` are not defined outside the curly braces. The declaration `int n1,n2,n3` declares a set of new, local variables that have nothing to do with the parameters passed to the function. (Fortunately, in ANSI C this is illegal.) This declaration causes the parameters to be hidden throughout the entire function. The proper declaration is:

```
int ave(n1, n2, n3)
int n1, n2, n3;
{
```

Programming Exercises

Exercise 1: Write a procedure that counts the number of words in a string. (Your documentation should describe exactly how you define a word.) Write a program to test your new procedure.

Exercise 2: Write a function `begins(string1,string2)` which returns true if `string1` begins `string2`. Write a program to test the function.

Exercise 3: Write a function `count(number, array, length)` that will count the number of times `number` appears in `array`. The array has `length` elements. The function should be recursive. Write a test program to go with the function.

Exercise 4: Write a function that will take a character string and return a primitive hash code by adding up the value of each character in the string.

Exercise 5: Write a function that returns the maximum value of an array of numbers.

Exercise 6: Write a function that scans a string for the character "-" and replaces it with "_".

9

The C Preprocessor

The speech of man is like embroidered tapestries, since like them this has to be extended in order to display its patterns, but when it is rolled up it conceals and distorts them.

—Themistocles

In the early days, when C was still being developed, it soon became apparent that C needed a facility for handling named constants, macros, and include files. The solution was to create a preprocessor that recognized these constructs in the programs before they were passed to the C compiler. The preprocessor is nothing more than a specialized text editor. Its syntax is completely different from C's and it has no understanding of C constructs.

The preprocessor was very useful, and soon it was merged into the main C compiler. On some systems, like UNIX, it is still a separate program, automatically executed by the compiler wrapper `cc`. Some of the newer compilers, like Turbo C, have the preprocessor built-in.

#define Statement

Program 9-1 initializes two arrays (**data** and **twice**). Each array contains 10 elements. Suppose we wanted to change the program to use 20 elements. Then we would have to change the array size (two places) and the index limit (one place). Aside from being a lot of work, multiple changes can lead to errors.

Program 9-1.

```
int data[10];     /* some data */
int twice[10];    /* twice some data */

main()
{
    int index;    /* index into the data */

    for (index = 0; index < 10; index++) {
        data[index] = index;
        twice[index] = index * 2;
    }
    return (0);
}
```

We would like to be able to write a generic program where we can define a constant for the size of the array and let C adjust the dimensions of our two arrays. By using the **#define** statement we can do just that. Program 9-2 is a new version of Program 9-1.

Program 9-2.

```
#define SIZE 20     /* work on 20 elements */

int data[SIZE];     /* some data */
int twice[SIZE];    /* twice some data */

main()
{
    int index;    /* index into the data */

    for (index = 0; index < SIZE; index++) {
    data[index] = index;
    twice[index] = index * 2;
    }
    return (0);
}
```

The line `#define SIZE 20` acts as a command to a special text editor to *globally change* `SIZE` to 20. This takes the drudgery and guesswork out of making changes.

All preprocessor commands begin with a hash mark (#) in column one. Although C is free format, the preprocessor is not, and it depends on the hash mark being in the first column. As we will see, the preprocessor knows nothing about C and can be (and is) used to edit things other than C programs.

WARNING

> The preprocessor is not part of the C compiler. It uses an entirely different syntax and requires an entirely different mind set to use it well. Most problems you will see occurred because the preprocessor was treated like C.

A preprocessor directive terminates at the end of line. This is different from C, where a semicolon (`;`) is used to end a statement. Putting a semicolon at the end of a preprocessor directive can lead to unexpected results. A line may be continued by putting a backslash (\) at the end. The simplest use of the preprocessor is to define a replacement macro. For example, the command:

```
#define FOO bar
```

will cause the preprocessor to replace the word "FOO" with the word "bar" everywhere it occurs. It is common programming practice to use all uppercase letters for macro names. This makes it very easy to tell the difference between a variable (all lowercase) and a macro (all uppercase).

The general form of a simple define statement is:

#define *name substitute-text*

where *name* can be any valid C identifier and *substitute-text* can be anything. It is possible to use the following definition:

```
#define FOR_ALL for(i = 0; i < ARRAY_SIZE; i++)
```

and use it like this:

```
/*
 * Clear the array
 */
FOR_ALL {
    data[i] = 0;
}
```

However, it is considered bad programming practice to define macros in this manner. They tend to obscure the basic control flow of the program. In this example, a programmer who wants to know what the loop does would have to search the beginning of the program for the definition **FOR_ALL**.

It is even worse to define macros that do large-scale replacement of basic C programming constructs. For example, you can define the following:

```
#define BEGIN {
#define END }
. . .
    if (index == 0)
    BEGIN
        printf("Starting\n");
    END
```

The problem is that you are no longer programming in C, but in a half-C/half-Pascal mongrel. The Bourne shell uses preprocessor directives to define a language that looks a lot like Algol-68.

Here's a sample section of code:

```
IF (x GREATER_THAN 37) OR (Y LESS_THAN 83) THEN
    CASE value OF
        SELECT 1:
            start();
        SELECT 3:
            backspace();
        OTHERWISE:
            error();
    ESAC
FI
```

NOTE

Most programmers encountering this program first curse, then use the editor to turn the source back into a reasonable version of C.

The preprocessor can cause unexpected problems because it does not check for correct C syntax. For example, Program 9-3 generates an error on line 11.

Program 9-3.

```
1: #define BIG_NUMBER 10 ** 10
2:
3: main()
4: {
5:     /* index for our calculations */
6:     int   index;
```

```
 7:
 8:     index = 0;
 9:
10:     /* syntax error on next line */
11:     while (index < BIG_NUMBER) {
12:         index = index * 8;
13:     }
14:     return (0);
15: }
16:
```

The problem is in the **#define** statement on line 1, but the error message points to line 11. The definition in line 1 causes the preprocessor to expand line 11 to look like:

```
while (index < 10 ** 10)
```

Because `**` is an illegal operator, this generates a syntax error.

Question 9–1: The following program generates the answer 47 instead of the expected answer 144. Why? (See the hint below.)

```
#include <stdio.h>

#define FIRST_PART      7
#define LAST_PART       5
#define ALL_PARTS       FIRST_PART + LAST_PART

main() {
    (void)printf("The square of all the parts is %d\n",
        ALL_PARTS * ALL_PARTS);
    return (0);
}
```

Hint: The answer may not be readily apparent. Luckily, C allows you to run your program through the preprocessor and view the output. In UNIX, the command:

```
% cc -E prog.c
```

will send the output of the preprocessor to the standard output.

In DOS, the command:

```
% cpp prog.c
```

will do the same thing.

Running this program through the preprocessor gives us:

```
# 1 "first.c"
# 1 "/usr/include/stdio.h" 1


... Listing of data in include file <stdio.h>

# 2 "first.c" 2

main() {
    (void)printf("The square of all the parts is %d\n",
        7 + 5 * 7 + 5);
    return (0);
}
```

Question 9–2: The following program generates a warning (when passed through `lint`) that `counter` is used before it is set. This is a surprise to us because the **for** loop should set it. We also get a very strange warning, "null effect," for line 11.

```
 1: /* warning, spacing is VERY important */
 2:
 3: #include <stdio.h>
 4:
 5: #define MAX=10
 6:
 7: main()
 8: {
 9:     int  counter;
10:
11:     for (counter =MAX; counter > 0; counter--)
12:         (void)printf("Hi there\n");
13:
14:     return (0);
15: }
16:
```

Hint: Take a look at the preprocessor output.

Question 9–3: The following program computes the wrong value for `size`. Why?

```
#include <stdio.h>

#define SIZE    10;
#define FUDGE   SIZE -2;
main()
{
    int size;/* size to really use */

    size = FUDGE;
```

```
    (void)printf("Size is %d\n", size);
    return (0);
}
```

Hint: Use `lint` and the output of the preprocessor.

Question 9–4: The following program is supposed to print the message "Fatal Error:Abort" and exit when it receives bad data. But when it gets good data, it exits. Why?

```
#include <stdio.h>
#include <stdlib.h>      /* ANSI Standard only */

#define DIE \
    (void)printf("Fatal Error:Abort\n");exit(8);

main() {
        /* a random value for testing */
        int value;

        value = 1;
        if (value < 0)
            DIE;

        (void)printf("We did not die\n");
        return (0);
}

```

Conditional Compilation

One of the problems programmers have is writing code that can work on many different machines. In theory, C code is portable; in actual practice, many machines have little quirks that must be accounted for. For example, this book covers both the portable C compiler and ANSI C. Although they are almost the same, things like procedure prototypes are found in ANSI C but not in portable C.

The preprocessor allows the programmer great flexibility in changing the way code is generated through the use of conditional compilation. Suppose we want to put debugging code in the program while we are working on it, but remove it in the production version. We could do this by including the code in a **#ifdef/#endif** section:

```
#ifdef DEBUG
    printf("In compute_hash, value %d hash %d\n",
        value, hash);
#endif /* DEBUG */
```

NOTE

> You do not have to put the `/* DEBUG */` after the `#endif`; however, it is very useful as a comment.

If the beginning of the program contains the directive:

```
#define DEBUG        /* Turn debugging on */
```

the `printf` will be included. If the program contains the directive:

```
#undef DEBUG         /* Turn debugging off */
```

the `printf` will be omitted.

Strictly speaking, the `#undef DEBUG` is unnecessary. If there is no `#define DEBUG` statement, then `DEBUG` is undefined. The `#undef DEBUG` statement is used to indicate explicitly that `DEBUG` is used for conditional compilation and is now turned off.

The directive **#ifndef** will cause the code to be compiled if the symbol is *not* defined. **#else** reverses the sense of the conditional. For example:

```
#ifdef DEBUG
    printf("Test version. Debugging is on\n");
#else DEBUG
    printf("Production version\n");
#endif DEBUG
```

A programmer may wish to remove a section of code temporarily. One common method is to comment out the code by enclosing it in `/* */`. This can cause problems, as shown by the following example:

```
1:  /***** Comment out this section
2:      section_report();
3:      /* Handle the end of section stuff */
4:      dump_table();
5:  **** end of commented out section */
```

This generates a syntax error for the fifth line. Why?

A better method is to use the **#ifdef** construct to remove the code:

```
#ifdef UNDEF
    section_report();
    /* Handle the end of section stuff */
    dump_table();
#endif UNDEF
```

(Of course, the code will be included if anyone defines the symbol `UNDEF`; however, anyone who does should be shot.)

The compiler switch **–Dsymbol** allows symbols to be defined on the command line. For example, the command:

```
% cc -DDEBUG -g -o prog prog.c
```

will compile the program `prog.c` and include all the code in between `#ifdef DEBUG` and `#endif DEBUG` even though there is no `#define DEBUG` in the program. The Turbo C equivalent is:

```
% tcc -DDEBUG -g -eprog.exe prog.c
```

The general form of the option is **–Dsymbol=** or **–Dsymbol=value**. For example, the following sets **MAX** to 10:

```
% cc -DMAX=10 -o prog prog.c
```

Notice that the programmer can override the command-line options with directives in the program. For example, the directive:

```
#undef DEBUG
```

will result in **DEBUG** being undefined whether or not you use **-DDEBUG**.

Most C compilers automatically define some system-dependent symbols. For example, Turbo C defines the symbols `__TURBOC__` and `__MSDOS__`. The ANSI Standard compiler defines the symbol `__STDC__`. Most UNIX compilers define a name for the system (i.e., SUN, VAX, Celerity, etc.); however, they are rarely documented. The symbol `unix` is always defined for all UNIX machines.

Include Files

The **#include** directive allows the program to use source code from another file.

For example, we have been using the directive:

```
#include <stdio.h>
```

in our programs. This tells the preprocessor to take the file *stdio.h* and insert it in the program. Files that are included in other programs are called *header files*. (Most **#include** directives come at the head of the program). The angle brackets (<>) indicate that the file is a standard header file. On UNIX, these files are located in */usr/include*. On DOS, they are located in the Turbo C directory (installation dependent).

Standard include files are used for defining data structures and macros used by library routines. For example, `printf` is a library routine that prints data on the standard output. The **FILE** structure used by **printf** and its related routines is defined in *stdio.h.*

Sometimes the programmer may want to write her own set of include files. Local include files are particularly useful for storing constants and data structures when a program spans several files. They are especially useful for information passing when a team of programmers are working on a single project. (See Chapter 17, *Modular Programming.*)

Local include files may be specified by using double quotes (") around the filename, for example:

```
#include "defs.h"
```

The filename **"defs.h"** can be any valid filename. This can be a simple file, **"defs.h"**; a relative path, **"../../data.h"**; or an absolute path, **"/root/include/const.h"**. (On DOS you should use backslash (\) instead of slash (/) as a directory separator.)

Include files may be nested, and that can cause problems. Suppose you define several useful constants in the file *const.h*. If the files *data.h* and *io.h* both include *const.h* and you put the following in your program:

```
#include "data.h"
#include "io.h"
```

you will generate errors because the preprocessor will set the definitions in *const.h* twice. Defining a constant twice is not a fatal error; however, defining a data structure or union twice is and must be avoided.

One way around this problem is to have *const.h* check to see if it has already been included and does not define any symbol that has already been defined. The directive **#ifndef** *symbol* is true if the symbol is *not* defined. It is the reverse of **#ifdef**.

Look at the following code:

```
#ifndef _CONST_H_INCLUDED_
/* define constants */
#define _CONST_H_INCLUDED_
#endif  _CONST_H_INCLUDED_
```

When *const.h* is included, it defines the symbol **_CONST_H_INCLUDED_**. If that symbol is already defined (because the file was included earlier), the **#ifndef** conditional hides all defines so they don't cause trouble.

NOTE

It is possible to put code in a header file but it is considered poor programming practice.

Parameterized Macros

So far we have discussed only simple **#defines** or macros. Macros can take parameters. The following macro will compute the square of a number:

```
#define SQR(x)  ((x) * (x))          /* Square a number */
```

When used, the macro will replace x by the text of the following argument:

`SQR(5)` expands to `((5) * (5))`

It is a good rule always to put parentheses, (), around the parameters of a macro. Program 9-4 illustrates the problems that can occur if this rule is not followed.

Program 9-4.

```
#include <stdio.h>
#define SQR(x) (x * x)

main()
{
    int counter;     /* counter for loop */

    for (counter = 0; counter < 5; counter++) {
        (void)printf("x %d, x squared %d\n",
            counter+1, SQR(counter+1));
    }
    return (0);
}
```

Question 9–5: What does Program 9-4 output? Try running it on your machine. Why did it output what it did? Try checking the output of the preprocessor.

The *keep-it-simple* system of programming prevents us from using the increment (++) and decrement (--) operators except on a line by themselves. When used in an expression, they are considered side effects, and this can lead to unexpected results, as illustrated by Program 9-5.

Program 9-5.

```
#include <stdio.h>
#define SQR(x) ((x) * (x))

main()
{
    int counter;    /* counter for loop */

    counter = 0;
    while (counter < 5)
        (void)printf("x %d square %d\n",
            counter, SQR(counter++));
    return (0);
}
```

Question 9–6: Why will Program 9-5 not produce the expected output? How much will the counter go up each time?

Question 9–7: The following program tells us that we have an undefined variable `number`, but our only variable name is `counter`.

```
#include <stdio.h>
#define RECIPROCAL (number) (1.0 / (number))

main()
{
    float   counter;

    for (counter = 0.0; counter < 10.0;
         counter += 1.0) {

        (void)printf("1/%f = %f\n",
                counter, RECIPROCAL(counter);
    }
    return (0);
}
```

Advanced Features

This book does not cover the complete list of C preprocessor directives. Among the more advanced features are an advanced form of the **#if** directive for conditional compilations and the **#pragma** directive for inserting compiler-dependent commands into a file. See your C reference manual for more information on these features.

Summary

The C preprocessor is a very useful part of the C language. It has a completely different look and feel, though, and it must be treated apart from the main C compiler.

Problems in macro definitions often do not show up where the macro is defined, but result in errors much further down in the program. By following a few simple rules, you can decrease the chances of having problems:

1. Put parentheses () around everything. In particular, they should enclose **#define** constants and macro parameters.
2. When defining a macro with more than one statement, enclose the code in curly braces ({ }).
3. The preprocessor is not C. Don't use = and `;`.

Finally, if you got this far, be glad that the worst is over.

Answers

Answer 9–1: After the program has been run through the preprocessor, the `printf` statement is expanded to look like:

```
printf("The square of all the parts is %d\n",
        7 + 5 * 7 + 5);
```

The equation `7 + 5 * 7 + 5` evaluates to 47. It is a good rule to put parentheses around all expressions in macros. By changing the definition of `ALL_PARTS` to:

```
#define ALL_PARTS (FIRST_PART + LAST_PART)
```

the program will execute correctly.

Answer 9–2: The preprocessor is a very simple-minded program. When it defines a macro, everything past the identifier is part of the macro. In this case, the definition of **MAX** is literally `= 10`. When the **for** statement is expanded, the result is:

```
for (counter==10; counter > 0; counter--)
```

C allows you to compute a result and throw it away. (This will generate a null effect warning in `lint`.) For this statement, the program checks to see if `counter` is 10, and then discards the answer. Removing the = from the definition will correct the problem.

Answer 9–3: As with the previous problem, the preprocessor does not respect C syntax conventions. In this case, the programmer used a semicolon (`;`) to end the statement, but the preprocessor included it as part of the definition for `SIZE`. The assignment statement for `SIZE` expanded is:

```
size = 10; -2;;
```

The two semicolons at the end do not hurt us, but the one in the middle is the killer. This line tells C to do two things:

1. Assign 10 to size.
2. Compute the value –2 and throw it away (this results in the null effect warning).

Removing the semicolons will fix the problem.

Answer 9–4: The output of the preprocessor looks like:

```
void exit();
main() {
    int value;

    value = 1;
    if (value < 0)
        printf("Fatal Error:Abort\n");exit(8);
    (void)printf("We did not die\n");
    return (0);
}
```

The problem is that two statements follow the **if** line. Normally, they would be put on two lines. Let's look at this program properly indented:

```
#include <stdio.h>
#include <stdlib.h>     /* ANSI Standard only */


main() {
    int value;  /* a random value for testing */

    value = 1;
    if (value < 0)
```

```
            (void)printf("Fatal Error:Abort\n");

        exit(8);

        (void)printf("We did not die\n");
        return (0);
    }
```

From this, it is obvious why we always exit. The fact that there were two statements after the **if** was hidden from us by using a single preprocessor macro.

The cure for this problem is to put curly braces ({ }) around all multi-statement macros; for example:

```
#define DIE     {printf("Fatal Error:Abort\n");exit(8);}
```

Answer 9–5: The program prints:

```
x 1 x squared 1
x 2 x squared 3
x 3 x squared 5
x 4 x squared 7
x 5 x squared 9
```

The problem is with the `SQR(counter+1)` expression. Expanding this we get:

```
SQR(counter+1)
(counter + 1 * counter + 1)
```

So our SQR macro does not work. Putting parentheses around the parameters solves this problem.

```
#define SQR(x)  ((x) * (x))
```

Answer 9–6: The answer is that the counter is incremented by two each time through the loop. This is because the macro call:

```
SQR(counter++)
```

is expanded to:

```
((counter++) * (counter++))
```

Answer 9–7: The only difference between a parameterized macro and one without parameters is the parentheses immediately following the macro name. In this case, a space follows the definition of `RECIPROCAL`, so it is *not* a parameterized macro. Instead, it is a simple text replacement macro that will replace `RECIPROCAL` with:

```
(number) (1.0 / number)
```

Removing the space between `RECIPROCAL` and `(number)` will correct the problem.

Programming Exercises

Exercise 1: C does not have a Boolean type. Create one using **#define** to define values for BOOLEAN, TRUE, and FALSE.

Exercise 2: Write a macro that returns TRUE if its parameter is divisible by 10 and FALSE otherwise.

Exercise 3: Write a macro `is_digit` that returns TRUE if its argument is a decimal digit.

Exercise 4: Write a second macro `is_hex` that returns true if its argument is a hex digit (0-9, A-F, a-f). The second macro should reference the first.

Exercise 5: Write a preprocessor macro that swaps two integers. (For the real hacker, write one that does not use a temporary variable declared outside the macro.)

10

Bit Operations

Bit Operators
Bitmapped Graphics

To be or not to be, that is the question.
—Shakespeare, on Boolean algebra

This chapter discusses bit-oriented operations. A bit is the smallest unit of information. Normally, it is represented by the values 1 and 0. Bit manipulations are used to control the machine at the lowest level. Some programmers will never need to use bit operations. Others, who are writing device drivers, or doing pixel-level graphic programming, for instance, need to be able to manipulate bits. If you plan on programming only at a higher level, this chapter may safely be skipped.

Eight bits together form a byte, represented by the C data type **char**.

A byte might contain the following bits:

```
01100100
```

This can also be written as the hexadecimal number 0x64. C uses the prefix "0x" to indicate a hexadecimal (base 16) number. Hexadecimal is convenient for representing binary data because each hexadecimal digit represents four binary bits.

Table 10-1 gives the hexadecimal to binary conversion.

Table 10-1. Hex and Binary

Hex	Binary	Hex	Binary
0	0000	8	1000
1	0001	9	1001
2	0010	A	1010
3	0011	B	1011
4	0100	C	1100
5	0101	D	1101
6	0110	E	1110
7	0111	F	1111

So the hexadecimal number 0xAF represents the binary number 10101111.

Bit Operators

Bit operators allow the programmer to work on individual bits. For example, a short integer holds 16 bits (on most machines). The bit operators treat each of these as an independent bit. By contrast, an add operator treats the 16 bits as a single 16-bit number.

Bit operators allow the programmer to set, clear, test, and perform other operations on bits. The bit operators are shown in Table 10-2.

Table 10-2. Bitwise Operators

Operator	Meaning
&	Bitwise and
|	Bitwise or
^	Bitwise exclusive or
~	Complement
<<	Shift left
>>	Shift right

These operators work on any integer or character data type.

The and Operator

The *and* operator compares two bits. If they both are 1, the result is 1. The results of the *and* operator are defined according to Table 10-3.

Table 10-3. and Operator

Bit 1	Bit 2	Bit 1 & Bit 2
0	0	0
0	1	0
1	0	0
1	1	1

When two 8-bit variables (**char** variables) are "anded" together, the *and* operator works on each bit. The following program segment illustrates this operation:

```
char    c1, c2;
c1 = 0x45;
c2 = 0x71;
(void)printf("Result of %x & %x = %x\n", c1, c2, c2 & c2);
```

The output of this program is:

```
Result of 45 & 71 = 41
```

This is because:

```
      c1 = 0x45 binary 01000101
&     c2 = 0x71 binary 01110001
-------------------------------
=          0x41 binary 01000001
```

The bitwise *and* (&) is similar to the logical *and* (&&). In the logical *and*, if both operands are true (nonzero), the result is true (one). In bitwise *and* (&), if the corresponding bits of both the operands are true (ones), then the corresponding bits of the results are true (ones).

However, & and && are different operators, as the following program illustrates:

```
#include <stdio.h>
main()
{
    int i1, i2; /* two random integers */

    i1 = 4;
    i2 = 2;      /* set values */

    /* Nice way of writing the conditional */
    if ((i1 != 0) && (i2 != 0))
```

```
        (void)printf("Both are not zero #1\n");

    /* Shorthand way of doing the same thing */
    /* Correct C code, but rotten style */
    if (i1 && i2)
        (void)printf("Both are not zero #2\n");

    /* Incorrect use of bitwise and resulting in an error */
    if (i1 & i2)
        (void)printf("Both are not zero #3\n");
    return (0);
}
```

Why does test #3 fail to print `Both are not zero #3`? The operator & is a bitwise *and.*

	i1=4	00000100
	i2=2	00000010
&		00000000

The result of the bitwise *and* is zero, and the conditional is false. If the programmer had used the first form:

```
if ((i1 != 0) && (i2 != 0))
```

and made the mistake of using & instead of &&:

```
if ((i1 != 0) & (i2 != 0))
```

the program would still have executed correctly.

(i1 != 0)	is true (result = 1)
(i2 != 0)	is true (result = 1)

1 bitwise and 1 is 1 so the expression is true.

NOTE

> Soon after discovering the bug illustrated by this program, I told my office mate, "I now understand the difference between *and* and *and and,*" and he understood me. How we understand language has always fascinated me, and the fact that I could utter such a sentence and have someone understand it without trouble amazed me.

You can use the bitwise *and* operator to test if a number is even or odd. In base 2, the last digit of all even numbers is zero and the last digit of all odd numbers is one. The following macro uses the bitwise *and* to pick off this last digit. If it is zero (an even number), the result of the macro is true. For example:

```
#define EVEN(x)   (((x) & 1) == 0)
```

Bitwise or

The *inclusive or* operator (also known as just the *or* operator) compares two operands, and if one or the other bit is a 1, the result is a 1. Table 10-4 shows a truth table for *or*.

Table 10-4. or Operator

Bit 1	Bit 2	Bit 1 | Bit 2
0	0	0
0	1	1
1	0	1
1	1	1

On a byte this would be:

```
          i1=0x47   01000111
          i2=0x53   01010011
    ------------------------
    or         57   01010111
```

The Bitwise Exclusive or

The *exclusive or* (also known as *xor*) operator results in a 1 when either of its two operands is a 1, but not both. Table 10-5 shows a truth table for *xor*.

Table 10-5. Exclusive or

Bit 1	Bit 2	Bit 1 ^ Bit 2
0	0	0
0	1	1
1	0	1
1	1	0

On a byte this would be:

```
     $i1=0x47$  01000111
     $i2=0x53$  01010011
-----------------------
xor         14  00010100
```

The Ones Complement Operator (not)

The *not* operator (also called the invert operator, or bit flip) is a unary operator that returns the inverse of its operand. The truth table for the *not* operator is shown in Table 10-6.

Table 10-6. not Operator

Bit	~Bit
0	1
1	0

On a byte this is:

```
  i=0x45 01000101
 ~i=0xBA 10111010
```

The Left and Right Shift Operators

The left shift operator moves the data left a specified number of bits. Any bits that are shifted out the left side disappear. New bits coming in from the right are zeros. The right shift does the same thing in the other direction. For example:

```
    i=0x1C  00011100
i<<1=0x38  00111000
i>>2=0x07  00000111
```

Setting, Clearing, and Testing Bits

A character contains eight bits. Each of these can be treated as a separate flag.

Bit operations can be used to pack eight single-bit values in a single byte. For example, suppose we are writing a low-level communications program. We are going to store the characters in an 8K buffer for later use. With each character, we will also store a set of status flags. The flags are shown in Table 10-7.

Table 10-7. Communications Status Values

Name	Description
`ERROR`	True if any error is set.
`FRAMING_ERROR`	A framing error occurred for this character.
`PARITY_ERROR`	Character had the wrong parity.
`CARRIER_LOST`	The carrier signal went down.
`CHANNEL_DOWN`	Power was lost on the communication device.

We could store each of these flags in a character variable. That would mean that for each character buffered, we would need 5 bytes of status storage. By assigning each status flag its own bit within an 8-bit status character, we cut our storage requirements down to one-fifth of our original need.

We assign our flags the bit numbers shown in Table 10-8.

Table 10-8. Bit Assignments

Bit	Name
0	`ERROR`
1	`FRAMING_ERROR`
2	`PARITY_ERROR`
3	`CARRIER_LOST`
4	`CHANNEL_DOWN`

Bits are numbered 76543210. The constants for each bit are defined in Table 10-9.

Table 10-9. Bit Values

Bit	Binary Value	Hex Constant
7	10000000	0x80
6	01000000	0x40
5	00100000	0x20
4	00010000	0x10
3	00001000	0x08
2	00000100	0x04
1	00000010	0x02
0	00000001	0x01

The definitions could be:

```
/* True if any error is set */
#define ERROR            0x01
/* A framing error occurred for this character */
#define FRAMING_ERROR    0x02
/* Character had the wrong parity */
#define PARITY_ERROR     0x04
/* The carrier signal went down */
#define CARRIER_LOST     0x08
/* Power was lost on the communication device */
#define CHANNEL_DOWN     0x10
```

This method of defining bits is somewhat confusing. Can you tell (without looking at the table) which bit number is represented by the constant 0x10? Look at how we can use the left shift operator (<<) to represent bits:

1<<0 is equal to bit 0 because $00000001_2 << 0 = 00000001_2$

1<<1 is equal to bit 1 because $00000001_2 << 1 = 00000010_2$

Although it is hard to tell what bit is represented by 0x10, it's easy to tell what bit is meant by 1<<4.

Our flags can be defined as:

```
/* True if any error is set */
#define ERROR            (1<<0)
/* A framing error occurred for this character */
#define FRAMING_ERROR    (1<<1)
/* Character had the wrong parity */
#define PARITY_ERROR     (1<<2)
/* The carrier signal went down */
#define CARRIER_LOST     (1<<3)
/* Power was lost on the communication device */
#define CHANNEL_DOWN     (1<<4)
```

Now that we have defined the bits, we can manipulate them. To set a bit, use the | operator. For example:

```
char    flags = 0;  /* start all flags at 0 */
flags |= CHANNEL_DOWN; /* Channel just died */
```

To test a bit, we use the & operator to "mask out" the bits:

```
if ((flags & ERROR) != 0)
    (void)printf("Error flag is set\n");
else
    (void)printf("No error detected\n");
```

Clearing a bit is a little harder. Suppose we want to clear the bit **PARITY_ERROR**. In binary this bit is 00000100. We want to create a mask which has all bits set *except* for the bit we want to clear (11111011). This is done with the *not* operator (~). The mask is then *and*ed with the number to clear the bit.

PARITY_ERROR	00000100
~PARITY_ERROR	11111011
flags	00000101
flags & ~PARITY_ERROR	00000001

In C this is:

```
flags &= ~PARITY_ERROR; /* Who cares about parity */
```

Question 10–1: In the following program, the **HIGH_SPEED** flag works, but the **DIRECT_CONNECT** flag does not. Why?

```
#include <stdio.h>

#define HIGH_SPEED (1<<7)    /* modem is running fast */
/* we are using a hardwired connection */
#define DIRECT_CONNECT (1<<8)

char flags = 0;          /* start with nothing */

main()
{
    flags |= HIGH_SPEED;     /* we are running fast */
    flags |= DIRECT_CONNECT;/* because we are wired together */

    if ((flags & HIGH_SPEED) != 0)
        (void)printf("High speed set\n");

    if ((flags & DIRECT_CONNECT) != 0)
        (void)printf("Direct connect set\n");
    return (0);
}
```

Bitmapped Graphics

More and more computers now have graphic devices. For the PC, there are graphics devices like EGA and CGA cards. For UNIX, there are windowing systems like the X Window System and Sunview.

In bitmapped graphics, each pixel on the screen is represented by a single bit in memory. For example, Figure 10-1 shows a bitmap as it appears on the screen as a cursor and the same 14 × 14 bitmap enlarged so you can see the individual bits.

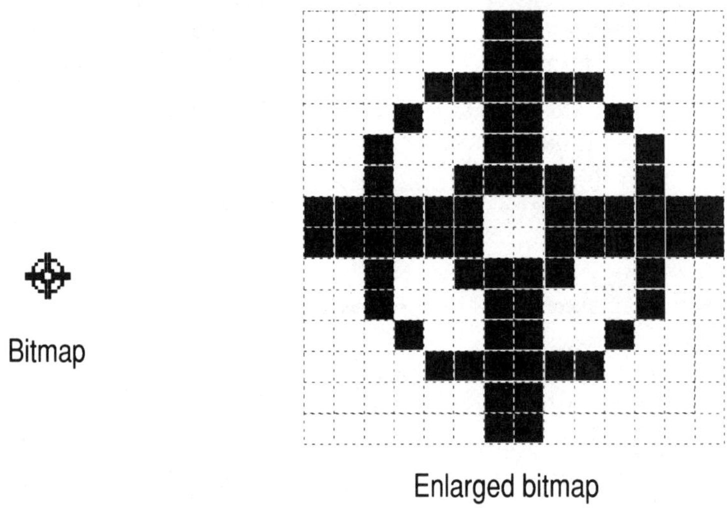

Figure 10-1. Bitmaps

Suppose we have a small graphic device containing a 16 × 16 black-and-white pixel display. We want to set the bit at 4,7. The bitmap for this device is shown as an array of bits in Figure 10-2.

But we have a problem. There is no data type for an array of bits in C. The closest we can come is an array of bytes. Our 16 × 16 array of bits now becomes a 2 × 16 array of bytes, as shown in Figure 10-3.

To set the pixel at bit number 4,7 we need to set the fourth bit of byte 0,7, as follows.

```
bit_array[0][7] |= (0x80 >> (4));
```

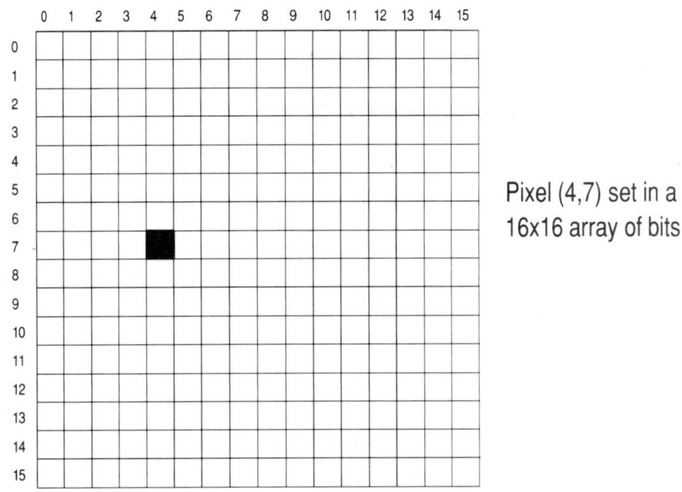

Pixel (4,7) set in a
16x16 array of bits

Figure 10-2. Array of Bits

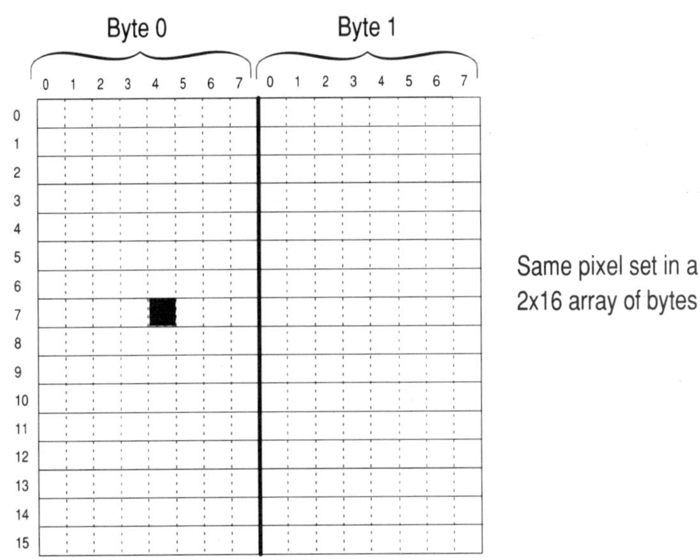

Figure 10-3. Array of Bytes

The constant 0x80 is the leftmost bit. We can generalize this process to produce a macro that turns on the bit (pixel) located at (x,y). We need to compute two values: the coordinate of the byte and the number of the bit within the byte.

Our bit address is (x,y). Bytes are groups of eight bits so our bit address is (x/8, y).

The bit within the byte is not so simple. We want to generate a mask consisting of the single bit we want to set. For the leftmost bit, this should be 10000000_2 or 0x80. This occurs when (x%8) == 0. The next bit is 01000000_2 or (0x80 >> 1) and occurs when (x%8) == 1. So in order to generate our bitmask, we use the expression (0x80 >> (x%8)).

Now that we have the byte location and the bit mask, all we have to do is set the bit. The following macro will set a given bit in a bitmapped graphics array named `graphics`:

```
#define SET_BIT(x,y) graphics[(x)/8][y] |= (0x80 >> ((x)%8))
```

Program 10-1 draws a diagonal line across a graphics array and then prints it out on the terminal.

Program 10-1.

```
#include <stdio.h>

#define X_SIZE 40 /* size of array in the X direction */
#define Y_SIZE 60 /* size of the array in Y direction */
/*
 * We use X_SIZE/8 since we pack 8 bits per byte
 */
char graphics[X_SIZE / 8][Y_SIZE];     /* the graphics data */

#define SET_BIT(x,y) graphics[(x)/8][y] |= (0x80 >>((x)%8))

main()
{
    int   loc;          /* current location we are setting */
    void  print_graphics(void); /* print the data */

    for (loc = 0; loc < X_SIZE; loc++)
        SET_BIT(loc, loc);

    print_graphics();
    return (0);
}
/********************************************************
 * print_graphics -- print the graphics bit array       *
 *                as a set of X and .'s.                *
 ********************************************************/
void print_graphics(void)
{
    int x;      /* current x BYTE */
    int y;      /* current y location */
    int bit;    /* bit we are testing in the current byte */
```

```
        for (y = 0; y < Y_SIZE; y++) {
            /* Loop for each byte in the array */
            for (x = 0; x < X_SIZE / 8; x++) {
                /* Handle each bit */
                for (bit = 0x80; bit > 0; bit = (bit >> 1)) {
                    if ((graphics[x][y] & bit) != 0)
                        (void) printf("X");
                    else
                        (void) printf(".");
                }
            }
            (void) printf("\n");
        }
    }
```

The program defines a bitmapped graphic array:

```
    char graphics[X_SIZE / 8][Y_SIZE];    /* the graphics data */
```

The constant `X_SIZE/8` is used because we have `X_SIZE` bits across which translates to `X_SIZE/8` bytes.

The main **for** loop:

```
    for (loc = 0; loc < X_SIZE; loc++)
            SET_BIT(loc, loc);
```

draws a diagonal line across the graphics array.

Since we do not have a bitmapped graphics device, we will simulate it with the subroutine `print_graphics`.

The loop:

```
    for (y = 0; y < Y_SIZE; y++) {
        ....
```

prints each row. The loop:

```
    for (x = 0; x < X_SIZE / 8; x++) {
        ...
```

goes through every byte in the row. There are eight bits in each byte handled by the loop:

```
    for (bit = 0x80; bit > 0; bit = (bit >> 1))
```

which uses an unusual loop counter. This loop causes the variable `bit` to start with bit 7 (the leftmost bit). For each iteration of the loop, the bit is moved to the right one bit by `bit = (bit >> 1)`. When we run out of bits, the loop exits.

The loop counter, **bit**, cycles through the values in Table 10-10.

Table 10-10. Values for bit loop Operator

Binary	Hex
1000 0000	0x80
0100 0000	0x40
0010 0000	0x20
0001 0000	0x10
0000 1000	0x08
0000 0100	0x04
0000 0010	0x02
0000 0001	0x01

Finally, at the heart of the loops is the code:

```
if ((graphics[x][y] & bit) != 0)
    (void) printf("X");
else
    (void) printf(".");
```

This tests an individual bit and writes **X** if it is set or a "**.**" if it is not.

Answers

Answer 10–1: **DIRECT_CONNECT** is defined to be bit number 8 by the expression (1<<8); however, the eight bits in a character variable are numbered 76543210. There is no bit number 8. A solution to this problem is to make **flags** a short integer with 16 bits.

Programming Exercises

Exercise 1: Write a set of macros, **CLEAR_BIT** and **TEST_BIT**, to go with the **SET_BIT** operation defined in Program 10-1. Write a main program to test these macros.

Exercise 2: Write a program to draw a 10 × 10 bitmapped square.

Exercise 3: Change Program 10-1 so it draws a white line across a black background.

Exercise 4: Write a program that counts the number of bits set in an integer. For example, the number 5 (decimal), which is 0000000000000101 (binary), has two bits set.

Exercise 5: Write a program that takes a 32-bit integer (**long int**) and splits it into eight 4-bit values. (Be careful of the sign bit.)

Exercise 6: Write a program that will take all the bits in a number and shift them to the left end. For example, 01010110 (binary) would become 11110000 (binary).

11

Advanced Types

Total grandeur of a total edifice,
Chosen by an inquisitor of structures.
—Wallace Stevens

C provides the programmer with a rich set of data types. Through the use of structures, unions, and enumerated types, the programmer can extend the language with new types.

Structures

Suppose we are writing an inventory program for a warehouse. The warehouse is filled with bins that contain various parts. All the parts in a bin are identical so we don't have to worry about mixed bins.

For each bin we need to know:

- The name of the part it holds (string 30 characters long).
- The quantity on hand (integer).
- The price (integer cents).

In previous chapters we have used arrays for storing a group of similar data types, but in this example we have a mixed bag: two integers and a string.

Instead of an array, we will use a new data type called a *structure*. In an array, all the elements are of the same type and are numbered. In a structure, each element or *field* is named and has its own data type.

The general form of a structure definition is:

> struct *structure-name* {
> *field-type field-name* /* *comment* */
> *field-type field-name* /* *comment* */
> . . . .
> } *variable-name* ;

For example, we want to define a bin to hold printer cables. The structure definition is:

```
struct bin {
    char    name[30];       /* name of the part */
    int     quantity;       /* how many are in the bin */
    int     cost;           /* The cost of a single part  (in cents) */
} printer_cable_bin;        /* where we put the print cables */
```

This definition actually tells C two things. The first is what a `struct bin` looks like. This statement defines a new data type that can be used in declaring other variables. The variable `printer_cable_bin` is also declared by this statement. Since the structure of a `bin` has been defined, we can use it to declare additional variables:

```
struct bin terminal_cable_box;  /* Place to put terminal cables */
```

The *structure-name* part of the definition may be omitted:

```
struct {
    char    name[30];      /* name of the part */
    int     quantity;      /* how many are in the bin */
    int     cost;          /* The cost of a single part  (in cents) */
} printer_cable_bin;       /* where we put the print cables */
```

The variable `printer_cable_bin` still has to be defined, but no data type has been created. The data type for this variable is an *anonymous structure*.

The *variable-name* may also be omitted. The following example would define a structure type, but no variables:

```
struct bin {
    char    name[30];    /* name of the part */
    int     quantity;    /* how many are in the bin */
    int     cost;        /* The cost of a single part  (in cents) */
};
```

In an extreme case, both the *variable-name* and the *structure-name* may be omitted. This creates a section of correct, but totally useless code.

We have defined the variable `printer_cable_bin` containing three named fields: `name`, `quantity`, and `cost`. To access them, we use the syntax:

variable .field

For example, if we just found out that the price of the cables went up to $12.95, we would do the following:

```
printer_cable_bin.cost = 1295;    /* $12.95 is the new price */
```

To compute the value of everything in the bin, we can use the following:

```
total_cost = printer_cable_bin.cost * printer_cable_bin.quantity;
```

Structures may be initialized at declaration time by putting the list of elements in curly braces ({ }):

```
/*
 * Printer cables
 */
struct bin {
    char    name[30];    /* name of the part */
    int     quantity;    /* how many are in the bin */
    int     cost;        /* The cost of a single part  (in cents) */
} printer_cable_bin = {
    "Printer Cables",    /* Name of the item in the bin */
    0,                   /* Start with empty box */
    1295                 /* cost -- $12.95  */
};
```

Unions

A structure is used to define a data type with several fields. Each field takes up a separate storage location. For example, the structure:

```
struct rectangle {
    int width;
    int height;
};
```

appears in memory.

A *union* is similar to a structure; however, it defines a single location that can be given many different field names:

```
union value {
    long int i_value;    /* integer version of value */
    float f_value;       /* floating version of value */
};
```

The fields `i_value` and `f_value` share the same space.

You might think of a structure as a large box divided up into several different compartments, each with its own name. A union is a box, not divided at all, with several different labels placed on the single compartment inside.

Figure 11-1 illustrates a structure with two fields. Each field is assigned a different section of the structure. A union contains only one compartment which is assigned different names.

In a structure, the fields do not interact. Changing one field does not change any others. In a union, all fields occupy the same space, so only one may be active at a time. In other words, if you put something in `i_value`, assigning something to `f_value` wipes out the old value of `i_value`.

Program 11-1 shows how a union can be used.

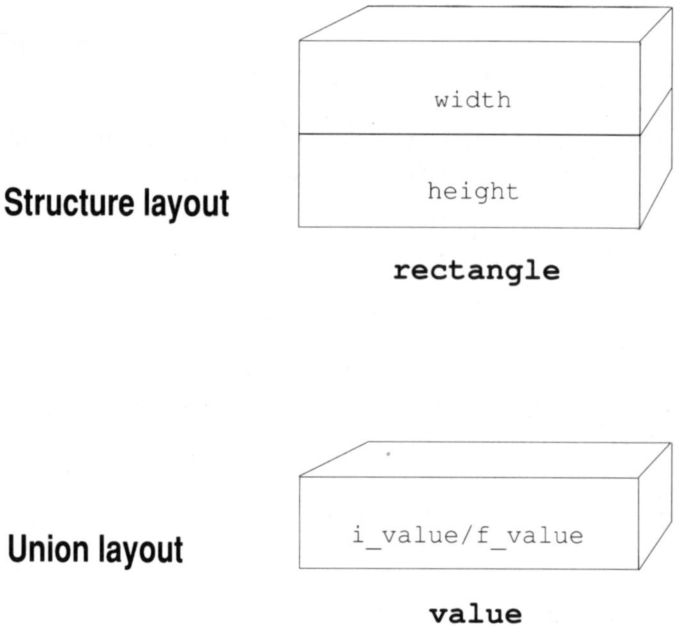

Figure 11-1. Layout of Structure and Union

Program 11-1.

```
/*
 * Define a variable to hold an integer or
 * a real number (but not both)
 */
union value {
    long int i_value;   /* The real number */
    float f_value;      /* The floating-point number */
} data;
int i;                  /* Random integer */
float f;                /* Random floating-point number */
main()
{
    data.f_value = 5.0;
    data.i_value = 3;   /* data.f_value overwritten */
    i = data.i_value;   /* legal */
    f = data.f_value;   /* not legal, will generate unexpected results */
    data.f_value = 5.5; /* put something in f_value/clobber i_value */
    i = data.i_value;   /* not legal, will generate unexpected results */
}
```

typedef

C allows the programmer to define her own variable types through the **typedef** statement. It provides a way for the program to extend C's basic types. The general form of the **typedef** statement is:

typedef *type-declaration*

where *type-declaration* is the same as a variable declaration except a type name is used instead of a variable-name. For example:

```
typedef int boolean;
```

defines a new type `boolean` that is the same as an integer. So the declaration:

```
boolean flag;
```

is the same as:

```
int flag;
```

At first glance, this is not much different than:

```
#define boolean int
boolean flag;
```

However, **typedefs** can be used to define more complex objects that are beyond the scope of a simple **#define** statement. For example:

```
typedef int group[10];
```

There is now a new type named `group` denoting an array of ten integers, for example:

```
main()
{
    typedef int group[10];      /* Create a new type "group" */
    group totals;               /* Use the new type for a variable */
    for (i = 0; i < 10; i++)
        totals[i] = 0;
}
```

enum Type

The enumerated data type is designed for variables that contain only a limited set of values. These values are referenced by name (tag). The compiler assigns each tag an integer value internally; for example, the days of the week. We could use the directive **#define** to create values for the **week_days**, as follows:

```
#define week_day int    /* define the type for week_days */
#define SUNDAY 0
#define MONDAY 1
#define TUESDAY 2
#define WEDNESDAY 3
#define THURSDAY 4
#define FRIDAY 5
#define SATURDAY 6
/* now to use it */
week_day today = TUESDAY;
```

This method is cumbersome. A better method is to use the **enum** type:

```
enum week_day {SUNDAY, MONDAY, TUESDAY, WEDNESDAY, THURSDAY,
    FRIDAY, SATURDAY};
/* now use it */
enum week_day today = TUESDAY;
```

The general form of an **enum** statement is:

enum *enum-name* { *tag-1*, *tag-2*, . . .} *variable-name*

Like structures, the *enum-name* or the *variable-name* may be omitted. The tags may be any valid C identifier; however, they are usually all uppercase.

One of the additional advantages of using an **enum** type is that C will restrict the values that can be used to the ones listed in the **enum** declaration. The following will result in a compiler error:

```
today = 5;  /* 5 is not a week_day */
```

One of the disadvantages of using **enum** is that **enum** variables cannot be used to index an array. The following will result in an error:

```
enum week_day today = TUESDAY;
char day_names[7][] = {
    "Sunday",
    "Monday",
    "Tuesday",
    "Wednesday",
    "Thursday",
```

```
        "Friday",
        "Saturday"
    };
        /*
         * the following line generates a warning
         * because today is not an integer
         */
        (void)printf("Today is %s\n", day_names[today]);
```

In order to get around this problem, we need to tell C to treat **today** as an integer. This is accomplished through the *cast* or *typecast operation*. The expression **(int)today** tells C, "I know that **today** is not an integer, but treat it like one." To fix our problem, we use the statement:

```
(void)printf("Today is %s\n", day_names[(int)today]);
```

Casts are also useful in expressions to make sure the variables have the correct type. In general, you can change the type of almost any expression:

(*type*) *expression*

This is particularly useful when working with integers and floating-point numbers:

```
int won, lost;          /* # games won/lost so far */
float   ratio;          /* win/lose ratio */
won = 5;
lost = 3;
ratio = won / lost; /* ratio will get 1.0 (a wrong value) */
/* The following will compute the correct ratio */
ratio = ((float) won) / ((float) lost);
```

Bit Fields or Packed Structures

Packed structures allow us to declare structures in a way that takes up a minimum amount of storage. For example, the following structure takes up six bytes (on a 16-bit machine):

```
struct item {
    unsigned int list;  /* true if item is in the list */
    unsigned int seen;  /* true if this item has been seen */
    unsigned int number;    /* item number */
};
```

The storage layout for this structure can be seen in Figure 11-2. Each structure uses six bytes of storage (two bytes for each integer).

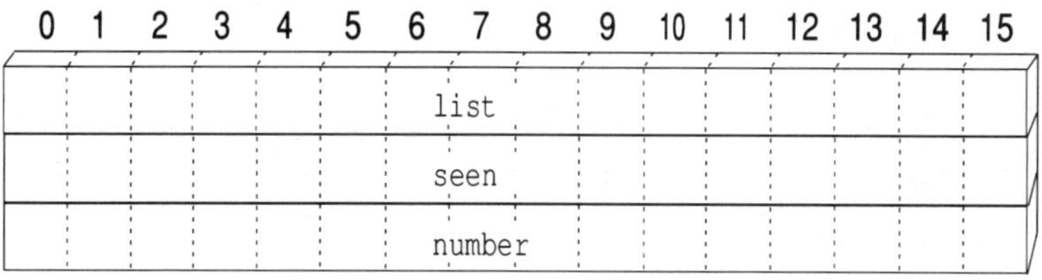

Figure 11-2. Unpacked Structure

However, the fields **list** and **seen** can only have two values, 0 and 1. So only one bit is needed to represent them. We never plan on having more than 16383 items (0x3fff or 14 bits). We can redefine this structure using bit fields, so it takes only two bytes, by following each field with a colon and the number of bits to be used for that field:

```
struct item {
    unsigned int list:1;    /* true if item is in the list */
    unsigned int seen:1;    /* true if this item has been seen */
    unsigned int number:14; /* item number */
};
```

In this example, we tell the compiler to use one bit for **list**, one bit for **seen** and 14 bits for **number**. Using this method, we can pack our data into only two bytes, as seen in Figure 11-3.

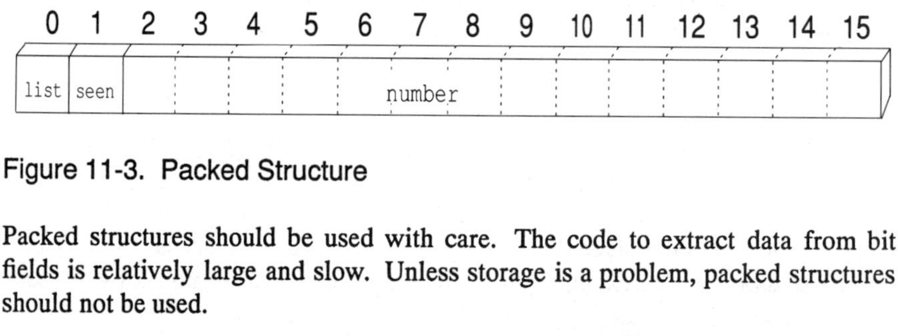

Figure 11-3. Packed Structure

Packed structures should be used with care. The code to extract data from bit fields is relatively large and slow. Unless storage is a problem, packed structures should not be used.

In Chapter 9, *The C Preprocessor*, we needed to store character data and five status flags for 8,000 characters. In this case, using a different byte for each flag would eat up a lot of storage (five bytes for each incoming character). We used bitwise operations to pack the five flags into a single byte. Alternatively, a packed structure could have accomplished the same thing:

```
struct char_and_status {
    char character;     /* character from device */
    int error:1;        /* True if any error is set */
    int framing_error:1;/* A framing error occurred */
```

```
        int parity_error:1; /* Character had the wrong parity */
        int carrier_lost:1; /* The carrier signal went down */
        int channel_down:1; /* Power was lost on the channel */
};
```

Using packed structures for flags is clearer and less error prone than using bitwise operators. However, bitwise operators give the programmer additional flexibility. You should use the one that is clearest and easiest for you to use.

Arrays of Structures

Structures and arrays can be combined. For example, suppose we want to record the time a runner completes each lap of a four-lap race. We define a structure to store the time:

```
struct time {
    int hour;   /* hour (24 hour clock ) */
    int minute; /* 0-59 */
    int second; /* 0-59 */
};
#define MAX_LAPS 4 /* we will have only 4 laps */
/* the time of day for each lap*/
struct time lap[MAX_LAPS];
```

We can use this structure as follows:

```
/*
 * Runner just past the timing point
 */
lap[count].hour = hour;
lap[count].minute = minute;
lap[count].second = second;
count++;
```

This array can also be initialized at run time.

Initialization of an array of structures is similar to the initialization of multi-dimensional arrays:

```
struct time start_stop[2] = {
    {10, 0, 0},
    {12, 0, 0}
};
```

Suppose we want to write a program to handle a mailing list. Mailing labels are 5 lines high and 60 characters wide. We need a structure to store names and addresses. The mailing list will be sorted by name for most printouts, and sorted in zip code order for actual mailings. Our mailing list structure looks like this:

```
struct mailing {
    char name[60];      /* last name, first name */
    char address1[60];/* Two lines of street address */
    char address2[60];
    char city[40];
    char state[2];      /* Two character abbreviation */
    long int zip;       /* numeric zip code */
};
```

We can now declare an array to hold our mailing list:

```
/* Our mailing list */
struct mailing list[MAX_ENTRIES];
```

Summary

Structures and unions are some of the more powerful features of the C language. No longer are you limited to C's built-in data type—you can create your own. As we will see in later chapters, structures can be combined with pointers to create very complex and powerful data structures.

Programming Exercises

Exercise 1: Write a program that will take a list of names and addresses, sort them, and produce a set of mailing labels.

Exercise 2: Design a structure to store time and date. Write a function to find the difference between two times in minutes.

Exercise 3: Design an airline reservation data structure that contains the following data:

- Flight number
- Originating airport code (three characters)
- Destination airport code (three characters)

- Starting time
- Arrival time

Exercise 4: Write a program that lists all the planes that leave from two airports specified by the user.

12

Simple Pointers

The choice of a point of view is the initial act of culture.
—Ortega y Gasset

There are things and there are pointers to things, as shown in Figure 12-1.

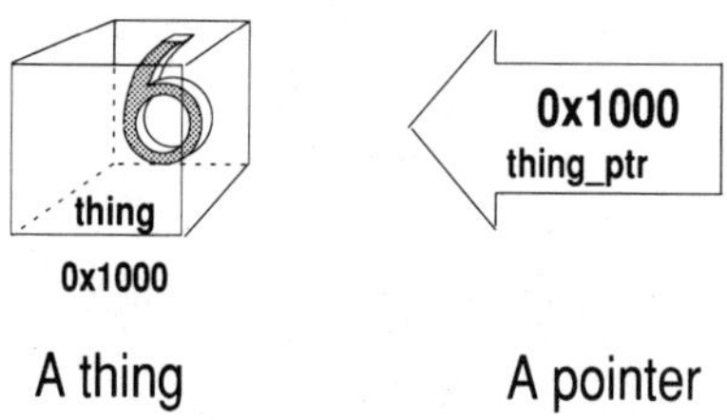

Figure 12-1. A Thing and A Pointer to a Thing

In this book, we will use a box to represent a thing. The name of the variable is written on the bottom of the box. In this case, our variable is named `thing`. The value of the variable is 6.

The address of `thing` is `0x1000`. Addresses are automatically assigned by the C compiler to every variable. Normally, you don't have to worry about the addresses of variables, but it's important to understand that they're there.

Our pointer (`thing_ptr`) points to the variable `thing`. Pointers are also called *address variables* since they contain the addresses of other variables. In this case, our pointer contains the address `0x1000`. Since it is the address of `thing`, we say that `thing_ptr` points to `thing`.

Variables and pointers are much like street addresses and houses. For example, your address might be "214 Green Hill Lane." Houses come in many different shapes and sizes. Addresses are approximately the same size (street, city, state, zip). So while "1600 Pennsylvania Ave." might point to a very big white house and "8347 Undershoe Street" might be a one room shack, both addresses are the same size.

The same is true in C. While things may be big and small, pointers come is one size (relatively small).* Many novice programmers get pointers and their contents confused. In order to limit this problem, all pointer variables in this book end with the extension `_ptr`. You might want to follow this convention in your own programs. Although it's not as common as it should be, this notation is extremely useful.

Several pointers may point to the same thing. Consider the directory of a small town, as shown in the following table.

Building	**Address**
City Hall	1 Main Street
Fire Station	1 Main Street
Police Station	1 Main Street
Gas Station	2 Main Street

In this case, we have a government building which serves many functions. Although it has one address, there are three different pointers to it.

As we will see in this chapter, pointers can be used as a quick and simple way to access arrays. In later chapters we will discover how pointers can be used to create new variables and complex data structures such as linked lists and trees. As you go through the rest of the book, you will be able to understand these data structures as well as create your own.

*This is not strictly true in Turbo C. Because of the strange architecture of the 8086, Turbo C is forced to use both *near* pointers (16 bits) and *far* pointers (32 bits). See the Turbo C manual for details.

A pointer is declared by putting an asterisk (*) in front of the variable name in the declaration statement:

```
int thing, other; /* define a thing and another thing */
int *thing_ptr;  /* define a pointer to a thing */
```

The operators that are used in conjunction with pointers are shown in Table 12-1.

Table 12-1. Pointer Operators

Operator	Meaning
*	Dereference (given a pointer, get the thing referenced).
&	Address of (given a thing, point to it).

The operator ampersand (&) returns the address of a thing which is a pointer. The operator asterisk (*) returns the object which a pointer points to. These operators can easily cause confusion. Let's look at some typical uses of the various pointer operators.

`thing`
: is a thing. The declaration `int thing` does *not* contain an *, so `thing` is not a pointer. For example:

```
thing = 4;
```

`&thing`
: is a pointer to a thing. `thing` is an object. The & (address of operator) gets the address of an object (a pointer), so `&thing` is a pointer. For example:

```
thing_ptr = &thing;   /* Point to the thing */
*thing_ptr = 5;       /* Set "thing" to 5 */
```

`thing_ptr`
: is a thing pointer. The * in the declaration indicates this is a pointer. Also, we have put the extension `_ptr` onto the name.

`*thing_ptr`
: is a thing. The variable `thing_ptr` is a pointer. The * (dereference operator) tells C to look at the data pointed to, not the pointer itself. Note that this points to any integer. It may or may not point to the specific variable `thing`. For example:

```
*thing_ptr = 5;     /* Assign 5 to an integer */
                    /* We may or may not be pointing */
                    /* to the specific integer "thing" */
```

These pointer operations are summarized in Figures 12-2 and 12-3.

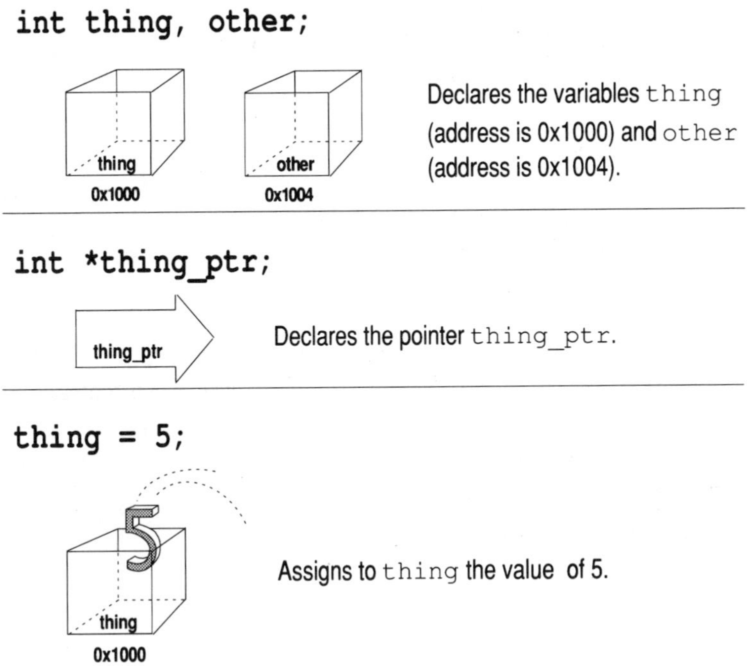
int thing, other;
thing
0x1000
other
0x1004
Declares the variables thing (address is 0x1000) and other (address is 0x1004).
int *thing_ptr;
thing_ptr
Declares the pointer thing_ptr.
thing = 5;
5
thing
0x1000
Assigns to thing the value of 5.

Figure 12-2. Pointer Operations

The following examples show how to misuse the pointer operations.

`*thing` is illegal. It asks C to get the object pointed to by the variable **`thing`**. Since **`thing`** is not a pointer, this is an invalid operation.

`&thing_ptr` is legal, but strange. **`thing_ptr`** is a pointer. The **`&`** (address of operator) gets a pointer to the object (in this case **`thing_ptr`**). The result is a pointer to a pointer.

Program 12-1 illustrates a simple use of pointers. It declares one object, **`thing_var`**, and a pointer, **`thing_ptr`**. **`thing_var`** is set explicitly by the line:

```
thing_var = 2;
```

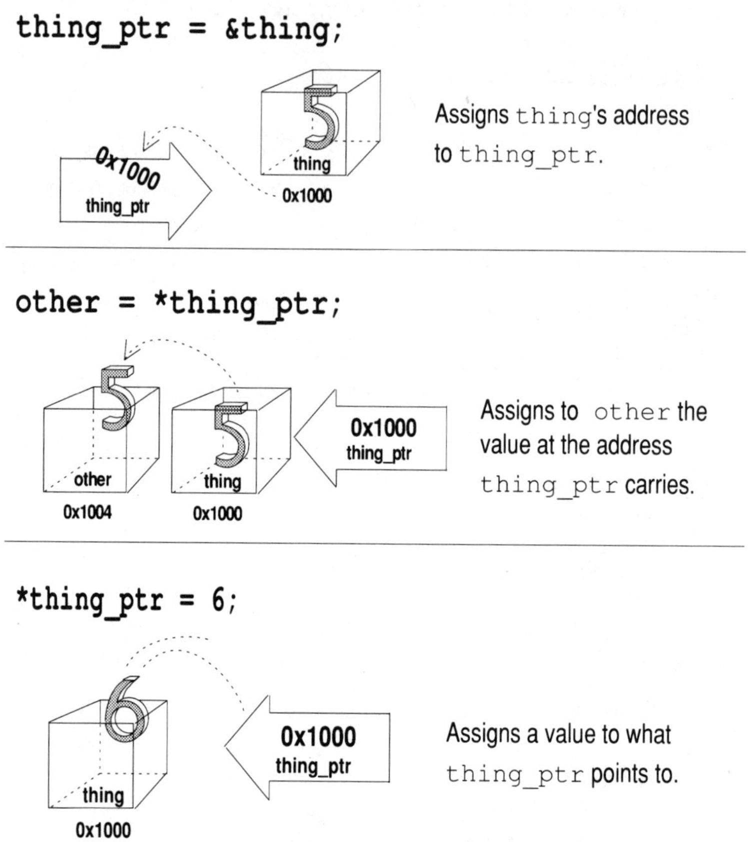
thing_ptr = &thing;
0x1000
thing_ptr
5
thing
0x1000
Assigns thing's address to thing_ptr.
other = *thing_ptr;
5
other
0x1004
5
thing
0x1000
0x1000
thing_ptr
Assigns to other the value at the address thing_ptr carries.
*thing_ptr = 6;
6
thing
0x1000
0x1000
thing_ptr
Assigns a value to what thing_ptr points to.

Figure 12-3. Pointer Operations, Continued

The line:

```
thing_ptr = &thing_var;
```

causes C to set **thing_ptr** to the address of **thing_var**. From this point on, **thing_var** and ***thing_ptr** are the same.

Program 12-1.

```
#include <stdio.h>
main()
{
    int   thing_var;  /* define a variable for thing */
    int  *thing_ptr;  /* define a pointer to thing */

    thing_var = 2;       /* assigning a value to thing */
    (void)printf("Thing %d\n", thing_var);

    thing_ptr = &thing_var; /* make the pointer point to thing */
    *thing_ptr = 3;      /* thing_ptr points to thing_var so */
                         /* thing_var changes to 3 */
    (void)printf("Thing %d\n", thing_var);

    /* another way of doing the printf */
    (void)printf("Thing %d\n", *thing_ptr);
    return (0);
}
```

It is possible for several pointers to point to the same thing:

```
1:      int something;
2:
3:      int       *first_ptr;      /* one pointer */
4:      int       *second_ptr;     /* another pointer */
5:
6:      something = 1;           /* give the thing a value */
7:
8:      first_ptr = &something;
9:      second_ptr = first_ptr;
```

In line 8 we use the `&` operator to change something, a thing, into a pointer that can be assigned to `first_ptr`. Because `first_ptr` and `second_ptr` are both pointers, we can do a direct assignment in line 9.

After executing this program fragment, we have the situation shown in Figure 12-4.

It is important to note that while we have three variables, there is only one integer (`something`). The following are all equivalent:

```
something = 1;
*first_ptr = 1;
*second_ptr = 1;
```

C passes parameters using "call by value." That is, the parameters go only one way into the function. The only result of a function is a single return value. This is illustrated in Figure 12-5.

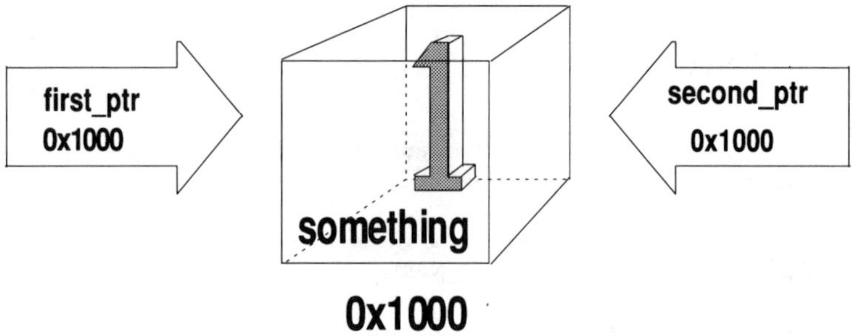

Figure 12-4. Two Pointers and a Thing

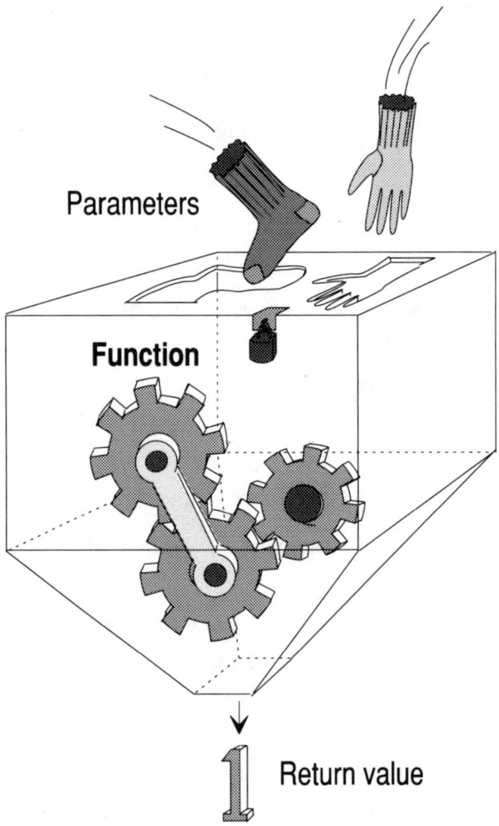

Figure 12-5. Function Call

However, pointers can be used to get around this restriction.

Imagine that there are two people, Sam and Joe, and whenever they meet, Sam can only talk and Joe can only listen. How is Sam ever going to get any information from Joe? Simple, all Sam has to do is tell Joe, "I want you to leave the answer in the mailbox at 335 West 5th Street."

C uses a similar trick to pass information from a function to its caller. In Program 12-2, `main` wants the function `inc_count` to increment the variable `count`. Passing it directly would not work, so a pointer is passed instead ("Here's the address of the variable I want you to increment"). Note that the prototype for `inc_count` contains an `int *`. This indicates that the single parameter given to this function is a pointer to an integer, not the integer itself.

Program 12-2.

```
#include <stdio.h>
main()
{
    int  count = 0;      /* number of times through */

    void inc_count(int *);/* update the counter */

    while (count < 10)
        inc_count(&count);

    return (0);
}

void inc_count(int *count_ptr)
{
    (*count_ptr)++;
}
```

This is represented graphically in Figure 12-6. Note that the parameter is not changed, but what it points to is changed.

Finally, there is a special pointer called `NULL`. It points to nothing. (The actual numeric value is 0.) The standard include file, *stdio.h*, defines the constant `NULL`. The `NULL` pointer is represented graphically in Figure 12-7.

```
while (count < 10)
     inc_count(&count);
```

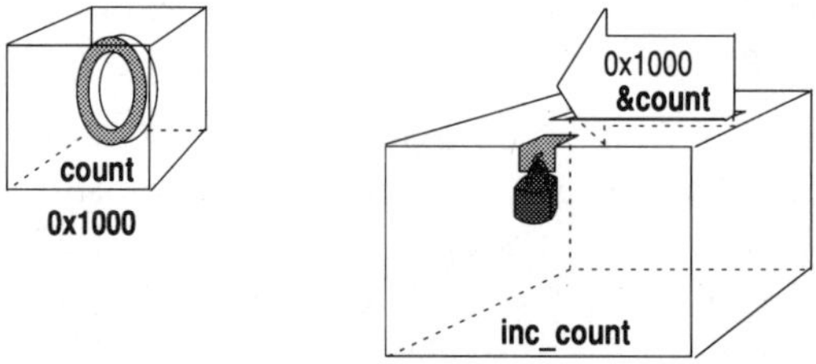

Calls the function `inc_count`, sending `&count` as a parameter. `count`'s address is now in the function.

```
(void) inc_count(count_ptr)
int *count_ptr;
```

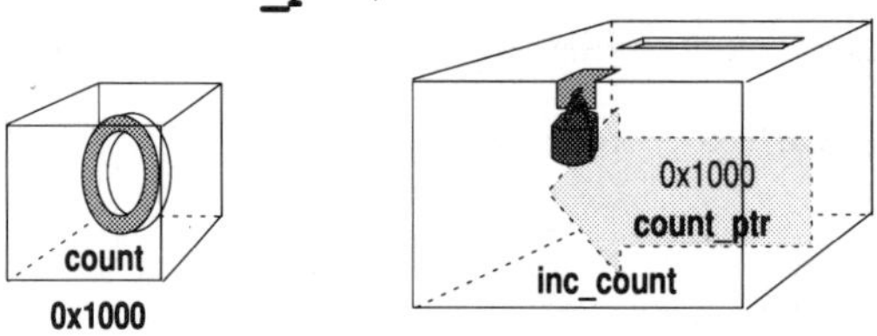

Declaration of the function, giving the local name `count_ptr` to the parameter `&count`.

```
(*count_ptr)++;
```

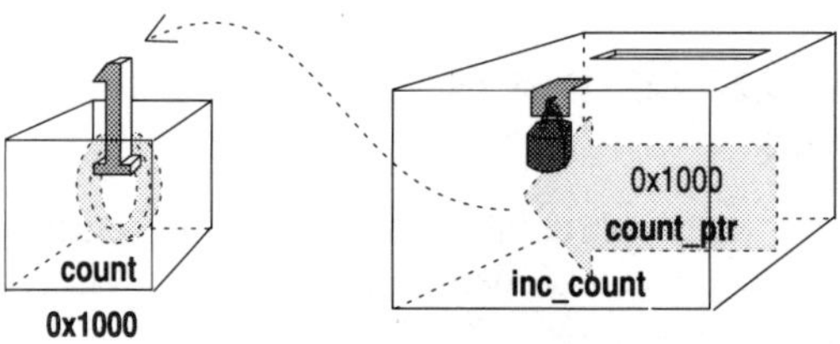

Increments the value at the address that `count_ptr` carries.

Figure 12-6. Call of inc_count

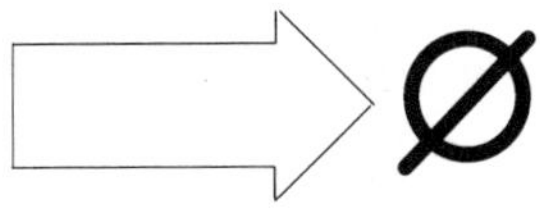

Figure 12-7. NULL

Pointers and Arrays

C allows pointer arithmetic (addition and subtraction). Suppose we have the following:

```
char array[5];
char *array_ptr = &array[0];
```

In this example, `*array_ptr` is the same as `array[0]`, `*(array_ptr+1)` is the same as `array[1]`, `*(array_ptr+2)` is the same as `array[2]`, and so on. Note the use of parentheses. This is represented graphically in Figure 12-7.

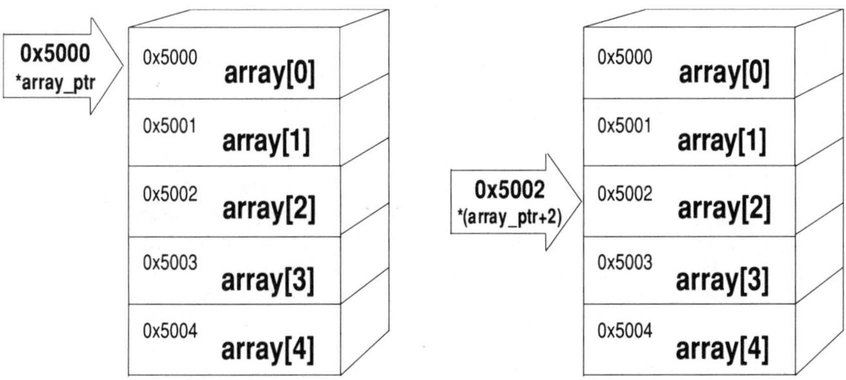

Figure 12-8. Pointers into an Array

However, `(*array_ptr)+1` is *not* the same as `array[1]`. The `+1` is outside the parentheses, so it is added after the dereference. So `(*array_ptr)+1` is the same as `array[0]+1`.

At first glance this may seem like a complex way of representing simple array indices. We are starting with simple pointer arithmetic. In later chapters we will use more complex pointers to handle more difficult functions efficiently.

Because pointers are merely memory addresses, the elements of an array are assigned to consecutive addresses. For example, **array[0]** may be placed at address 0xff000024. Then **array[1]** would be placed at address 0xff000025, and so on. Program 12-3 prints out the elements and addresses of a simple character array.

Program 12-3.

```
#define ARRAY_SIZE 10    /* Number of characters in array */
/* Array to print */
char array[ARRAY_SIZE] = "012345678";

main()
{
    int index;  /* Index into the array */

    for (index = 0; index < ARRAY_SIZE; index++) {
        (void)printf(
            "&array[index]=0x%x (array+index)=0x%x array[index]=0x%x\n",
            &array[index], (array+index), array[index]);
    }
    return (0);
}
```

NOTE

When printing pointers in Turbo C, the special conversion **%p** should be used instead of the **%x** used in the following example.

When run, this program prints:

```
&array[index]=0x20090 (array+index)=0x20090 array[index]=0x30
&array[index]=0x20091 (array+index)=0x20091 array[index]=0x31
&array[index]=0x20092 (array+index)=0x20092 array[index]=0x32
&array[index]=0x20093 (array+index)=0x20093 array[index]=0x33
&array[index]=0x20094 (array+index)=0x20094 array[index]=0x34
&array[index]=0x20095 (array+index)=0x20095 array[index]=0x35
&array[index]=0x20096 (array+index)=0x20096 array[index]=0x36
&array[index]=0x20097 (array+index)=0x20097 array[index]=0x37
&array[index]=0x20098 (array+index)=0x20098 array[index]=0x38
&array[index]=0x20099 (array+index)=0x20099 array[index]=0x0
```

Characters take up one byte, so the elements in a character array will be assigned consecutive addresses. A **short int** takes up two bytes, so in an array of **short int**, the addresses increase by two. Does this mean that **short_array+1** will not work for anything other than characters? No. C automatically scales pointer arithmetic so that it works correctly. In this case **short_array+1** will point to element number 1.

C provides a shorthand for dealing with arrays. Rather than writing:

```
array_ptr = &array[0];
```

we can write:

```
array_ptr = array;
```

C blurs the distinction between pointers and arrays by treating them the same in many cases. Here we use the variable **array** as a pointer, and C automatically did the necessary conversion.

Program 12-4 counts the number of elements that are nonzero and stops when a zero is found. No limit check is provided, so there must be at least one zero in the array.

Program 12-4.

```
#include <stdio.h>

int array[10] = {4, 5, 8, 9, 8, 1, 0, 1, 9, 3};
int index;

main()
{
    index = 0;
    while (array[index] != 0)
        index++;

    (void) printf("Number of elements before zero %d\n",
                  index);
    return (0);
}
```

Program 12-5 is a version of Program 12-4 that uses pointers.

Program 12-5.

```
#include <stdio.h>

int array[10] = {4, 5, 8, 9, 8, 1, 0, 1, 9, 3};
int *array_ptr;

main()
{
    array_ptr = array;

    while ((*array_ptr) != 0)
        array_ptr++;
```

```
    (void) printf("Number of elements before zero %d\n",
                  array_ptr - array);
    return (0);
}
```

Program 12-4 uses the expression `(array[index] != 0)`. This requires the compiler to generate an index operation, which takes longer than a simple pointer dereference, `((*array_ptr) != 0)`.

The expression at the end of this program, `array_ptr - array`, computes how far `array_ptr` is into the array.

When passing an array to a procedure, C will automatically change the array into a pointer. In fact, if you put `&` before the array, C will issue a warning. Program 12-6 illustrates the various ways that an array can be passed to a subroutine.

Program 12-6.

```
#define MAX 10
main()
{
    int  array[MAX];

    void init_array_1();
    void init_array_2();

    /* one way of initializing the array */
    init_array_1(array);

    /* another way of initializing the array */
    init_array_1(&array[0]);

    /* works, but the compiler generates a warning */
    init_array_1(&array);

    /* Similar to the first method but  */
    /*    function is different */
    init_array_2(array);

    return (0);
}
/********************************************************
 * init_array_1 -- Zero out an array                    *
 *                                                      *
 * Parameters                                           *
 *      data -- the array to zero                       *
 ********************************************************/
void init_array_1(int data[])
{
    int  index;
```

```
    for (index = 0; index < MAX; index++)
        data[index] = 0;
}

/********************************************************
 * init_array_2 -- Zero out an array                    *
 *                                                      *
 * Parameters                                           *
 *      data_ptr -- pointer to array to zero            *
 ********************************************************/
void init_array_2(int *data_ptr)
{
    int index;

    for (index = 0; index < MAX; index++)
        *(data_ptr + index) = 0;
}
```

Splitting

Suppose we are given a string of the form "Last/First." We want to split this into two strings, one containing the first name and one containing the last.

Program 12-7 reads in a single line, stripping the newline character from it. The function `strchr` is called to find the location of the slash (/). (The function `strchr` is actually a standard function. We have duplicated it for this example so you can see how it works.)

At this point `last_ptr` points to the first character of the last name and `first_ptr` points to slash. We then split the string by replacing the slash (/) with an end of string (NUL or `\0`). Now `last_ptr` points to just the last name and `first_ptr` points to a null string. Moving `first_ptr` to the next character makes it point to the beginning of the first name.

The sequence of steps in splitting the string is illustrated in Figure 12-9.

Program 12-7 contains the full program, which demonstrates how pointers and character arrays may be used for simple string processing.

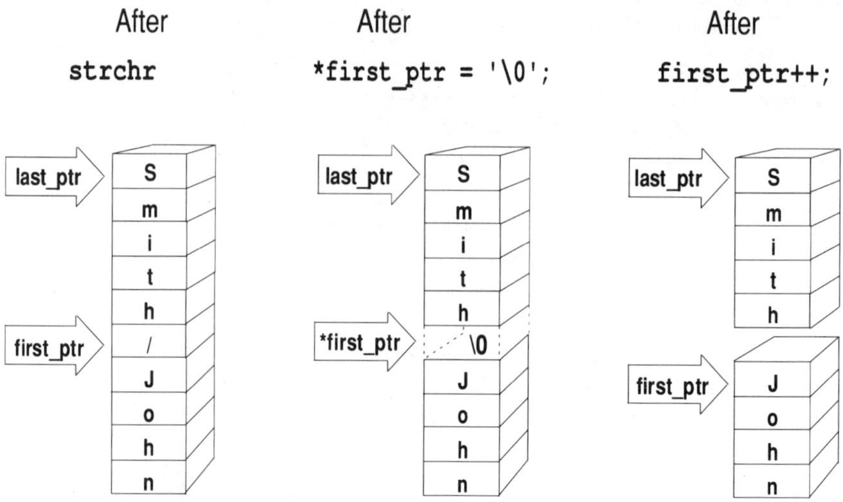

Figure 12-9. Splitting a String

Program 12-7.

```
/********************************************************
 * split -- split an entry of the form Last/First       *
 *      into two parts.                                  *
 ********************************************************/
#include <stdio.h>
#include <string.h>

/* Our version of the library function */
char *strchr(char *, char);

main()
{
    char line[80];       /* The input line */
    char *first_ptr;     /* pointer to the first name */
    char *last_ptr;      /* pointer to the last name */

    (void)fgets(line, sizeof(line), stdin);

    /* Get rid of trailing newline */
    line[strlen(line)-1] = '\0';

    last_ptr = line;     /* last name is at beginning of line */

    first_ptr = strchr(line, '/');      /* Find slash */

    /* Check for an error */
    if (first_ptr == NULL) {
```

```
        (void)fprintf(stderr,
            "Error: Unable to find slash in %s\n", line);
        exit (8);
    }

    *first_ptr = '\0';  /* Zero out the slash */

    first_ptr++;        /* Move to first character of name */

    (void)printf("First:%s Last:%s\n", first_ptr, last_ptr);
    return (0);
}
/********************************************************
 * strchr -- find a character in a string               *
 *      Duplicate of a standard library function,       *
 *      put here for illustrative purposes.             *
 *                                                      *
 * Parameters                                           *
 *      string_ptr -- string to look through            *
 *      find -- character to find                       *
 *                                                      *
 * Returns                                              *
 *      pointer to 1st occurrence of character          *
 *      in string or NULL for error                     *
 ********************************************************/
char *strchr(char * string_ptr, char find)
{
    while (*string_ptr != find) {

        /* Check for end */

        if (*string_ptr == '\0')
            return (NULL);        /* not found */

        string_ptr++;
    }
    return (string_ptr);         /* Found */
}
```

Question 12–1: The following program is supposed to print out:

```
Name: tmp1
```

but instead we get:

```
Name: !_@$#ds80
```

(Your results may vary.) Why?

```
#include <stdio.h>
#include <string.h>

main()
```

```
{
    char *tmp_name(void); /* get name of a temporary file */

    (void)printf("Name: %s\n", tmp_name());
    return (0);
}
/********************************************************
 * tmp_name -- return a temporary filename.              *
 *              Each time it is called, a new name       *
 *              will be returned.                        *
 *                                                       *
 * Returns                                               *
 *      pointer to a temporary name                      *
 ********************************************************/
char *tmp_name(void)
{
    char name[30];  /* the name */
    static int sequence = 0;  /* sequence number for last digit */

    sequence++; /* bump sequence number */
    (void)strcpy(name, "tmp");

    /* turn a numeric sequence number into an ascii digit */
    name[3] = sequence + '0';

    /* store end of string */
    name[4] = '\0';

    /* return pointer */
    return (name);
}
```

Pointers and Structures

In Chapter 11, *Advanced Types*, we defined a structure for a mailing list:

```
struct mailing {
    char name[60];      /* last name, first name */
    char address1[60];/* Two lines of street address */
    char address2[60];
    char city[40];
    char state[2];      /* Two character abbreviation */
    long int zip;       /* numeric zip code */
} list[MAX_ENTRIES];
```

Mailing lists must frequently be sorted by name and zip code. We could sort the entries themselves, but each entry is 226 bytes long. That's a lot of data to move around. One way around this problem is to declare an array of pointers, and then sort the pointers:

```
/* Pointer to the data */
struct mailing *list_ptrs[MAX_ENTRIES];
int current;     /* current mailing list entry */
    for (current = 0; current = number_of_entries; current++)
        list_ptrs = &list[current];
    /* Sort list_ptrs by zip code */
```

Now instead of having to move a 226-byte structure around, we are moving 4-byte pointers. Our sorting is much faster. Imagine that you had a warehouse full of big heavy boxes and you needed to locate any box quickly. You could put them in alphabetical order, but that would require a lot of moving. Instead you assign each location a number, write down the name and number on index cards, and sort the cards by name.

Command-line Arguments

The procedure `main` actually takes two arguments. They are called `argc` and `argv`:

```
main(int argc, char *argv[])
{
```

(It's easy to remember which comes first when you realize that they are in alphabetical order.)

The parameter `argc` is the number of arguments on the command line (including the program name). The array `argv` contains the actual arguments. For example, if the program `args` were run with the command line:

```
args this is a test
```

then:

```
   argc =    5
argv[0] =   "args"
argv[1] =   "this"
argv[2] =   "is"
argv[3] =   "a"
argv[4] =   "test"
```

NOTE

The UNIX shell expands wildcard characters like *, ?, and [ ] before sending the command line to the program. See your **sh** or **csh** manual for details.

Turbo C will expand wildcard characters if the file *WILDARG.OBJ* is linked with your program. See the Turbo C manual for details.

Almost all UNIX commands use a standard command-line format. This standard has carried over into other environments. A standard UNIX command has the form:

command options file1 file1 file3 **. . .**

Options are preceded by a dash (–) and are usually a single letter. For example, the option **–v** might turn on verbose mode for a particular command. If the option takes a parameter, it follows the letter. For example, the switch **–m1024** sets the maximum number of symbols to 1024 and **–ooutfile** sets the output filename to *outfile*.

Let's look at writing a program that can read the command line arguments and act accordingly. This program will format and print files. Part of the documentation for the program is given here:

print_file [–v] [–l*length*] [–o*name*] [*file1*] [*file2*] **. . .**

where:

–v	specifies verbose options. Turns on a lot of progress information messages.
–l*length*	sets the page size to *length* lines. (Default = 66)
–o*name*	sets the output file to *name*. (Default = *print.out*)
file1, *file2*, ...	is a list of files to print. If no files are specified, then the file *print.in* is printed.

We can use a **while** loop to cycle through the command-line options. The actual loop is:

```
while ((argc > 1) && (argv[1][0] == '-')) {
```

There is always one argument, the program name. The expression **(argc > 1)** checks for additional arguments. The first one will be numbered 1. The first character of the first argument is **argv[1][0]**. If this is a dash, we have an option.

At the end of the loop is the code:

```
argc--;
argv++;
}
```

This consumes an argument. The number of arguments is decremented to indicate one less option, and the pointer to the first option is incremented, shifting the list to the left one place. (Note: after the first increment, `argv[0]` no longer points to the program name.)

The **switch** statement is used to decode the options. Character 0 of the argument is the dash (–). Character 1 is the option character, so we use the expression:

```
switch (argv[1][1]) {
```

to decode the option.

The option **–v** has no arguments; it just causes a flag to be set.

The option **–o** takes a filename. Rather than copy the whole string, we set the character pointer `out_file` to point to the name part of the string. By this time we know the following:

```
argv[1][0]    ='-'
argv[1][1]    ='o'
argv[1][2]    = first character of the filename
```

We set `out_file` to point to the string with the statement:

```
out_file = &argv[1][2];
```

The `–l` option takes an integer argument. The library function `atoi` is used to convert the string into an integer. From the previous example, we know that `argv[1][2]` is the first character of the string containing the number. This string is passed to `atoi`.

Finally, all the options are parsed and we fall through to the processing loop. This merely executes the function `do_file` for each file argument. Program 12-8 contains the `print` program.

Program 12-8.

```
/********************************************************
 * print -- format files for printing                   *
 ********************************************************/
#include <stdio.h>
#include <stdlib.h>       /* ANSI Standard only */

int verbose = 0;          /* verbose mode (default = false) */
char *out_file = "print.out";   /* output filename */
char *program_name;       /* name of the program (for errors) */
```

```
int line_max = 66;       /* number of lines per page */

main(int argc, char *argv[])
{
    void do_file(char *); /* print a file */
    void usage(void);     /* tell user how to use the program */

    /* save the program name for future use */
    program_name = argv[0];

    /*
     * loop for each option.
     *   Stop if we run out of arguments
     *   or we get an argument without a dash.
     */
    while ((argc > 1) && (argv[1][0] == '-')) {
        /*
         * argv[1][1] is the actual option character.
         */
        switch (argv[1][1]) {
            /*
             * -v verbose
             */
            case 'v':
                verbose = 1;
                break;
            /*
             * -o<name>  output file
             *    [0] is the dash
             *    [1] is the "o"
             *    [2] starts the name
             */
            case 'o':
                out_file = &argv[1][2];
                break;
            /*
             * -l<number> set max number of lines
             */
            case 'l':
                line_max = atoi(&argv[1][2]);
                break;
            default:
                (void)fprintf(stderr,"Bad option %s\n", argv[1]);
                usage();
        }
        /*
         * move the argument list up one
         * move the count down one
         */
        argv++;
        argc--;
    }
```

```
    /*
     * At this point all the options have been processed.
     * Check to see if we have no files in the list
     * and if so, we need to process just standard in.
     */
    if (argc == 1) {
        do_file("print.in");
    } else {
        while (argc > 1) {
          do_file(argv[1]);
          argv++;
          argc--;
        }
    }
    return (0);
}
/********************************************************
 * do_file -- dummy routine to handle a file            *
 *                                                      *
 * Parameter                                            *
 *      name -- name of the file to print               *
 ********************************************************/
void do_file(char *name)
{
    (void)printf("Verbose %d Lines %d Input %s Output %s\n",
        verbose, line_max, name, out_file);
}
/********************************************************
 * usage -- tell the user how to use this program and   *
 *              exit                                    *
 ********************************************************/
void usage(void)
{
    (void)fprintf(stderr,"Usage is %s [options] [file-list]\n",
                                program_name);
    (void)fprintf(stderr,"Options\n");
    (void)fprintf(stderr,"  -v          verbose\n");
    (void)fprintf(stderr,"  -l<number>  Number of lines\n");
    (void)fprintf(stderr,"  -o<name>    Set output filename\n");
    exit (8);
}
```

This is one way of parsing the argument list. The use of the **while** loop and **switch** statement is simple and easy to understand. This method does have a limitation. The argument must immediately follow the options. For example, "`-odata.out`" will work, but "`-o  data.out`" will not. An improved parser would make the program more friendly, but this works only for simple programs.

Answers

Answer 12–1: The problem is that the variable `name` is a temporary variable. The compiler allocates space for the name when the function is entered and reclaims the space when the function exits. The function assigns `name` the correct value and returns a pointer to it. However, the function is over, so `name` disappears and we have a pointer with an illegal value.

The solution is to declare `name` **static**. That way, it is a permanent variable and will not disappear at the end of the function.

Question 12–2: After fixing the function, we try using it for two filenames. The program below should print out:

```
Name: tmp1
Name: tmp2
```

but it doesn't. What does it print and why?

```
#include <stdio.h>
#include <string.h>

main()
{
    char *tmp_name(void); /* get name of a temporary file */
    char *name1;
    char *name2;

    name1 = tmp_name();
    name2 = tmp_name();
    (void)printf("Name: %s\n", name1);
    (void)printf("Name: %s\n", name2);
    return (0);
}
/********************************************************
 * tmp_name -- return a temporary filename.             *
 *              Each time it is called a new name       *
 *              will be returned.                       *
 *                                                      *
 * Returns                                              *
 *      pointer to a temporary name                     *
 ********************************************************/
char *tmp_name(void)
{
    static char name[30];  /* the name */
    static int sequence = 0;  /* sequence number for last digit */

    sequence++; /* bump sequence number */
    (void)strcpy(name, "tmp");

    /* turn a numeric sequence number into an ascii digit */
    name[3] = sequence + '0';
```

```
        /* store end of string */
        name[4] = '\0';

        /* return pointer */
        return (name);
}
```

Answer 12–2: The first call to `tmp_name` returns a pointer to `name`. There is only one `name`. The second call to `tmp_name` changes `name` and returns a pointer to it. So we have two pointers, and they point to the same thing, `name`.

Several library functions return pointers to **static** strings. A second call to one of these routines will overwrite the first value. A solution to this problem is to copy the values below:

```
char name1[100];
char name2[100];
(void)strcpy(name1, tmp_name());
(void)strcpy(name2, tmp_name());
```

Programming Problems

Exercise 1: Write a program that uses pointers to set each element of an array to zero.

Exercise 2: Write a function that takes a single string as its argument and returns a pointer to the first nonwhite character in the string.

13

File Input/Output

Conversion Routines
Binary and ASCII Files
Binary I/O
Buffering Problems
Unbuffered I/O
Designing File Formats

I the heir of all the ages, in the foremost files of time.
—Tennyson

A *file* is a collection of related data. C treats a file as a series of bytes. Many files reside on disk; however, devices like terminals, printers, and magnetic tapes are also considered files.

The C library contains a large number of routines for manipulating files. The declarations for the structures and functions used by the file functions are stored in the standard include file `<stdio.h>`. Before doing anything with the filesystem, you must put the line:

```
#include <stdio.h>
```

at the beginning of your program.

The declaration for a file variable is:

FILE **file-variable* ;   /* *comment* */

For example:

```
#include <stdio.h>
FILE *in_file;  /* file containing the input data */
```

Before a file can be used, it must be opened using the function `fopen`. `fopen` returns a pointer to the file structure for the file. The format for `fopen` is:

file_variable = fopen(*name*, *mode*);

where:

file-variable is a file variable.

name is the actual name of the file (*data.txt*, *temp.dat*, etc.).

mode indicates if the file is to be read or written. *mode* is `w` for writing and `r` for reading.

The function `fclose` will close the file. The format of `fclose` is:

status = fclose(*file-variable*);

or:

(void)fclose(*file-variable*);

The variable *status* will be zero if the `fclose` was successful or nonzero for an error. If you don't care about the status, the second form closes the file and discards the return value.

C provides three pre-opened files. These are listed in Table 13-1.

Table 13-1. Standard Files

File	Description
stdin	Standard input (open for reading).
stdout	Standard output (open for writing).
stderr	Standard error (open for writing).

The function `fgetc` will read a single character from a file. If there is no more data in the file, it will return the constant `EOF` (`EOF` is defined in *stdio.h*). Note that `fgetc` returns an integer, not a character. This is necessary because the `EOF` flag must be a noncharacter value.

Program 13-1 counts the number of characters in the file *input.txt*.

Program 13-1.

```
#include <stdio.h>
#define FILE_NAME "input.txt"
#include <stdlib.h>      /* ANSI Standard C file */

main()
{
    int             count = 0;  /* number of characters seen */
    FILE           *in_file;    /* input file */

    /* character or EOF flag from input */
    int             ch;

    in_file = fopen(FILE_NAME, "r");
    if (in_file == NULL) {
        (void)printf("Can not open %s\n", FILE_NAME);
        exit(8);
    }

    while (1) {
        ch = fgetc(in_file);
        if (ch == EOF)
            break;
        count++;
    }
    (void) printf("Number of characters in %s is %d\n",
                  FILE_NAME, count);

    (void) fclose(in_file);
    return (0);
}
```

A similar function, **fputc**, exists for writing a single character. Its format is:

fputc(*character*, *file*);

The functions **fgets** and **fputs** work on one line at a time. The format of the **fgets** call is:

string_ptr = fgets(*string*, *size*, *file*);

where:

string_ptr is equal to *string* if the read was successful or **NULL** if end of file or an error is detected.

string is a character array where the function places the string.

size is the size of the character array. **fgets** will read until it gets a line (complete with ending **\n**) or it reads *size*–1 characters. It will then end the string with a null (**\0**).

Problems can occur if the size specified is too big. C provides a convenient way of making sure that the size parameter is just right through the use of the **sizeof** operator.

The **sizeof** operator returns the size in bytes of its argument. For example:

```
long int array[10];      /* (Each element contains 4 bytes) */
char string[30];
```

Then **sizeof(string)** is 30.

NOTE

> This is not the same as length. **sizeof** returns the number of bytes in **string** (used or not). A **long int** takes up 4 bytes so **sizeof(array)** is 40.

The **sizeof** operator is particularly useful when using the **fgets** routine. By using **sizeof**, you don't have to worry about how big a string is or, worse, what happens if someone changes the dimension of the string.

For example:

```
char    string[100];
. . .
(void)fgets(string, sizeof(string), in_file);
```

fputs is similar to **fgets** except it writes a string instead of reading it. The format of the **fputs** function is:

string_ptr = fputs(*string*, *file*);

The parameters to **fputs** are similar to the ones for **fgets**. **fputs** needs no size because it gets the size of the line to write from the length of the string. (It keeps writing until it hits a null, **'\0'**.)

Conversion Routines

So far we have just discussed writing characters and strings. In this section, we will discuss some of the more sophisticated I/O operations and conversions.

In order to write a number to a printer or terminal, you must convert it to characters. The printer only understands characters, not numbers. For example, the number 567 must be converted to three characters: 5, 6, and 7 in order to be printed.

The function **fprintf** will convert data and write it to a file. The general form of the **fprintf** function is:

count = fprintf(*file*, *format*, *parameter-1*, *parameter-2*, . . .);

where:

count is the number of characters sent or –1 if an error occurred.

format describes how the arguments are to be printed.

parameter-1, *parameter-2*, . . .
are parameters to be converted and sent.

fprintf has two sister functions: **printf** and **sprintf**. **printf()** is equivalent to **fprintf**, with a first argument of **stdout()**. **sprintf** is similar to **fprintf** except that the first argument is a string. For example:

```
char string[40];          /* the filename */
/* current file number for this segment */
int file_number = 0;
(void)sprintf(string, "file.%d", file_number);
file_number++;
out_file = fopen(string, "w");
```

WARNING

The return value of **sprintf** differs from system to system. The ANSI standard defines it as the number of characters stored in the string; however, some implementations of UNIX C define it to be a pointer to the string.

scanf has similar sister functions: **fscanf** and **sscanf**. The format for **fscanf** is:

number = fscanf(*file*, *format*, &*parameter-1*, . . .);

where:

number is the number of parameters successfully converted.

file is a file opened for reading.

format describes the data to be read.

parameter-1 is the first parameter to be read.

sscanf is similar, except that a string is scanned instead of a file.

`scanf` is very fussy about where the end-of-line characters occur in the input. Frequently, the user has to type extra returns to get `scanf` unstuck.

We have avoided this problem by using `fgets` to read a line from the file and then use `sscanf` to parse it. `fgets` always gets a single line without trouble. For example:

```
char line[100];      /* Line from the keyboard */
int count, total;    /* Number of entries & total value */
int scan_count;      /* Number of parameters scanned */

(void)fgets(line, sizeof(line), stdin);

/* Warning: Works for ANSI standard 'sscanf' only */
scan_count = sscanf(line,"%d %d", &count, &total);

switch (scan count) {
    case 0:
        printf("Didn't find any number\n");
        break;
    case 1:
        printf("Found 'count' (%d), but not 'total'\n",
            count);
        break;
    case 2:
        printf("Found both 'count' (%d) and 'total' (%d)\n",
            count, total);
        break;
    default:
        printf("This should not be possible\n");
        printf("Do you have an old style sscanf that\n");
        printf("returns a pointer instead of a count?\n");
        break;
}
```

Question 13–1: No matter what filename we give the following program, our program can't find it. Why?

```
#include <stdio.h>
#include <stdlib.h>      /* ANSI Standard only */

main()
{
    char            name[100];  /* name of the file to use  */
    FILE            *in_file;   /* file for input */

    (void) printf("Name? ");
    (void) fgets(name, sizeof(name), stdin);

    in_file = fopen(name, "r");
    if (in_file == NULL) {
        (void) fprintf(stderr, "Could not open file\n");
```

```
            exit(8);
        }
        (void) printf("File found\n");
        (void) fclose(in_file);
        return (0);
    }
```

Binary and ASCII Files

We have been working with ASCII files. ASCII stands for *A*merican *S*tandard *C*ode for *I*nformation *I*nterchange. It is a set of 95 printable characters and 33 control codes. ASCII files are readable text. When you write a program, the *prog*.c file is in ASCII.

Terminals, keyboards, and printers deal with character data. When you want to write a number like 1234 to the screen, it must be converted to four characters (`'1'`, `'2'`, `'3'`, and `'4'`) and written. Similarly, when you read a number from the keyboard, the data must be converted from characters to integers. This is done by the `sscanf` routine.

The ASCII character `'0'` has the value of 48, `'1'` has the value of 49, and so on. When you want to convert a single digit from ASCII to integer, you must subtract this number. For example:

```
int integer;
char ch;
ch
= '5';
integer = ch - 48;
(void)printf("Integer %d\n", integer);
```

Rather than remember that `'0'` is 48, you can just subtract `'0'`:

```
integer = ch - '0';
```

Computers work on binary data. When reading numbers from an ASCII file, the program must process the character data through a conversion routine like `sscanf`. This is expensive. Binary files require no conversion. They also generally take up less space than ASCII files. The drawback is they cannot be directly printed on a terminal or printer. (If you've ever seen a long printout coming out of the printer displaying pages with a few characters at the top that look like "!E#(@$%@^Aa^AA^^JHC%^X," then you know what happens when you try to print a binary file.)

ASCII files are portable (for the most part). They can be moved from machine to machine with very little trouble. Binary files are almost certainly nonportable. Unless you are an expert programmer, it is almost impossible to make a portable binary file.

Which file type should you use? In most cases, ASCII. If you have small to medium amounts of data, the conversion time will not seriously affect the performance of your program. (Who cares if it takes 0.5 seconds to start up instead of 0.3?) ASCII files make it easy to check the data for correctness.

Only when you are using large amounts of data will the space and performance problems force you to use the binary format.

The End-of-line Puzzle

Back in the dark ages BC (Before Computers), there existed a magical device called a Teletype Model 33. This amazing machine contained a shift register made out of a motor, with a rotor, and a keyboard ROM consisting solely of levers and springs. It contained a keyboard, a printer, and a paper tape reader/punch. It could transmit messages over the phones using a modem at the rate of 10 characters a second.

The Teletype had a problem. It took two-tenths of a second to move the printhead from the right side to the left. Two-tenths of a second is two character times. If a second character came while the printhead was in the middle of a return, it was lost.

The Teletype people solved this problem by making end-of-line two characters: <carriage return> to position the printhead at the left margin and <line feed> to move the paper up one line.

When the early computers came out, some designers realized that using two characters for end of line wasted storage (at this time storage was very expensive). Some picked <line feed> for their end of line, some <carriage return>. Some of the diehards stayed with the two-character sequence.

UNIX uses <line feed> for end of line. The newline character, `\n`, is code 0xA (LF or <line feed>).

DOS uses the two characters: <line feed><carriage return>. Compiler designers had a problem. What do we do about the old C programs which thought that newline was just <line feed>? The solution was to add code to the I/O library that stripped out the <carriage return> characters from ASCII input files and changed <line feed> to <line feed> <carriage return> on output.

In MS-DOS it makes a difference whether or not a file is opened as ASCII or binary. The flag `b` is used to indicate a binary file:

```
/* open ASCII file for reading */
ascii_file = fopen("name", "r");
/* open binary file for reading */
binary_file = fopen("name", "rb");
```

Question 13–2: The routine `fputc` can be used to write out a single byte of a binary file. The following program writes out numbers 0 to 127 to a file called *test.out*. It works just fine on UNIX, creating a 128-byte long file; however, on DOS, the file contains 129 bytes. Why?

```
#include <stdio.h>
#include <stdlib.h>       /* ANSI Standard only */
main()
{
    int cur_char;     /* current character to write */
    FILE *out_file; /* output file */

    out_file = fopen("test.out", "w");
    if (out_file == NULL) {
        (void)fprintf(stderr,"Can not open output file\n");
        exit (8);
    }

    for (cur_char = 0; cur_char < 128; cur_char++) {
        (void)fputc(cur_char, out_file);
    }
    (void)fclose(out_file);
    return (0);
}
```

Hint: Here is a hex dump of the DOS file:

```
000:0001 0203 0405 0607 0809 0d0a 0b0c 0d0e
010:0f10 1112 1314 1516 1718 191a 1b1c 1d1e
020:1f20 2122 2324 2526 2728 292a 2b2c 2d2e
030:2f30 3132 3334 3536 3738 393a 3b3c 3d3e
040:3f40 4142 4344 4546 4748 494a 4b4c 4d4e
050:4f50 5152 5354 5556 5758 595a 5b5c 5d5e
060:5f60 6162 6364 6566 6768 696a 6b6c 6d6e
070:6f70 7172 7374 7576 7778 797a 7b7c 7d7e
080:7f
```

UNIX programmers don't have to worry about the C library automatically fixing their ASCII files. In UNIX, a file is a file and ASCII is no different from binary. In fact you can write a half ASCII, half binary file if you want to. The `b` is not used and is illegal on most UNIX machines.

Binary I/O

Binary I/O is accomplished through two routines: `fread` and `fwrite`. The syntax for `fread` is:

read_size = fread (*data_ptr*, 1, *size*, *file*);

where:

read_size is the size of the data that was read. If this is less than *size*, then an end of file or error will occur.

data_ptr is the pointer to the data to be read.

size is the number of bytes to be read.

file is the input file.

For example:

```
struct {
        int     width;
        int     height;
} rectangle;
if (fread((char *)&rectangle, 1, sizeof(rectangle), in_file) !=
        sizeof(rectangle)) {
        fprintf(stderr,"Unable to read rectangle\n");
        exit (8);
}
```

In this example we are reading in the structure rectangle. The `&` operator makes it into a pointer. The cast `(char *)` keeps `lint` happy. The `sizeof` operator is used to determine how many bytes to read in, as well as to check that the read was successful.

`fwrite` has a calling sequence similar to `fread`:

write_size = fwrite (*data_ptr*, 1, *size*, *file*);

NOTE

In order to make programming simpler and easier, we always use one as the second parameter to `fread` and `fwrite`. For a full description of these functions, see your C reference manual.

Buffering Problems

Buffered I/O does not write immediately to the file. Instead, the data is kept in a buffer until there is enough for a big write, or until it is flushed. The following program is designed to print out a progress message as each section is finished:

```
(void)printf("Starting");
do_step_1();
(void)printf("Step 1 complete");
do_step_2();
(void)printf("Step 2 complete");
do_step_3();
(void)printf("Step 3 complete\n");
```

Instead of writing the messages as each step is completed, the `printf` function puts them in a buffer. Only when the program is finished does the buffer get flushed and all the messages come spilling out at once.

The routine `fflush` will force the flushing of the buffers. Properly written, our example should be:

```
(void)printf("Starting");
(void)fflush(stdout);
do_step_1();
(void)printf("Step 1 complete");
(void)fflush(stdout);
do_step_2();
(void)printf("Step 2 complete");
(void)fflush(stdout);
do_step_3();
(void)printf("Step 3 complete\n");
(void)fflush(stdout);
```

Unbuffered I/O

In buffered I/O, data is buffered and then sent to the file. In unbuffered I/O, the data is immediately sent to the file.

If you drop a number of paperclips on the floor, you can pick them up in buffered or unbuffered mode. In buffered mode, you use your right hand to pick up a paper clip and transfer it to your left hand. The process is repeated until your left hand is full, then you dump a handful of paperclips into the box on your desk.

In unbuffered mode, you pick up a paperclip and dump it immediately into the box. There is no left-hand buffer.

In most cases, buffered I/O should be used instead of unbuffered. In unbuffered I/O, each read or write requires a system call. Any call to the operating system is expensive. Buffered I/O minimizes these calls.

Unbuffered I/O should be used only when reading or writing large amounts of binary data or when direct control of a device or file is required.

Back to our paperclip example—if we were picking up small items like paperclips, we would probably use a left-hand buffer. But if we were picking up cannon balls (which are much larger), no buffer would be used.

The `open` system call is used for opening an unbuffered file. The macro definitions used by this call differ from system to system. We are using both UNIX and MS-DOS, so we have used conditional compilation (**#ifdef/#endif**) to bring in the correct files:

```
#ifndef __MSDOS__          /* if we are not MS-DOS */
#define __UNIX__           /* then we are UNIX */
#endif __MSDOS__
#ifdef __UNIX__
#include <sys/types.h>  /* file defines for UNIX filesystem */
#include <sys/stat.h>
#include <fcntl.h>
#endif __UNIX__
#ifdef __MSDOS__
#include <stdlib.h>
#include <fcntl.h>      /* file defines for DOS filesystem */
#include <sys\stat.h>
#include <io.h>
#endif __MSDOS__
int     file_descriptor;
file_descriptor = open(name, flags);         /* existing file */
file_descriptor = open(name, flags, mode);  /*new file */
```

where:

file_descriptor is an integer that is used to identify the file for the read, write, and close calls. If file descriptor is less than zero, an error occurred.

name is the name of the file.

flags are defined in the *fcntl* header file. Flags are described in Table 13-2.

mode is the protection mode for the file. Normally, this is 0666 for most files.

Table 13-2. Open Flags

Flag	Meaning
O_RDONLY	Open for reading only.
O_WRONLY	Open for writing only.
O_RDWR	Open for reading and writing.
O_APPEND	Append new data at the end of the file.
O_CREAT	Create file (mode required when this flag present).
O_TRUNC	If the file exists, truncate it to zero length.
O_EXCL	Fail if file exists.
O_BINARY	Open in binary mode (UNIX does not have this flag).

For example, to open the existing file *data.txt* in text mode for reading, we use the following:

```
data_fd = open("data.txt", O_RDONLY);
```

The next example shows how to create a file called *output.dat* for writing only:

```
out_fd = open("output.dat", O_CREAT|O_WRONLY);
```

Notice that we combined flags using the or operator (|). This is a quick and easy way of merging multiple flags.

When any program is initially run, there are three files already opened. These are described in Table 13-3.

Table 13-3. Standard Unbuffered Files

File Number	Description
0	Standard in.
1	Standard out.
2	Standard error.

The format of the `read` call is:

read_size = read (*file_descriptor*, *buffer*, *size*);

where:

read_size is the number of bytes read. Zero indicates end of file, and a negative number indicates an error.

file_descriptor is the file descriptor of an open file.

buffer is the pointer to the place to read the data.

size is the size of the data to be read.

The format of a `write` call is:

write_size = write (*file_descriptor*, *buffer*, *size*);

where:

write_size is the number of bytes written. A negative number indicates an error.

file_descriptor is the file descriptor of an open file.

buffer is the pointer to the data to be written.

size is the size of the data to be written.

Finally, the `close` call will close the file:

flag = close (*file_descriptor*)

where:

flag is zero for success, negative for error.

file_descriptor is the file descriptor of an open file.

Program 13-2 copies a file. Unbuffered I/O is used because of the large buffer size. It makes no sense to use buffered I/O to read 1K of data into a buffer and then transfer it into a 16K buffer.

Program 13-2.

```
/****************************************
 * copy -- copy one file to another.    *
 *                                      *
 * Usage                                *
 *      copy <from> <to>                *
 *                                      *
 * <from> -- the file to copy from      *
 * <to>   -- the file to copy into      *
 ****************************************/
#include <stdio.h>
#ifndef __MSDOS__           /* if we are not MS-DOS */
#define __UNIX__            /* then we are UNIX */
#endif __MSDOS__

#include <stdlib.h>        /* ANSI Standard C file */

#ifdef __UNIX__
#include <sys/types.h>  /* file defines for UNIX filesystem */
```

```
#include <sys/stat.h>
#include <fcntl.h>
#endif __UNIX__

#ifdef __MSDOS__
#include <fcntl.h>      /* file defines for DOS filesystem */
#include <sys\stat.h>
#include <io.h>
#endif __MSDOS__

void  exit();                   /* lib routine */

#define BUFFER_SIZE (16 * 1024) /* use 16K buffers */

main(int argc, char *argv[])
{
    char  buffer[BUFFER_SIZE];  /* buffer for data */
    int   in_file;              /* input file descriptor */
    int   out_file;             /* output file descriptor */
    int   read_size;            /* number of bytes on last read */

    if (argc != 3) {
        (void) fprintf(stderr, "Error:Wrong number of arguments\n");
        (void) fprintf(stderr, "Usage is: copy <from> <to>\n");
        exit(8);
    }
    in_file = open(argv[1], O_RDONLY);
    if (in_file < 0) {
        (void) fprintf("Error:Unable to open %s\n", argv[1]);
        exit(8);
    }
    out_file = open(argv[2], O_WRONLY | O_TRUNC | O_CREAT, 0666);
    if (out_file < 0) {
        (void) fprintf("Error:Unable to open %s\n", argv[2]);
        exit(8);
    }
    while (1) {
        read_size = read(in_file, buffer, sizeof(buffer));

        if (read_size == 0)
            break;              /* end of file */

        if (read_size < 0) {
            (void) fprintf(stderr, "Error:Read error\n");
            exit(8);
        }
        (void) write(out_file, buffer, (unsigned int) read_size);
    }
    (void) close(in_file);
    (void) close(out_file);
    return (0);
}
```

Question 13–3: Why does this program dump core instead of printing an error message, if it can't open the input file?

Several things should be noted about this program. First of all, the buffer size is defined as a constant, so it is easily modified. Rather than have to remember that 16K is 16384, the programmer used the expression (16 * 1024). This form of the constant is obviously 16K.

If the user improperly uses the program, an error message results. To help get it right, the message tells how to use the program.

We may not read a full buffer for the last read. That is why *read_size* is used to determine the number of bytes to write.

Designing File Formats

Suppose you are designing a program to produce a graph. The height, width, limits, and scales are to be defined in a graph configuration file. You are also assigned to write a user-friendly program that asks the operator questions and writes a configuration file so he does not have to learn the text editor. How should you design a configuration file?

One way would be as follows:

height (in inches)
width (in inches)
x lower limit
x upper limit
y lower limit
y upper limit
x scale
y scale

A typical plotter configuration file might look like:

```
10.0
7.0
0
100
30
300
0.5
2.0
```

This file does contain all the data, but in looking at it, it is difficult to tell what, for example, is the value of the y lower limit. A solution is to comment the file.

That is, to have the configuration program write out not only the data, but a string describing the data.

```
10.0   height (in inches)
7.0    width (in inches)
0      x lower limit
100    x upper limit
30     y lower limit
300    y upper limit
0.5    x scale
2.0    y scale
```

Now the file is user readable. But suppose that one of the users runs the plot program and types in the wrong filename, and the program gets the lunch menu for today instead of a plot configuration file. The program is probably going to get very upset when it tries to construct a plot whose dimensions are "BLT on white" versus "Meatloaf and gravy."

The result is that you wind up with egg on your face. There should be some way of identifying this file as a plot configuration file. One method of doing this is to put the words "Plot Configuration File" on the first line of the file. Then, when someone tries to give your program the wrong file, it will print an error message.

This takes care of the wrong file problem, but what happens when you are asked to enhance the programs and add optional logarithmic plotting? You could simply add another line to the configuration file, but what about all those old files? It's not reasonable to ask everyone to throw them away. The best thing to do (from a user's point of view) is to accept old format files. You can make this easier by putting a version number in the file.

A typical file now looks like:

```
Plot    Configuration File V1.0
log     Logarithmic or Normal plot
10.0    height (in inches)
7.0     width (in inches)
0       x lower limit
100     x upper limit
30      y lower limit
300     y upper limit
0.5     x scale
2.0     y scale
```

In binary files, it is common practice to put an identification number in the first four bytes of the file. This is called the *magic number*. The magic number should be different for each type of file.

One method for choosing a magic number is to start with the first four letters of the program name (i.e., *list*) and convert them to hex: 0x6c607374. Then add 0x80808080 to the number, producing a magic number of 0xECE0F3F4.

This algorithm generates a magic number that is probably unique. The high bit is set on each byte to make the byte non-ASCII and avoid confusion between ASCII and binary files.

When reading and writing a binary file containing many different types of structures, it is easy to get lost. For example, you might read a name structure when you expected a size structure. This is usually not detected until later in the program. In order to locate this problem early, the programmer can put magic numbers at the beginning of each structure.

Now if the program reads the name structure and the magic number is not correct, it knows something is wrong.

Magic numbers for structures do not need to have the high bit set on each byte. Making the magic number just four ASCII characters, makes it easy to pick out the beginning of structures in a file dump.

Answers

Answer 13–1: The problem is that `fgets` gets the entire line including the newline character (`\n`). If you have a file named *sam*, the program will read *sam\n* and try to look for a file by that name. Because there is no such file, the program reports an error.

The fix is to strip the newline character from the name:

```
name[strlen(name)-1] = ' ';     /* get rid of last character */
```

The error message in this case is poorly designed. True, we did not open the file, but the programmer could supply the user with more information. Are we trying to open the file for input or output? What is the name of the file we are trying to open? We don't even know if the message we are getting is an error, a warning, or just part of the normal operation. A better error message is:

```
(void)fprintf(stderr,"Error:Unable to open %s for input\n", name);
```

Notice that this message would also help us detect the programming error. When we typed in `sam`, the error would be:

```
Error:Unable to open sam
for input
```

This clearly shows us that we are trying to open a file with a newline in its name.

Answer 13–2: The problem is that we are writing an ASCII file, but we wanted a binary file. On UNIX, ASCII is the same as binary, so the program will run fine. On DOS, the end-of-line problem causes us problems. When we write a newline character (0x0a) to the file, a carriage return (0x0D) is added to it. (Remember that end of line on DOS is <carriage-return><linefeed>, or 0x0d, 0x0a.) Because of this editing, we get an extra carriage return (0x0d) in the output file.

In order to write binary data (without output editing) we need to open the file with the binary option:

```
out_file = fopen("test.out", "wb");
```

Answer 13–3: The problem is with the `fprintf` call. The first parameter of an `fprintf` should be a file, instead it is the format string. Trying to use a format string where the program was expecting a file causes a core dump.

Programming Problems

Exercise 1: Write a program that reads a file and counts the number of lines in it.

Exercise 2: Write a program to copy a file, expanding all tabs to multiple spaces.

Exercise 3: Write a program that reads a file containing a list of numbers and writes two files, one with all numbers divisible by three and another containing all the other numbers.

Exercise 4: Write a program that reads an ASCII file containing a list of numbers and writes a binary file containing the same list. Write a program that goes the other way so you can check your work.

Exercise 5: Write a program that copies a file and removes all characters with the high bit set (`((ch & 0x80) != 0)`).

Exercise 6: Design a file format to store a person's name, address, and other information. Write a program to read this file and produce a set of mailing labels.

14

Debugging and Optimization

Bloody instructions which, being learned, return to plague the inventor.
—Shakespeare, on debugging

Debugging

The hardest part of a program is not the design and writing, but the debugging phase. It is here that you find out how your program really works (instead of how you think it works).

In order to eradicate a bug, you need two things: a way of reproducing it and information from the program that lets you locate and correct the problem.

In some cases finding the bug is easy. You discover the bug yourself, the test department produces a clear and easy test plan that displays the bug, or else the output always comes out bad.

In some cases, especially interactive programs, reproducing the bug may be 90% of the problem. It is especially true when dealing with bug reports sent in by users in the field. A typical call from a user might be:

> User: That database program you gave me is broken.
>
> Programmer: What's wrong?
>
> User: Sometimes when I'm doing a sort, it gets things in the wrong order.
>
> Programmer: What command were you using?
>
> User: The `sort` command.
>
> Programmer (patiently): Tell me exactly what you typed, keystroke by keystroke to get it to fail.
>
> User: I don't remember it exactly. I was doing a lot of sorts.
>
> Programmer: If I come over can you show me the bug?
>
> User: Of course..

Two minutes later the programmer is in the user's office and utters the fatal words, "Show me." The user types away and the program stubbornly works, no matter what the user does to it.

The programmer gives up and goes back to her office only to find a message from the user: "It failed five minutes after you left."

Program 14-1 is a short database lookup program. It asks the user for input and checks it against a hardcoded list of names. Although very simple, its structure is typical of much larger and more complex interactive programs.

Program 14-1.

```
/********************************************************
 * Database -- A very simple database program to        *
 *                look up names in a hardcoded list.    *
 *                                                      *
 * Usage:                                               *
 *      database                                        *
 *                Program will ask you for a name.      *
 *                Enter the name; it will tell you if   *
 *                it is the list.                       *
 *                                                      *
 *                A blank name terminates the program.  *
 ********************************************************/
#define STRING_LENGTH 80        /* Length of typical string */
#include <stdio.h>
```

```
main()
{
    char name[STRING_LENGTH];    /* a name to lookup */

    int lookup(char *); /* lookup a name */

    while (1) {
        (void)printf("Enter name: ");
        (void)fgets(name, sizeof(name), stdin);

        /* Check for blank name  */
        /* (remember 1 character for newline) */
        if (strlen(name) <= 1)
            break;

        /* Get rid of newline */
        name[strlen(name)-1] = '\0';

        if (lookup(name))
            (void)printf("%s is in the list\n", name);
        else
            (void)printf("%s is not in the list\n", name);
    }
    return (0);
}
/********************************************************
 * lookup -- lookup a name in a list                    *
 *                                                      *
 * Parameters                                           *
 *      name -- name to lookup                          *
 *                                                      *
 * Returns                                              *
 *      1 -- name in the list                           *
 *      0 -- name not in the list                       *
 ********************************************************/
int lookup(char *name)
{
    /* List of people in the database */
    /* Note: Last name is a NULL for end of list */
    static char *list[] = {
        "John",
        "Jim",
        "Jane",
        "Clyde",
        NULL
    };

    int index;             /* index into list */

    for (index = 0; list[index] != NULL; index++) {
        if (strcmp(list[index], name) == 0)
            return (1);
```

```
    }
    return (0);
}
```

A typical execution of this program is:

```
Enter name: Sam
Sam is not in the list
Enter name: John
John is in the list
Enter name:
```

When we release this program, of course, the users immediately start complaining about mysterious problems that go away whenever the programmer is around. Wouldn't it be nice to have a little gremlin that sits on the shoulder, copying down everything the user types? Unfortunately, gremlins are not available; however, we can change this program so it produces a *save file* that contains every keystroke the user typed in.

Our program uses the statement:

```
(void)fgets(name, sizeof(name), stdin);
```

to read the user's data.

Let's write a new routine, `extended_fgets`, and use it instead of `fgets`. It will not only get a line, but will also save the user's response in a save file. Program 14-2 is a revision of Program 14-1 that includes `extended_fgets`.

Program 14-2.

```
#include <stdio.h>
/*
 * The main program will open this file if -S is on
 * the command line.
 */
FILE *save_file = NULL;
/********************************************************
 * extended_fgets -- get a line from the input file     *
 *                  and record it in a save file if needed. *
 *                                                      *
 * Parameters                                           *
 *      line -- the line to read                        *
 *      size -- sizeof(line) -- maximum number of       *
 *                      characters to read              *
 *      file -- file to read data from                  *
 *              (normally stdin)                        *
 *                                                      *
 * Returns                                              *
 *      NULL -- error or end of file in read            *
 *      otherwise line (just like fgets)                *
 ********************************************************/
```

```
char *extended_fgets(char *line, int size, FILE *file)
{

    char *result;               /* result of fgets */

    result = fgets(line, size, file);

    /* did someone ask for a save file */
    if (save_file != NULL)
        (void)fputs(line, save_file);

    return (result);
}
```

We also change our main program to handle a new option, `-Sfile`, to specify a *save file*. (Typically, uppercase letters are used for debugging and other less used options.) Our new main program is shown in Program 14-3.

Program 14-3.

```
/********************************************************
 * Database -- A very simple database program to        *
 *              lookup names in a hardcoded list.       *
 *                                                      *
 * Usage:                                               *
 *      database [-S<file>]                             *
 *                                                      *
 *      -S<file>        Specify save file for           *
 *                      debugging purposes              *
 *                                                      *
 *              Program will ask you for a name.        *
 *              Enter the name; it will tell you if     *
 *              it is the list.                         *
 *                                                      *
 *              A blank name terminates the program.    *
 ********************************************************/
#include <stdio.h>

FILE *save_file = NULL; /* Save file if any */
char *extended_fgets(char *, int, FILE *);

main(int argc, char *argv[])
{
    char name[80];       /* a name to lookup */
    char *save_file_name; /* Name of the save file */

    int lookup(char *); /* lookup a name */

    while ((argc > 1) && (argv[1][0] == '-')) {
        switch (argv[1][1]) {
            case 'S':
                save_file_name = &argv[1][2];
```

```
                save_file = fopen(save_file_name, "w");
                if (save_file == NULL)
                    (void)fprintf(stderr,
                        "Warning:Unable to open save file %s\n",
                        save_file_name);
                break;
            default:
                (void)fprintf(stderr,"Bad option: %s\n", argv[1]);
                exit (8);
        }
        argc--;
        argv++;
    }


    while (1) {
        (void)printf("Enter name: ");
        (void)extended_fgets(name, sizeof(name), stdin);

        /* ... Rest of program ... */
```

Now we have a complete record of what the user typed. Looking at the input, we see that the user typed:

```
Sam
 John
```

The second name begins with a space and although "John" is in the list, "<space>John" is not. In this case we found the error by inspecting the input; however, more complex programs have much more complex input. We could type all that in when debugging, or we could add another feature to `extended_fgets` that would add *playback file* to it. When enabled, input will not be taken from the keyboard, but instead will be taken from the file. Program 14-4 contains the revised `extended_fgets`.

Program 14-4.

```
#include <stdio.h>
FILE *save_file = NULL;          /* Save input in this file */
FILE *playback_file = NULL;      /* Playback data from this file */
/********************************************************
 * extended_fgets -- get a line from the input file     *
 *                 and record it in a save file if needed *
 *                                                      *
 * Parameters                                           *
 *      line -- the line to read                        *
 *      size -- sizeof(line) -- maximum number of       *
 *                      characters to read              *
 *      file -- file to read data from                  *
 *              (normally stdin)                        *
 *                                                      *
 * Returns                                              *
```

```
 *      NULL -- error or end of file in read            *
 *      otherwise line (just like fgets)                *
 ********************************************************/
char *extended_fgets(char *line, int size, FILE *file)
{
    extern FILE *save_file;      /* file to save strings in */
    extern FILE *playback_file; /* file for alternate input */

    char *result;                /* result of fgets */

    if (playback_file != NULL) {
        result = fgets(line, size, file);
        /* echo the input to the standard out so the user sees it */
        (void)fputs(line, stdout);
    } else
        result = fgets(line, size, file);

    /* did someone ask for a save file */
    if (save_file != NULL)
        (void)fputs(line, save_file);

    return (result);
}
```

We also add a playback option to the command line `-Pfile`. This allows us to automatically type the commands that caused the error. Our main program, revised to support the `-P` option, is Program 14-5.

Program 14-5.

```
/********************************************************
 * Database -- A very simple database program to        *
 *             lookup names in a hardcoded list.        *
 *                                                      *
 * Usage:                                               *
 *      database [-S<file>] [-P<file>]                  *
 *                                                      *
 *      -S<file>        Specify save file for           *
 *                      debugging purposes.             *
 *                                                      *
 *      -P<file>        Specify playback file for       *
 *                      debugging or demonstration.     *
 *                                                      *
```

```
 *                                                      *
 *             Program will ask you for a name.         *
 *             Enter the name; it will tell you if      *
 *             it is the list.                          *
 *                                                      *
 *             A blank name terminates the program.     *
 ********************************************************/
#include <stdio.h>

FILE *save_file = NULL; /* Save file if any */
FILE *playback_file = NULL;     /* Playback file if any */
char *extended_fgets(char *, int, FILE *);

main(int argc, char *argv[])
{
    char name[80];       /* a name to lookup */
    char *save_file_name; /* Name of the save file */
    char *playback_file_name; /* Name of the playback file */

    int lookup(char *); /* lookup a name */

    while ((argc > 1) && (argv[1][0] == '-')) {
        switch (argv[1][1]) {
            case 'S':
                save_file_name = &argv[1][2];
                save_file = fopen(save_file_name, "w");
                if (save_file == NULL)
                    (void)fprintf(stderr,
                        "Warning:Unable to open save file %s\n",
                        save_file_name);
                break;
            case 'P':
                playback_file_name = &argv[1][2];
                playback_file = fopen(playback_file_name, "r");
                if (playback_file == NULL) {
                    (void)fprintf(stderr,
                        "Error:Unable to open playback file %s\n",
                        playback_file_name);
                    exit (8);
                }
                break;
            default:
                (void)fprintf(stderr,"Bad option: %s\n", argv[1]);
                exit (8);
        }
        argc--;
        argv++;
    }

    /* ... rest of program ... */
```

Now when a user calls up with an error report, we can tell him, "Try it again with the save file feature enabled, then send me a copy of your files." The user then runs the program and saves the input into the file *save.txt*:

```
% database -Ssave.txt
Enter name: Sam
Sam is not in the list
Enter name:  John
John is in the list
Enter name:
```

He sends us the file *save.txt*, and we run the program with the playback option enabled:

```
% database -Psave.txt
Enter name: Sam
Sam is not in the list
Enter name:  John
John is in the list
Enter name:
```

We now have a reliable way of reproducing the problem. In many cases, that's half the battle. Once we can reproduce the problem, we can proceed to find and fix the bugs.

A Copy Flip-flop

Once a programmer asked a user to send him a copy of his floppy. A next-day air package arrived at the programmer's desk containing a photocopy of the floppy. The user was not completely computer-illiterate. He knew it was a two-sided floppy, so he had photocopied both sides.

Before you start debugging, save the old, "working" copy of your program in a safe place. (If you are using a source control system like SCCS or RCS, your last working version should be checked in.) Many times while you are searching for a problem, you may find it necessary to try out different solutions or to add temporary debugging code. Sometimes you find you've been barking up the wrong tree and need to start over. That's when the last working copy becomes invaluable.

Once you have reproduced the problem, you must determine what caused it to happen. There are several methods for doing this, as described in the following sections.

Divide and Conquer

The *divide and conquer* method has already been briefly discussed in Chapter 5, *Decision and Control Statements*. It consists of putting in **printf** statements where you know the data is good (to make sure it is really good), where the data is bad, and several points in between. This way you can start zeroing in on the section of code that contains the error. More **printf** statements can further reduce the scope of the error until the bug is finally located.

Debug Only Code

The divide and conquer method uses temporary **printf** statements. They are put in as needed and taken out after they are used. The preprocessor conditional compilation directives can be used to put in and take out debugging code. For example:

```
#ifdef DEBUG
    (void)printf("Width %f Height %f\n", width, height);
#endif /* DEBUG */
```

The program can be compiled with **DEBUG** undefined for normal use and you can define it when debugging is needed.

Debug Command-line Switch

Rather than using a compile-time switch to create a special version of the program, you can permanently include the debugging code and add a special program switch that will turn on the debugging output. For example:

```
if (debug)
    (void)printf("Width %f Height %f\n", width, height);
```

where **debug** is a variable that is set if **–D** is present on the command line.

This has the advantage that only a single version of the program exists. Also the customer can turn on this switch in the field, save the output, and send it to you for analysis. The runtime switch should be used in all cases instead of conditional compilation unless there is some reason you do not want the customer to be able to get at the debugging information.

Some programs use the concept of a debug level. Level 0 outputs only minimal debugging information, level 1 more information, and on up to level 9 which outputs everything.

The `ghostscript`* program by Aladdin Enterprises implements the idea of debugging letters. The command option `-Z`*xxx* sets the debugging flags for each type of diagnostic output wanted. For example, `f` is the code for the fill algorithm, `p` is the code for the path tracer. If I wanted to trace both these sections, I would specify `-Zfp`.

The option is implemented by the following code:

```
/*
 * Even though we only put 1 zero, C will fill in the
 * rest of the arrays with zeros.
 */
char debug[128] = {0};     /* the debugging flags */
main(int argc, char *argv[])
{
    while ((argc > 1) && (argv[1][0] == '-')) {
        switch (argv[1][1]) {
            /* .... normal switch .... */
            /* Debug switch */
            case 'Z':
                debug_ptr = argv[1][2];
                /* loop for each letter */
                while (*debug_ptr != '\0') {
                    debug[*debug_ptr] = 1;
                    debug_ptr++;
                }
                break;
        }
        argc--;
        argv++;
    }
    /* rest of program */
}
```

This is used inside the program by:

```
if (debug['p'])
    (void)printf("Starting new path\n");
```

`ghostscript` is a large program (some 25,000 lines) and rather difficult to debug. This form of debugging allows the user to get a great deal of information easily.

---

*`ghostscript` is a PostScript-like interpreter available from the Free Software Foundation for a minimal copying charge. They can be reached at: Free Software Foundation, Inc., 675 Massachusetts Avenue, Cambridge, MA 02139 (617) 876-3296.

Going Through the Output

Enabling the debug printout is a nice way of getting information, but many times there is so much data that the information you want can easily get lost.

C allows you to *redirect* what would normally go to the screen to a file. For example:

```
buggy -D9 >tmp.out
```

will run the program **buggy** with a high level of debug set and send the output to the file *tmp.out*.

The text editor on your system makes a good file browser. You can use its search capabilities to look for the information you want to find.

Interactive Debuggers

Most compiler manufacturers provide you with an interactive debugger. They give you the ability to stop the program at any point, examine and change variables, and "single step" through the program. Since each debugger is different, a detailed discussion is not possible.

However, we are going to discuss one debugger, **dbx**. This program is available on many UNIX machines running the BSD versions of UNIX. SYSTEM V UNIX uses the debugger **sdb**, while on HP-UX the utility **cdb** is used. Turbo C has its own built-in debugger.

Although the exact syntax used by your debugger may be different, the principles shown here will work for all debuggers.

The basic list of **dbx** commands are:

`run` Start execution of a program.

`stop at` *`line-number`*
Insert a breakpoint at the given line number. When a running program reaches a breakpoint, execution stops and control returns to the debugger.

`stop in` *`function-name`*
: Insert a breakpoint at the first line of the named function. Commonly, the command `stop in main` is used to stop at the beginning of of the program.

`cont` — Continue execution after a breakpoint.

`print` *`expression`*
: Display the value of an expression.

`step` — Execute a single line in the program. If the current statement calls a function, the function is single-stepped.

`next` — Execute a single line in the program, but treat function calls as a single line. This command is used to skip over function calls.

`list` — List the source program.

`where` — Print the list of currently active functions.

We have a program that should count the number of threes and sevens in a series of numbers. Unfortunately, it keeps getting the wrong answer for the number of sevens. Our program is shown in Program 14-6.

Program 14-6.

```
#include <stdio.h>
int seven_count;        /* number of seven's in the data */
int data[5];            /* the data to count 3 and 7 in */
int three_count;        /* the number of threes in the data */

main() {
    int index;  /* index into the data */
    void get_data(int data[]);

    seven_count = 0;
    three_count = 0;
    get_data(data);

    for (index = 1; index <= 5; index++) {
        if (data[index] == 3)
            three_count++;
        if (data[index] == 7)
        seven_count++;
    }
    (void)printf("Three's %d Seven's %d\n",
            three_count, seven_count);
    return (0);
}
```

```
/********************************************************
 * get_data -- get 5 numbers from the command line      *
 ********************************************************/
void get_data(int data[])
{
    char line[100];     /* line of input */

    (void)printf("Enter 5 numbers\n");
    (void)fgets(line, sizeof(line), stdin);
    (void)sscanf(line, "%d %d %d %d %d",
        &data[1], &data[2], &data[3],
        &data[4], &data[5]);
}

```

When we run this program with the data 7 3 7 0 2, the results are:

```
Threes 1 Sevens 4
```

We start by invoking the debugger (**dbx**) with the name of the program we are going to debug (**count**). The debugger initializes itself, outputs the prompt (**dbx**), and waits for a command.

```
% dbx count
Reading symbolic information...
Read 72 symbols
(dbx)
```

We don't know where the variable is getting changed so we'll start at the beginning and work our way through until we get an error. At every step we'll display the variable **seven_count** just to make sure it's OK.

We need to stop the program at the beginning so we can single step through it. The command **stop in main** tells **dbx** to set a breakpoint at the first instruction of the function **main**. The command **run** tells **dbx** to start the program and run until it hits the first breakpoint.

```
(dbx) stop in main
(2) stop in main
```

The number **(2)** is used by **dbx** to identify the breakpoint. Now we need to start the program:

```
(dbx) run
Running: count
stopped in main at line 10 in file "/usr/sdo/count/count.c"
   10       seven_count = 0;
```

The message "stopped in main..." indicates that the program encountered a breakpoint and has now turned control over to debug.

We have reached the point where `seven_count` is initialized. The command `next` will execute a single statement, treating function calls as one statement. (The names of the command for your debugger may be different.) We go past the initialization and check to see if it worked:

```
(dbx) next
stopped in main at line 11 in file "/usr/sdo/count/count.c"
   11        three_count = 0;
(dbx) print seven_count
seven_count = 0
```

It did. We try the next few lines, checking all the time:

```
(dbx) next
stopped in main at line 12 in file "/usr/sdo/count/count.c"
   12        get_data(data);
(dbx) print seven_count
seven_count = 0
(dbx) next
Enter 5 numbers
3 7 3 0 2
stopped in main at line 14 in file "/usr/sdo/count/count.c"
   14        for (index = 1; index <= 5; index++) {
(dbx) print seven_count
seven_count = 2
```

`seven_count` somehow changed value to 2. The last statement we executed was `get_data(data)`, so something is going on in that function. We add a breakpoint at the beginning of `get_data` and start the program over with the `run` command:

```
(dbx) stop in get_data
(4) stop in get_data
(dbx) run
Running: count
stopped in main at line 10 in file "/usr/sdo/count/count.c"
   10        seven_count = 0;
```

We are at the beginning of `main`. We want to go onto the next breakpoint, so we issue the `cont` command to continue execution:

```
(dbx) cont
Running: count
stopped in get_data at line 31 in file "/usr/sdo/count/count.c"
   31        (void)printf("Enter 5 numbers\n");
```

We now start single stepping again until we find the error:

```
(dbx) print seven_count
seven_count = 0
(dbx) next
Enter 5 numbers
stopped in get_data at line 32 in file "/usr/sdo/count/count.c"
```

```
   32        (void)fgets(line, sizeof(line), stdin);
(dbx) print seven_count
seven_count = 0
(dbx) next
1 2 3 4 5
stopped in get_data at line 33 in file "/usr/sdo/count/count.c"
   35            &data[4], &data[5]);
(dbx) print seven_count
seven_count = 0
(dbx) next
stopped in get_data at line 36 in file "/usr/sdo/count/count.c"
   36    }
(dbx) print seven_count
seven_count = 5
(dbx) list 30,40
   30
   31        (void)printf("Enter 5 numbers\n");
   32        (void)fgets(line, sizeof(line), stdin);
   33        (void)sscanf(line, "%d %d %d %d %d",
   34            &data[1], &data[2], &data[3],
   35            &data[4], &data[5]);
   36    }
(dbx) quit
```

Note that we have a statement that takes up three lines (lines 33-35). The debugger lists only the last line (line 35) when single stepping.

At line 32 the data was good, but when we reached line 36 the data was bad, so the error is located at line 33 of the program, the `sscanf`. We've narrowed the problem down to one statement. By inspection we can see that we are using `data[5]`, an illegal member of the array `data`.

Debugging a Binary Search

The binary search algorithm is fairly simple. You want to see if a given number is in an ordered list. Check your number against the one in the middle of the list. If it is the number, you were lucky—stop. If your number was bigger, then you might find it in the top half of the list; try the middle of the top half. If it was smaller, try the bottom half. Keep trying and dividing the list in half until you find the number or the list gets down to a single number.

Program 14-7 uses a binary search to see if a number can be found in the file *numbers.dat*.

Program 14-7.

```
/********************************************************
 * search -- Search a set of numbers.                   *
 *                                                      *
 * Usage:                                               *
 *      search                                          *
 *              you will be asked numbers to lookup     *
 *                                                      *
 * Files:                                               *
 *      numbers.dat -- numbers 1 per line to search     *
 *                      (Numbers must be ordered)       *
 ********************************************************/
#include <stdio.h>
#define MAX_NUMBERS     1000          /* Max numbers in file */
#define DATA_FILE       "numbers.dat" /* File with numbers */

int data[MAX_NUMBERS];  /* Array of numbers to search */
int max_count;          /* Number of valid elements in data */
main()
{
    FILE *in_file;      /* Input file */
    int middle;         /* Middle of our search range */
    int low, high;      /* Upper/lower bound */
    int search;         /* number to search for */
    char line[80];      /* Input line */

    in_file = fopen(DATA_FILE, "r");
    if (in_file == NULL) {
        (void)fprintf(stderr,"Error:Unable to open %s\n", DATA_FILE);
        exit (8);
    }

    /*
     * Read in data
     */

    max_count = 0;
    while (1) {
        if (fgets(line, sizeof(line),  in_file) == NULL)
            break;

        /* convert number */
        (void)sscanf(line, "%d", data[max_count]);
        max_count++;
    }

    while (1) {
        (void)printf("Enter number to search for or -1 to quit:" );
        (void)fgets(line, sizeof(line), stdin);
        (void)sscanf(line, "%d", &search);
```

```
        if (search == -1)
            break;

        low = 0;
        high = max_count;

        while (1) {
            middle = (low + high) / 2;

            if (data[middle] == search) {
                (void)printf("Found at index %d\n", middle);
            }

            if (low == high) {
                (void)printf("Not found\n");
                break;
            }

            if (data[middle] < search)
                low = middle;
            else
                high = middle;
        }
    }
    return (0);
}
```

Our data file, *numbers.dat*, contains:

```
 4
 6
14
16
17
```

When we run this program, the results are:

```
% search
Segmentation fault (core dumped)
```

This is not good. It means that something went wrong in our program and it tried to read memory that wasn't there. A file called *core* was created when the error occurred. It contains a snapshot of our executing program. The debugger **dbx** can read this file and help us determine what happened:

```
% dbx search
Reading symbolic information...
Read 79 symbols
warning: core file read error: address not in data space
warning: core file read error: address not in data space
warning: core file read error: address not in data space
program terminated by signal SEGV (no mapping at the fault address)
(dbx)
```

The message "warning: core file..." is the debugger's way of telling you that the temporary variable space (the stack) has been trashed and contains bad data. The **where** command tells you which function is calling which function (also known as a stack trace). The current function is printed first, the function that called it, and so on until we reach the outer function **main**.

```
(dbx) where
number() at 0xdd7d87a
_doscan() at 0xdd7d329
sscanf(0xdfffadc, 0x200e3, 0x0) at 0xdd7ce7f
main(0x1, 0xdfffb58, 0xdfffb60), line 41 in "search.c"
(dbx)
```

This tells us that **main** called **sscanf**. The call was made from line 41 of **main**. **sscanf** called **_doscan**. Since **sscanf** is a standard library routine, we cannot get line number information. The instruction number is 0xdd7ce7f; however, this information is not too useful to us. **_doscan** called **number**. It was **number** that tried to perform the illegal memory access.

This does *not* mean that there is a bug in **number**. The problem could be caused by the parameters passed to it by **_doscan**, which could have gotten its parameters from **sscanf**, which got its parameters from **main**. Any one of the functions along this chain could contain an error that caused a bad pointer to be passed to another function.

Usually the standard library has been debugged, so we should probably look for the error in our code. Looking at the stack trace, we see that the last line of our program to be executed was line 41 of **main**.

Using the **list** command, we can examine that line.

```
(dbx) list 41
   41           (void)sscanf(line, "%d", data[max_count]);
(dbx)
```

This is the line that caused the problem.

Another way of finding the problem is to single step the program until the error occurs. First, we list a section of the program to find a convenient place to put the breakpoint, then start the execution and the single-step process:

```
(dbx) list 26,31
   22         int low, high;          /* Upper/lower bound */
   23         int search;             /* number to search for */
   24         char line[80];          /* Input line */
   25
   26         in_file = fopen(DATA_FILE, "r");
   27         if (in_file == NULL) {
   28             (void)fprintf(stderr,"Error:Unable to open %s\n",
                                                      DATA_FILE);
```

```
   29           exit (8);
   30       }
   31
(dbx) stop at 26
(1) stop at "search.c":26
(dbx) run
Running: search
stopped in main at line 26 in file "search.c"
   26       in_file = fopen(DATA_FILE, "r");
(dbx) step
stopped in main at line 27 in file "search.c"
   27       if (in_file == NULL) {
(dbx) step
stopped in main at line 35 in file "search.c"
   35       max_count = 0;
(dbx) step
stopped in main at line 37 in file "search.c"
   37           if (fgets(line, sizeof(line),  in_file) == NULL)
(dbx) step
stopped in main at line 41 in file "search.c"
   41           (void)sscanf(line, "%d", data[max_count]);
(dbx) step
signal SEGV (no mapping at the fault address) in number at 0xdd7d87a
number+0x520:           movl    a6@(0x1c),a0
(dbx) quit
```

This method also points at line 41 as the culprit. On inspection we notice that we forgot to put an ampersand (&) in front of the variable for `sscanf`. So we change line 41 from:

```
(void)sscanf(line, "%d", data[max_count]);
```

to:

```
(void)sscanf(line, "%d", &data[max_count]);
```

and try again. The first number in our list is 4, so we try it. This time our output looks like:

```
Enter number to search for or -1 to quit:4
Found at index 0
Found at index 0
Not found
Enter number to search for or -1 to quit:^C
```

The program should find the number, let us know it's at index 0, and then ask for another number. Instead we get two "found" messages and one "not found" message. We know that everything is running smoothly up until we get the first "found" message. After that things go downhill.

Getting back into the debugger, we use the `list` command to locate the found message and put a breakpoint there:

```
% dbx search
Reading symbolic information...
Read 79 symbols
(dbx) list 58,60
   58
   59              if (data[middle] == search) {
   60                  (void)printf("Found at index %d\n", middle);
   61              }
   62
   63              if (low == high) {
   64                  (void)printf("Not found\n");
   65                  break;
   66              }
   67
(dbx) stop at 60
(3) stop at "search.c":60
(dbx) run
stopped in main at line 60 in file "search.c"
   60                  (void)printf("Found at index %d\n", middle);
(dbx)
```

Now we start single-stepping to see what happens:

```
   60                  (void)printf("Found at index %d\n", middle);
(dbx) step
Found at index 0
stopped in main at line 63 in file "search.c"
   63              if (low == high) {
(dbx) step
stopped in main at line 68 in file "search.c"
   68              if (data[middle] < search)
(dbx) step
stopped in main at line 71 in file "search.c"
   71                  high = middle;
(dbx) step
stopped in main at line 57 in file "search.c"
   57              middle = (low + high) / 2;
(dbx) quit
```

The program doesn't exit the loop. Instead it continues with the search. Since the number has already been found, this results in strange behavior. We are missing a **break** after the `printf`.

We need to change:

```
if (data[middle] == search) {
    (void) printf("Found at index %d\n", middle);
}
```

to:

```
if (data[middle] == search) {
    (void) printf("Found at index %d\n", middle);
    break;
}
```

Making this fix, we try our program again:

```
% search
Enter number to search for or -1 to quit:4
Found at index 0
Enter number to search for or -1 to quit:6
Found at index 1
Enter number to search for or -1 to quit:3
Not found
Enter number to search for or -1 to quit:5
...Program runs forever (or until we abort it)...
```

We have a runaway program. This time instead of setting a breakpoint, we just start running the program. After a few seconds pass and we believe that we are stuck in the infinite loop, we stop the program with a CTRL-C to return to the shell prompt. Since we are running with the debugger, it returns control to **dbx**.

```
% dbx search
Reading symbolic information...
Read 80 symbols
(dbx) run
Running: search
Enter number to search for or -1 to quit:5
^C
interrupt in main at line 70 in file "search.c"
   70                      low = middle;
```

Now we can use the single-step command to step through our infinite loop, looking at key values along the way:

```
   70                      low = middle;
(dbx) step
stopped in main at line 57 in file "search.c"
   57                middle = (low + high) / 2;
(dbx) step
stopped in main at line 59 in file "search.c"
   59                if (data[middle] == search) {
(dbx) print middle
middle = 0
(dbx) print data[middle]
data[middle] = 4
(dbx) print search
search = 5
(dbx) step
stopped in main at line 64 in file "search.c"
   64                if (low == high) {
```

```
(dbx) step
stopped in main at line 69 in file "search.c"
   69              if (data[middle] < search)
(dbx) step
stopped in main at line 70 in file "search.c"
   70                  low = middle;
(dbx) step
stopped in main at line 57 in file "search.c"
   57              middle = (low + high) / 2;
(dbx) step
stopped in main at line 59 in file "search.c"
   59              if (data[middle] == search) {
(dbx) step
stopped in main at line 64 in file "search.c"
   64              if (low == high) {
(dbx) step
stopped in main at line 69 in file "search.c"
   69              if (data[middle] < search)
(dbx) step
stopped in main at line 70 in file "search.c"
   70                  low = middle;
(dbx) step
stopped in main at line 57 in file "search.c"
   57              middle = (low + high) / 2;
(dbx) step
stopped in main at line 59 in file "search.c"
   59              if (data[middle] == search) {
(dbx) step
stopped in main at line 64 in file "search.c"
   64              if (low == high) {
(dbx) step
stopped in main at line 69 in file "search.c"
   69              if (data[middle] < search)
(dbx) print low,middle,high
low = 0
middle = 0
high = 1
(dbx) print search
search = 5
(dbx) print data[0], data[1]
data[0] = 4
data[1] = 6
(dbx) quit
```

The problem is that we have reached a point where:

```
low=     0
middle=  0
high=    1
```

The item we are searching for falls exactly between elements 0 and 1. Our algorithm has an off-by-one error. Obviously, the middle element does not match. If it did, we'd exit with a "found" message. So there is no point including the middle element in our new search range. Our code to adjust the interval is:

```
if (data[middle] < search)
    low = middle;
else
    high = middle;
```

It should be:

```
if (data[middle] < search)
    low = middle +1;
else
    high = middle -1;
```

The full version of our corrected program is shown in Program 14-8.

Program 14-8.

```
/********************************************************
 * search -- Search a set of numbers.                    *
 *                                                       *
 * Usage:                                                *
 *      search                                           *
 *              you will be asked numbers to lookup      *
 *                                                       *
 * Files:                                                *
 *      numbers.dat -- numbers 1 per line to search      *
 *                     (Numbers must be ordered)         *
 ********************************************************/
#include <stdio.h>
#define MAX_NUMBERS     1000    /* Max numbers in file */
#define DATA_FILE       "numbers.dat"   /* File with numbers */

int data[MAX_NUMBERS];  /* Array of numbers to search */
int max_count;          /* Number of valid elements in data */
main()
{
    FILE *in_file;      /* Input file */
    int middle;         /* Middle of our search range */
    int low, high;      /* Upper/lower bound */
    int search;         /* number to search for */
    char line[80];      /* Input line */

    in_file = fopen(DATA_FILE, "r");
    if (in_file == NULL) {
        (void)fprintf(stderr,"Error:Unable to open %s\n", DATA_FILE);
        exit (8);
    }
```

```
    /*
     * Read in data
     */

    max_count = 0;
    while (1) {
        if (fgets(line, sizeof(line),  in_file) == NULL)
            break;

        /* convert number */
        (void)sscanf(line, "%d", &data[max_count]);
        max_count++;
    }

    while (1) {
        (void)printf("Enter number to search for or -1 to quit:" );
        (void)fgets(line, sizeof(line), stdin);
        (void)sscanf(line, "%d", &search);

        if (search == -1)
            break;

        low = 0;
        high = max_count;

        while (1) {
            if (low >= high) {
                (void)printf("Not found\n");
                break;
            }

            middle = (low + high) / 2;

            if (data[middle] == search) {
                (void)printf("Found at index %d\n", middle);
                break;
            }

            if (data[middle] < search)
                low = middle +1;
            else
                high = middle -1;
        }
    }
    return (0);
}
```

Interactive debuggers work well for most programs. Sometimes they need a little help. Consider Program 14-9. We try to debug it and find it fails when `point_number` is 735. We want to put a breakpoint before the calculation is made. When the debugger inserts a breakpoint into a program, the program will execute normally until it hits the breakpoint, then control will return to the debugger. This allows the user to examine and change variables as well as perform other debugging commands. When a `continue` command is typed, the program will continue execution as if nothing had happened. The problem is that there are 734 points before the one we want, and we don't want to stop for each of them.

Program 14-9.

```
float point_color(point_number)
int point_number;
{
    float correction;  /* color correction factor */
    extern float red,green,blue;/* current colors */

    correction = lookup(point_number);
    return (red*correction * 100.0 +
            blue*correction * 10.0 +
            green*correction);
}
```

How do we force the debugger to stop only when `part_number == 735`? We can do this by adding the following temporary code:

```
48:    if (part_number == 735)   /* ### Temp code ### */
49:        part_number = point_number;    /* ### Line to stop on ### */
```

Line 49 does nothing useful except serve a line that the debugger can stop on. We can put a breakpoint on that line with the command `stop at 49`. The program will process the first 734 points, then execute line 49, hitting the breakpoint. (Some debuggers have a conditional breakpoint. The advanced `dbx` command `stop at 49 if part_number == 735` would also work; however, your debugger may not have such advanced features.)

Runtime Errors

Runtime errors are usually the easiest to fix. Some types of runtime errors are:

- **Segmentation Violation.** This error indicates that the program tried to dereference a pointer containing a bad value.

- **Stack Overflow.** The program tried to use too many temporary variables. Sometimes this means the program is too big or is using too many big temporary arrays, but most of the time this is due to infinite recursion problems. Almost all UNIX systems automatically check for this error. Turbo C will check for stack overflow only if the compile-time option `-N` is used.

- **Divide by 0.** Divide by 0 is an obvious error. UNIX masks the problem by reporting an *integer* divide by zero with the error message "Floating exception (core dumped)."

In all cases, program execution will be stopped. On UNIX, an image of the running program, called a *core file*, is written out. This file can be analyzed by the debugger to determine why the program died. Our first run of Program 14-7 resulted in a core dump which we used (along with the `dbx where` command) to locate a problem.

One problem with runtime errors is that when they occur, the program execution stops immediately. The buffers for buffered files are not flushed. This can lead to some unexpected surprises. Consider Program 14-10.

Program 14-10.

```
#include <stdio.h>
main()
{
    int i,j;     /* two random integers */

    i = 1;
    j = 0;
    (void)printf("Starting\n");
    (void)printf("Before divide...");
    i = i / j;  /* divide by zero error */
    (void)printf("After\n");
    return(0);
}
```

When run, this program outputs the following:

```
Starting
Floating exception (core dumped)
```

This might lead you to think the divide had never started, when in fact it had. What happened to the message "Before divide..."? The `printf` statement executed, put the message in a buffer, and then the program died. The buffer never got a chance to be emptied.

By putting explicit flush buffer commands inside the code, we get a truer picture of what is happening. See Program 14-11.

Program 14-11.

```
#include <stdio.h>
main()
{
    int i,j;     /* two random integers */

    i = 1;
    j = 0;
    (void)printf("Starting\n");
    (void)fflush(stdout);
    (void)printf("Before divide...");
    (void)fflush(stdout);
    i = i / j;  /* divide by zero error */
    (void)printf("After\n");
    (void)fflush(stdout);
    return(0);
}
```

The `flush` statement makes the I/O less efficient, but more current.

The Confessional Method of Debugging

The confessional method of debugging is where the programmer explains the program to someone: an interested party, an uninterested party, a wall—it does not matter who, as long the programmer talks about it.

A typical confessional session goes like this:

> "Hey Bill, could you take a look at this. My program has a bug in it. The output should be 8.0 and I'm getting –8.0. The output is computed using this formula and I've checked out the payment value and rate, and the date must be correct unless there is something wrong with the leap year code which—Thank you Bill, you've found my problem."

Bill never says a word.

This type of debugging is also called a "walkthrough." Getting other people involved brings a fresh point of view to the process, and frequently, other people can spot problems that you have overlooked.

Optimization

And now a word on optimization: don't. Most programs do not need to be optimized. They run fast enough. Who cares if an interactive program takes 0.5 seconds to start up instead of 0.2?

The simplest way to get your program to run faster is to get a faster computer. Many times it is cheaper to buy a more powerful machine than it is to optimize a program, possibly introducing new errors into your code. Don't expect miracles from optimization. Usually most programs can only be sped up 10% to 20%.

Program 14-12 initializes a matrix (two-dimensional array).

Program 14-12.

```
#define X_SIZE 60
#define Y_SIZE 30

int matrix[X_SIZE][Y_SIZE];

void init_matrix(void)
{
    int x,y;      /* current element to zero */

    for (x = 0; x < X_SIZE; x++) {
        for (y = 0; y < Y_SIZE; y++) {
            matrix[x][y] = -1;
        }
    }
}
```

How can this function be optimized? First we notice we are using two local variables. By using the qualifier `register` on these variables, we tell the compiler that they are frequently used and should be placed in fast registers instead of relatively slow main memory. The number of registers varies from computer to computer. Slow machines like the PC have two registers, most UNIX systems have about 11, and supercomputers can have as many as 128. It is possible to declare more register variables than you have registers. C will put the extra variables in main memory.

Our program now looks like Program 14-13.

Program 14-13.

```
#define X_SIZE 60
#define Y_SIZE 30

int matrix[X_SIZE][Y_SIZE];

void init_matrix(void)
{
    register int x,y;     /* current element to zero */

    for (x = 0; x < X_SIZE; x++) {
        for (y = 0; y < Y_SIZE; y++) {
            matrix[x][y] = -1;
        }
    }
}
```

The outer loop is executed 60 times. This means that the overhead associated with starting the inner loop is executed 60 times. If we reverse the order of the loops, we will have to deal with the inner loop only 30 times.

In general, loops should be ordered so the innermost loop is the most complex and the outermost loop is the simplest, as in Program 14-14.

Program 14-14.

```
#define X_SIZE 60
#define Y_SIZE 30

int matrix[X_SIZE][Y_SIZE];

void init_matrix(void)
{
    register int x,y;     /* current element to zero */

    for (y = 0; y < Y_SIZE; y++) {
        for (x = 0; x < X_SIZE; x++) {
            matrix[x][y] = -1;
        }
    }
}
```

The Power of Powers of 2

Indexing an array requires a multiply. Look at the following line from the previous example:

```
matrix[x][y] = -1;
```

To get the location where the –1 will be stored, the program must perform the following steps:

1. Get the address of the matrix.
2. Compute **x * Y_SIZE**.
3. Compute **y**.
4. Add up all three parts to form the address.

In C this code looks like:

```
*(matrix + (x * Y_SIZE) + y) = -1;
```

However, we typically don't write a matrix access this way because C handles the details. But being aware of the details can help us generate more efficient code.

Almost all C compilers will convert multiples by a power of 2 (2, 4, 8, ...) into shifts, thus taking an expensive operation (multiply) and changing it into an inexpensive operation (shift).

For example:

```
i = 32 * j;
```

is compiled as:

```
i = j << 5; /* 2**5 == 32 */
```

Y_SIZE is 30, which is not a power of 2. By increasing it to 32, we waste some memory, but get a faster program, as shown in Program 14-15.

Program 14-15.

```
#define X_SIZE 60
#define Y_SIZE 32

int matrix[X_SIZE][Y_SIZE];

void init_matrix(void)
{
    register int x,y;     /* current element to zero */

    for (y = 0; y < Y_SIZE; y++) {
        for (x = 0; x < X_SIZE; x++) {
            matrix[x][y] = -1;
        }
    }
}
```

Since we are initializing consecutive memory locations, we can initialize the matrix by starting at the first location and storing a –1 in the next `X_SIZE * Y_SIZE` elements. (See Program 14-16.) Using this method, we cut the number of loops down to one. The indexing of the matrix has changed from a standard index (`matrix[x][y]`), requiring a shift and add, in to a pointer dereference (`*matrix_ptr`), and an increment (`matrix_ptr++`).

Program 14-16.

```
#define X_SIZE 60
#define Y_SIZE 30

int matrix[X_SIZE][Y_SIZE];

void init_matrix(void)
{
    register int index;          /* element counter */
    register int *matrix_ptr;

    matrix_ptr = &matrix[0][0];
    for (index = 0; index < X_SIZE * Y_SIZE; index++) {
        *matrix_ptr = -1;
        matrix_ptr++;
    }
}
```

But why have both a loop counter and a `matrix_ptr`? Couldn't we combine the two? In fact, we can, as shown in Program 14-17.

Program 14-17.

```
#define X_SIZE 60
#define Y_SIZE 30

int matrix[X_SIZE][Y_SIZE];

void init_matrix(void)
{
    register int *matrix_ptr;

    for (matrix_ptr = &matrix[0][0];
             matrix_ptr <= &matrix[X_SIZE-1][Y_SIZE-1];
             matrix_ptr++) {

        *matrix_ptr = -1;
    }
}
```

The function is now well-optimized. The only way we could make it better is to hand-code it into assembly language. This might make it faster; however, assembly language is highly non-portable and very error-prone.

The library routine `memset` can be used to fill a matrix or an array with a single character value. As shown in Program 14-18, we can use it to initialize the matrix in this program. Frequently used library subroutines like `memset` are often coded into assembly language and may make use of special processor-dependent tricks to do the job faster than could be done in C.

Program 14-18.

```
#define X_SIZE 60
#define Y_SIZE 30

int matrix[X_SIZE][Y_SIZE];
void init_matrix(void)
{
    (void)memset(matrix, -1, sizeof(matrix));
}
```

Now our function consists of only a single function call. It seems a shame to have to call a function just to call another function. We have to pay for the overhead of two function calls. It would be better if we called `memset` from the main function. Why don't we tell the user to rewrite his code using `memset` instead of `init_matrix`? Because he has several hundred `init_matrix` calls and doesn't want to do all that editing.

If we redefine our function as a macro, we have an `init_matrix` that looks like a function call. But, because it is a macro, it is expanded in-line, avoiding all the extra overhead associated with a function call. Look at Program 14-19.

Program 14-19.

```
#define X_SIZE 60
#define Y_SIZE 30

int matrix[X_SIZE][Y_SIZE];

#define init_matrix() \
    (void)memset(matrix, -1, sizeof(matrix));
```

Question 14–1: Why does `memset` successfully initialize the matrix to –1, but when we try to use it to set every element to 1, we fail?

```
#define X_SIZE 60
#define Y_SIZE 30

int matrix[X_SIZE][Y_SIZE];

#define init_matrix() \
    (void)memset(matrix, 1, sizeof(matrix));
```

How to Optimize

Our matrix initialization function illustrates several optimizing strategies. These are:

- **Loop ordering**. Nested loops should be ordered with the simplest loop outermost and the most complex loops innermost.
- **Reduction in strength**. This is a fancy way of saying use cheap operations instead of expensive ones. Table 14-1 lists the relative cost of common operations.

Table 14-1. Relative Cost of Operations

Operation	Relative Cost
`printf, scanf`	1000
Trigonometric functions (sin, cos, . . .)	500
Floating point (any operation)	100
Integer divide	30
Integer multiple	20
Function call	10
Simple array index	6
Shifts	5
Add/subtract	5
Pointer dereference	2
Bitwise and, or, not	1
Logical and, or, not	1

NOTE

Formatting functions like `printf`, `scanf`, and `sscanf` are extremely costly because they have to go through the format string one character at a time looking for a format conversion character (`%`). They then have to do a costly conversion between a character string and a number. These functions should be avoided in time-critical sections of code.

- **Powers of 2.** Use a power of 2 when doing integer multiply or divide. Most compilers will substitute a shift for the operation.
- **Pointers.** Pointers are faster than indexing an array. They are also more tricky to use.
- **Macros.** Using a macro eliminates the overhead associated with a function call. It also makes the code bigger and a little more difficult to debug. (See the next section "Case Study: Macros Versus Functions.")

Case Study: Macros Versus Functions

I once worked on writing a word processing program for a large computer manufacturer. We had a function, `next_char`, that was used to get the next character from the current file. It was used in thousands of places throughout the program. When we first tested the program with `next_char` written as a function, the program was unacceptably slow. Analyzing our program, we found that 90% of our time was spent in `next_char`. So we changed it to a macro. The speed doubled, however, our code size went up 40% and required a memory expansion card to work. So the speed was all right, but the size was still unacceptable. We finally had to write the routine as a function in hand-optimized assembly language to get both the size and the speed up to acceptable levels.

Case Study: Optimizing a Color Rendering Algorithm

I was once asked to optimize a program that did color rendering for a large picture. The problem was that the program took eight hours to process a single picture. This limited us to doing one run a day.

The first thing I did was to run the program on a machine with a floating-point accelerator. This brought the time down to about six hours. Next I got permission to use a high-speed RISC computer that belonged to another project, but was now sitting idle. That reduced the time to two hours.

I saved six hours solely by using faster machines. No code has changed yet.

There were two fairly simple functions that were being called only once from the innermost loop. Rewriting these functions as macros saved me about 15 minutes.

Next I changed all the floating-point operations I could from floating point to integer. The savings amounted to 30 minutes out of an hour and 45 minutes of runtime.

I noticed the program was spending about five minutes reading an ASCII file containing a long list of floating-point numbers used in the conversion process. Knowing that `scanf` is an extremely expensive function, I cut the initialization process down to almost nothing by making the file binary. Total runtime was now down to one hour and ten minutes.

By carefully inspecting the code and using every trick I knew, I saved another five minutes, leaving me five minutes short of my goal of an hour per run.

At this point my project was refocused and the program put in mothballs for use at some future date.

Answers

Answer 14–1: The problem is that **memset** is a *character* fill routine. An integer consists of 2 or 4 bytes (characters). Each byte is assigned the value 1. So a 2-byte integer will receive the value:

```
integer = 0x0101;
```

The 1-byte hex value for –1 is 0xFF. The two-byte hex value of –1 is 0xFFFF. So we can take two single byte –1 values, put them together, and come out with –1. This also works for 0. Any other number will produce the wrong answer. For example, 1 is 0x01. Two bytes of this is 0x0101 or 257.

Programming Problems

Exercise 1: Take one of your previous programs and run it using the interactive debugger to examine several intermediate values.

Exercise 2: Write a matrix multiply function. Create a test program that not only tests the function, but times it as well. Optimize it using pointers and determine the time savings.

Exercise 3: Write a program to sum the elements in an array. Optimize it.

Exercise 4: Write a program that counts the number of bits in a character array. Optimize it through the use of register integer variables. Time it on several different arrays of different sizes. How much time do you save?

Exercise 5: Write your own version of the library function **memcpy**. Optimize it. Most implementations of **memcpy** are written in assembly language and take advantage of all the quirks and tricks of the processor. How does your **memcpy** compare with theirs?

15

Floating Point

1 is equal to 2 for sufficiently large values of 1.
—Anonymous.

Computers handle integers very well. The arithmetic is simple, exact, and fast. Floating point is the opposite. Computers do floating-point arithmetic only with great difficulty.

This chapter discusses some of the problems that can occur with floating point. In order to understand the principles involved in floating-point arithmetic, we have defined a simple, decimal floating point. I suggest that you put aside your computer and work through these problems using pencil and paper so you can see firsthand the problems and pitfalls that occur.

The format used by computers is very similar to the one defined in this chapter, except that instead of using base 10, computers use base 2, 8, or 16. However, all the problems demonstrated here on paper can occur in a computer.

Floating-point Format

Floating-point numbers consist of three parts: a sign, a fraction, and an exponent. Our fraction is expressed as a four-digit decimal. The exponent is a single-decimal digit. So our format is:

$$\pm f.fff \times 10^{\pm e}$$

where:

$\pm$ is the sign (plus or minus).

$f.fff$ is the four-digit fraction.

$\pm e$ is the single-digit exponent.

Zero is $+0.000 \times 10^{+0}$. We can represent these numbers in the following notation:

$$\pm d.ddd E \pm e.$$

This format is similar to the floating-point format used in many computers. The IEEE has defined a floating-point standard (#742); however, not all machines use it. Table 15-1 contains some examples of floating point numbers:

Table 15-1. Floating-point Examples

Notation	Number
+1.000*E*+0	1.0
+3.300*E*+5	33000
−8.223*E*−3	0.008223
+0.000*E*+0	0.0

The floating-point operations defined in this chapter will be following a rigid set of rules. In order to minimize errors, we will be making use of a *guard digit*. That is an extra digit added to the end of our fraction during computation. Many computers use a guard digit in their floating-point units.

Floating Addition/Subtraction

To add two numbers like 2.0 and 0.3, you must perform the following steps:

1. Start with the following numbers.

+2.000*E*+0	The number 2.0
+3.000*E*–1	The number 0.3

2. Add guard digits to both numbers.

+2.0000*E*+0	The number 2.0
+3.0000*E*–1	The number 0.3

3. Shift the number with the smallest exponent to the right one digit and increment its exponent. Continue until the exponents of the two numbers match.

+2.0000*E*+0	The number 2.0
+0.3000*E*+0	The number 0.3

4. Add the two fractions. The result will have the same exponent as the two numbers.

+2.0000*E*+0	The number 2.0
+0.3000*E*+0	The number 0.3
+2.3000*E*+0	Result 2.3

5. Normalize the number by shifting it left or right until there is just one nonzero digit to the left of the decimal point. Adjust the exponent accordingly. In this example, the result is already normalized. A number like +0.1234*E*+0 would be normalized to +1.2340*E*–1.

6. Finally, if the guard digit is less than or equal to 5, round the next digit up; otherwise truncate the number.

+2.3000*E*+1	Round last digit
+2.300*E*+0	Result 2.3

7. For floating-point subtraction, change the sign of the second operand and add.

Multiplication

When we want to multiply two numbers such as 0.12 × 11.0, the following rules apply:

1. Add the guard digit.

$+1.2000E-1$	The number .12
$+1.1000E+1$	The number 11

2. Multiply the two fractions and add the exponents, (1.2 × 1.1 = 1.32) (–1 + 1 = 0).

$+1.2000E-1$	The number .12
$+1.1000E+1$	The number 11
$+1.3200E+0$	The number 1.32

3. Normalize the result. If the guard digit is less than or equal to 5, round the next digit up. Otherwise, truncate the number.

$+1.320E+0$	The number 1.32

Notice that in multiply, you didn't have to go through all that shifting. The rules for multiply are a lot shorter than those for add. Integer multiply is a lot slower than integer add. In floating point, multiply speed is a lot closer to that of add.

Division

To divide numbers like 100.0 by 30.0, we must perform the following steps:

1. Add the guard digit.

$+1.0000E+2$	The number 100.0
$+3.0000E+1$	The number 30.0

2. Divide the fractions, subtract the exponents.

$+1.0000E+2$	The number 100.0
$+3.0000E+1$	The number 30.0
$+0.3333E+1$	The number 3.333

3. Normalize the result.

$+3.3330E+0$	The number 3.333

4. If the guard digit is less than or equal to 5, round the next digit up. Otherwise, truncate the number.

   $+3.333E+0$ The number 3.333

Overflow and Underflow

There are limits to the size of the number a computer can handle. What are the results of the following calculation?

$$9.000E+9 \times 9.000E+9$$

Multiplying it out, we get:

$$8.1 \times 10^{19}$$

However, we are limited to a single-digit exponent, which is too small to hold 19. This is an example of *overflow* (sometimes called *exponent overflow*). Some computers will generate a trap when this occurs, thus interrupting the program and causing an error message to be printed. Others are not so nice and generate a wrong answer (like 8.100E+9). Computers that follow the IEEE floating-point standard will generate a special value called `+Infinity`.

Overflow is only one of the many problems with floating point. *Underflow* occurs when the numbers become too small for the computer to handle. In the following example:

$$1.000E-9 \times 1.000E-9$$

the result is:

$$1.0 \times 10^{-18}$$

Since –18 is too small to fit into one digit, we have underflow.

Roundoff Error

Floating point is not exact. Everyone knows that 1+1 is 2, but did you know that 1/3 + 1/3 != 2/3?

This can be shown by the following floating-point calculations:

2/3 as floating point is 6.667*E*–1
1/3 as floating point is 3.333*E*–1

$$
\begin{array}{r}
3.333E{-1} \\
+\ 3.333E{-1} \\
\hline
6.666E{-1}
\end{array}
\text{ or } 0.6666
$$

which is not:

6.667*E*–1

Every computer has a similar problem with its floating point. For example, the number 0.2 has no exact representation in binary floating point.

Floating point should never be used for money. Because we are used to dealing with dollars and cents, it is tempting to define the amount $1.98 as:

```
float amount = 1.98;
```

However, the more calculations you do with floating point, the bigger the round-off error. Banks, credit cards, and the IRS tend to be very fussy about money. Giving the IRS a check that's almost right is not going to make them happy. Money should be stored as an integer number of pennies.

Accuracy

How many digits of the fraction are accurate? At first glance you might be tempted to say all four digits. Those of you who have read the previous section on roundoff error might be tempted to change your answer to three.

The answer is: it depends on the calculation. Certain operations, like subtracting two numbers that are close to each other, will generate inexact results. For example, consider the following equation:

1 – 1/3 – 1/3 – 1/3

$$
\begin{array}{r}
1.000E{+0} \\
3.333E{-1} \\
3.333E{-1} \\
3.333E{-1} \\
\hline
\end{array}
$$

which expands to:

$$\begin{array}{l} 1.0000E{+}0 \\ 0.3330E{+}0 \\ 0.3330E{+}0 \\ \underline{0.3330E{+}0} \\ 0.0010E{+}0 \text{ or } 1.000E{-}3 \end{array}$$

The correct answer is $0.000E+0$ and we got $1.000E-3$. The very first digit of the fraction is wrong. This is an example of a problem called *roundoff error* that can occur during floating-point operations.

Minimizing Roundoff Error

There are many techniques for minimizing roundoff error. Guard digits have already been discussed. C goes even further and does all floating-point calculations in double precision. This is somewhat slow, but produces better results.

Advanced techniques for limiting the problems caused by floating point can be found in books on numerical analysis. They are beyond the scope of this text. The purpose of this chapter is to give you some idea of what sort of problems can be encountered.

Floating point by its very nature is not exact. People tend to think of computers as very accurate machines. They can be, but they can also give wildly wrong results. You should be aware of the places where errors can slip into your program.

Accuracy

There is a simple way of determining how accurate your floating point is (for simple calculations). The method used in the following program is to add 1.0+0.1, 1.0+0.01, 1.0+0.001, and so on until the second number gets so small that it makes no difference in the result.

C does all floating-point arithmetic in **double**. This means that the expression:

```
float number1, number2;
. . .
while (number1 + number2 != number1)
```

is equivalent to:

```
while (((double)number1) + ((double)number2) != ((double)number1))
```

Because the **float** numbers are stored as single precision, this equation may give a distorted picture of the accuracy of your machine. (In one case, 84 bits of accuracy were reported for a 32-bit format.) Program 15-1 computes both the accuracy of floating point as used in equations and floating point as stored in memory.

Program 15-1.

```
#include <stdio.h>
main()
{
    /* two numbers to work with */
    float number1, number2;
    float result;               /* result of calculation */
    int   counter;              /* loop counter and accuracy check */

    number1 = 1.0;
    number2 = 1.0;
    counter = 0;

    while (number1 + number2 != number1) {
        counter++;
        number2 = number2 / 10.0;
    }
    (void) printf("%2d digits accuracy in calculations\n", counter);

    number2 = 1.0;
    counter = 0;

    while (1) {
        result = number1 + number2;
        if (result == number1)
            break;
        counter++;
        number2 = number2 / 10.0;
    }
    (void) printf("%2d digits accuracy in storage\n", counter);
    return (0);
}
```

Running this on a Sun-3/60 with an MC68881 floating-point chip, we get:

```
20 digits accuracy in calculations
 8 digits accuracy in storage
```

Precision and Speed

A variable of type **double** has about twice the precision of a normal **float** variable. Most people assume that double-precision arithmetic takes longer than single precision. This is not always the case.

For the equation:

```
float answer, number1, number2;
answer = number1 + number2;
```

C must perform the following steps:

1. Convert `number1` from single to double precision.
2. Convert `number2` from single to double precision.
3. Double-precision add.
4. Convert result into single precision and store in `answer`.

If the variables were of type **double**, C would only have to perform the following steps:

1. Double-precision add.
2. Store result in `answer`.

As you can see, the second form is a lot simpler, requiring three less converts. In some cases, converting a program from single precision to double precision will make it run *faster*.

Many computers, including the PC and Sun/3 series machines, have a special chip called a floating-point processor which does all the floating-point arithmetic. Actual tests using the Motorola 68881 floating-point chip, used in the Sun/3, as well as floating point on the PC show that single precision and double precision run at the same speed.

Some C compilers have an option switch that will cause arithmetic with single-precision floating-point operations to be done in single precision (instead of the standard double precision). Some have no switch, but they generate single-precision code in violation of the standard.

Power Series

Many trigonometry functions are computed using a power series. For example, the series for sin is:

$$sin(x) = x - \frac{x^3}{3!} + \frac{x^5}{5!} - \frac{x^7}{7!} + \ldots$$

The question is how many terms do we need to get four-digit accuracy? Table 15-2 contains the terms for the sin(π/2).

Table 15-2. Terms for Sin(π/2)

	Term	Value	Total
1	x	1.571*E*+0	
2	$\frac{x^3}{3!}$	6.462*E*–1	9.248*E*–1
3	$\frac{x^5}{5!}$	7.974*E*–2	1.005*E*+0
4	$\frac{x^7}{7!}$	4.686*E*–3	9.998*E*–1
5	$\frac{x^9}{9!}$	1.606*E*–4	1.000*E*+0
6	$\frac{x^{11}}{11!}$	3.604*E*–6	1.00*E*+0

From this we conclude that six terms are needed. However, if we try to compute the sin(π), we get reference to Table 15-3.

Table 15-3. Terms for Sin(π)

	Term	Value	Total
1	x	3.142*E*+0	3.142*E*+0
2	$\frac{x^3}{3!}$	5.170*E*+0	–2.028*E*+0

Table 15-3. Terms for Sin(π) (continued)

	Term	Value	Total
3	$\frac{x^5}{5!}$	2.552*E*+0	5.241*E*–1
4	$\frac{x^7}{7!}$	5.998*E*–1	-7.570*E*–2
5	$\frac{x^9}{9!}$	8.224*E*–2	6.542*E*–3
6	$\frac{x^{11}}{11!}$	7.381*E*–3	–8.388*E*–4
7	$\frac{x^{13}}{13!}$	4.671*E*–4	–3.717*E*–4
8	$\frac{x^{15}}{15!}$	2.196*E*–5	–3.937*E*–4
9	$\frac{x^{17}}{17!}$	7.970*E*–7	–3.929*E*–4
10	$\frac{x^{19}}{19!}$	2.300*E*–8	–3.929*E*–4

π needs nine terms. So, different angles require a different number of terms. (A program for computing the sin to four-digits accuracy showing intermediate terms is included in Appendix D, *Program to Compute sine Using a Power Series*.)

Compiler designers have a dilemma when it comes to designing a sin function. If they know ahead of time the number of terms to use, they can optimize their algorithms for that number of terms. However, they lose accuracy for some angles. So a compromise must be struck between speed and accuracy.

Don't assume that because the number came from the computer, it is accurate. Many times, the library functions will generate bad answers—especially when working with excessively large or small values. Most of the time you will not have any problems with these functions, but you should be aware of their limitations.

Finally, there is the question of what is *sin* (1000000)? Our floating-point format is good for only four digits. The sine function is cyclical. That is, sin(0) = sin(2π) = sin(4π) .... So *sin* (1000000) is the same as *sin* (1000000*mod*2π). The value of this function depends on the value of the last digit (number 7). Our floating-point format is only good for four digits. So we have an error of ±100.

With such a large unknown, the value of the sin could be anything. So *sin* (1000000) is meaningless.

Give or Take Twelve Million

I attended a Physics class at Caltech taught by two professors. One was giving a lecture on the sun when he said, "... and the mean temperature of the inside of the sun is 13,000,000 to 25,000,000 degrees." At this point the other instructor broke in and asked "Is that Celsius or Kelvin (absolute zero or Celsius-273)?"

The lecturer turned to the board for a minute, then said, "What's the difference?" The moral of the story is that when your calculations have a possible error of 12,000,000, a difference of 273 doesn't mean very much.

Programming Problems

Exercise 1: Write a program that uses strings to represent floating-point numbers in the format used in this chapter. The program should have functions to read, write, add, subtract, multiply, and divide floating-point numbers.

16

Advanced Pointers

- Pointers and Structures
- Linked List
- Structure Pointer Operator
- Ordered Linked Lists
- Double-linked List
- Trees
- Data Structures for a Chess Program

A race that binds
Its body in chains and calls them Liberty,
And calls each fresh link progress.
—Robert Buchanan

One of the more useful and complex features of C is its use of pointers. With pointers you can create complex data structures like linked lists and trees. Figure 16-1 illustrates some of these data structures.

Up to now all our data structures have been allocated by the compiler as either permanent or temporary variables. With pointers we can create and allocate *dynamic data structures* that can grow or shrink as needed. In this chapter you will learn how to use some of the more common dynamic data structures.

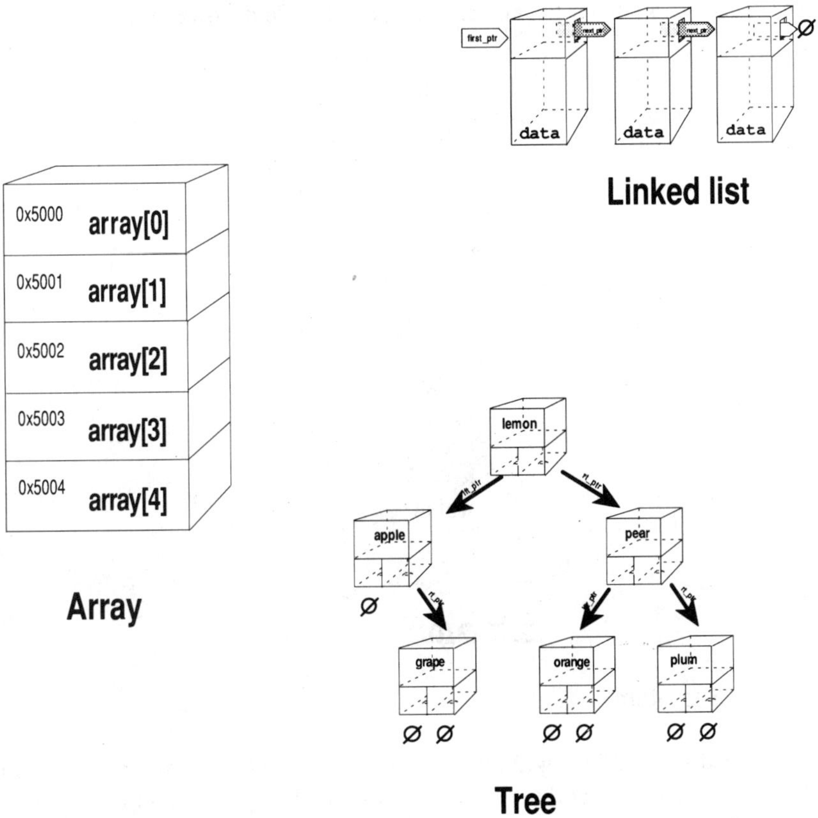

Figure 16-1. How Pointers May Be Used

Pointers and Structures

Structures may contain pointers, even a pointer to another instance of the same structure. In the following example:

```
struct item {
    struct item *next_ptr;
    int value;
}
```

the structure **item** is illustrated in Figure 16-2. This structure contains two fields, one named **value**, shown here as the section containing the number 2.

The other is a a pointer to another structure. The field **next_ptr** is shown as an arrow.

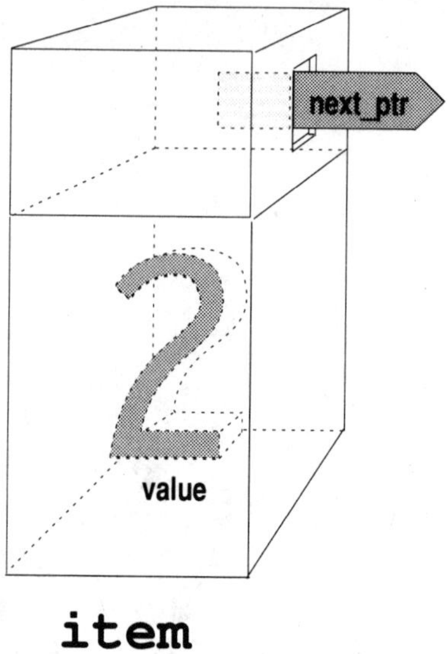

Figure 16-2. Item

The procedure **malloc** will allocate storage for a variable and return a pointer. It is used to create new things out of thin air (actually out of an area of memory called the *heap*). Up to now we've used pointers solely to point to named variables. So if we used a statement like:

```
int data;
int *number_ptr;
number_ptr = &data;
```

the thing we are pointing to has a name (**data**). The function **malloc** creates a new, unnamed variable and returns a pointer to it. The "things" created by **malloc** can only be referenced through pointers, never by name.

The UNIX version of **malloc** is defined as:

```
char *malloc(/* unsigned integer */)
```

The ANSI standard version is:

```
void *malloc(unsigned int);
```

The function **malloc** takes a single argument: the number of bytes to allocate. If **malloc** runs out of memory, it will return a null pointer.

In ANSI C, the declaration `void *` is used to indicate that `malloc` returns a generic pointer (a pointer that can point to any type of thing). So ANSI standard C uses **void** for two purposes:

- When used as a type in a function declaration, it indicates that the function returns no value.
- When used in a pointer declaration, it defines a generic pointer.

UNIX C does not have a generic pointer type, so it uses the next best thing, a character pointer.

NOTE

If `malloc` is used on UNIX to allocate anything other than a character string, it must be typecast to avoid type-conflict errors that `lint` will detect. However, `lint` will complain about possible pointer alignment errors. There is no way to silence these errors.

We will start using `malloc` by allocating space for simple structures. As we go on, we will see how to create bigger structures and link them together to form very complex data structures. Program 16-1 allocates storage for a character string 80 bytes long (`'\0'` included). The variable `string_ptr` will point to this storage.

Program 16-1.

```
#include <stdlib.h>      /* using ANSI C standard libraries */
main()
{
    char *string_ptr;

    string_ptr = malloc(80);
```

NOTE

If you are using the old UNIX C compiler, replace the line:

```
#include <stdlib.h>
```

with:

```
extern char *malloc()
```

Suppose we are working on a complex database that contains (among other things) a mailing list. The structure **person** is used to hold the data for each person:

```
struct person {
    char    name[30];             /* name of the person */
    char    address[30];          /* where he lives */
    char    city_state_zip[30];   /* Part 2 of address */
    int     age;                  /* his age */
    float   height;               /* his height in inches */
}
```

We could use an array to hold our mailing list, but an array is an inefficient use of memory. Every entry takes up space, whether or not it is used. What we need is a way to allocate space for only those entries that are used. We can use **malloc** to allocate space on an as-needed basis.

To create a new person, we use the code:

```
struct person *new_ptr;

new_ptr = (struct person *)malloc(sizeof(struct person));
```

The type cast **(struct person *)** is needed in UNIX C to change the character pointer into a person pointer. In ANSI C this is not necessary, but it does no harm. We determine the number of bytes to allocate by using the expression **sizeof(struct person)**. Without the **sizeof** operator, we would have to count the number of bytes in our structure, a difficult and error-prone operation.

free Function

The function **malloc** gets memory from the heap. To free that memory once you are done with it, use the function **free**. The general form of the **free** function is:

free(*pointer*);

where *pointer* is a pointer previously allocated by **malloc**.

The following is an example using **malloc** to get storage and **free** to dispose of it:

```
#define DATA_SIZE (16 * 1024)
void copy(void)
{
    char *data_ptr;          /* Pointer to large data buffer */
    data_ptr = malloc(DATA_SIZE);          /* Get the buffer */
```

```
    /*
     * Use the data buffer to copy a file
     */
    free(data_ptr);
}
```

But what happens if we forget to free our pointer? The buffer becomes dead. That is, the memory management system thinks it's being used, but no one is using it. If the **free** statement were removed from the function **copy**, then each succcssive call would eat up another 16K of memory.

The other problem that can occur is using memory that has been freed. When **free** is called, the memory is returned to the memory pool and can be re-used. Using a pointer after a **free** call is similar to an out-of-bounds error for an index to an array. You are using memory that belongs to someone else. This can cause unexpected results or program crashes.

Linked List

Suppose you are writing a program to send a list of names to another computer using a communications line. The operator types in the names during the day, then after work you dial up the other computer and send them. But, you don't know ahead of time how many names are going to be typed. By using a linked-list data structure, you can create a list of names that can grow as more names are entered. Also, as we will see later, linked lists may be combined with other data structures to handle extremely complex data.

A *linked list* is a chain of items where each item points to the next one in the chain. Think about the treasure hunt games you played when you were a kid. You were given a note that said, "Look in the mailbox." Racing to the mailbox you found your next clue, "Look in the big tree in the back yard," and so on until you found your treasure (or you got lost). In a treasure hunt, each clue points to the next one.

A linked list is shown in Figure 16-3.

The structure declarations for a linked list are:

```
struct linked_list {
    char    data[30];             /* data in this element */
    struct linked_list *next_ptr; /* pointer to next element */
};
struct linked_list *first_ptr = NULL;
```

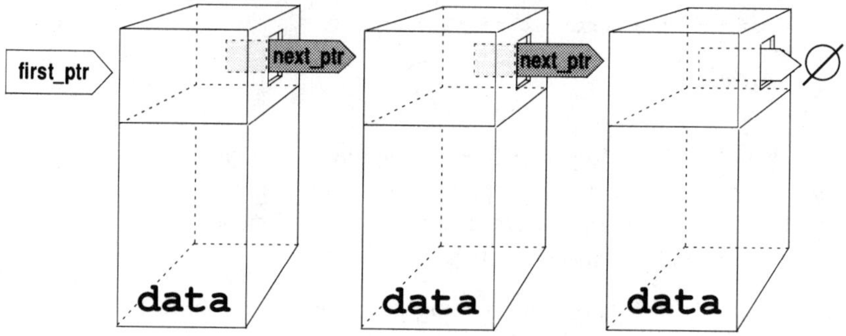

Figure 16-3. Linked List

The variable **first_ptr** points to the first element of the list. In the beginning, before we insert any elements into the list (it is empty), this variable is initialized to **NULL**.

In Figure 16-4, a new element is created and then inserted at the beginning of an existing list.

To insert a new element into a linked list in C, we execute the following steps:

1. Create a structure for the item.

```
new_ptr = (struct linked_list *)malloc(sizeof(struct linked_list));
```

2. Store the item in the new element.

```
(*new_ptr).data = item;
```

3. Make the first element of the list point to the new element.

```
(*new_ptr).next_ptr = first_ptr;
```

4. The new element is now the first element.

```
first_ptr = new_ptr;
```

(1) Create new element.

(2) Store item in new element.

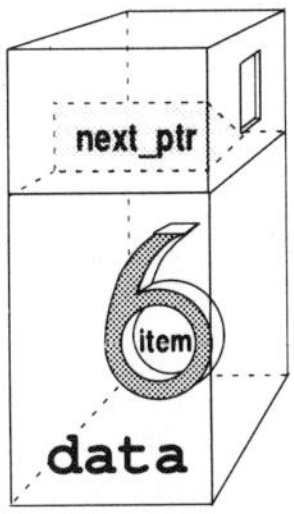

(3) Make `next_ptr` point to the first element.

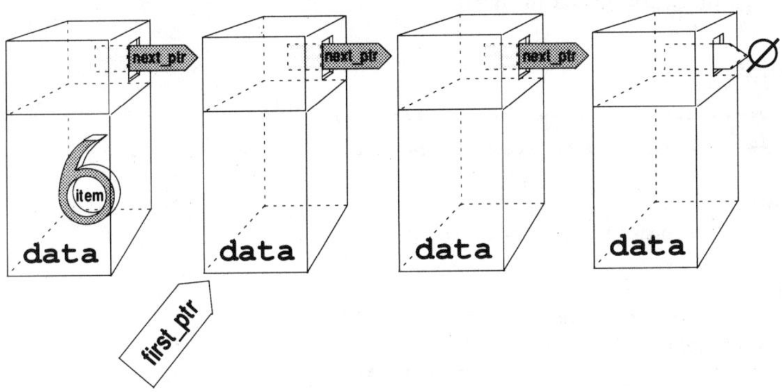

(4) Change `first_ptr` to point to the new element, thus breaking the link between `first_ptr` and the old first element.

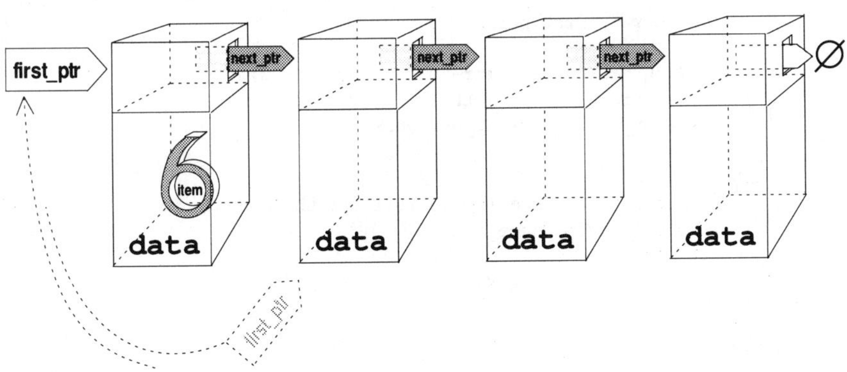

Figure 16-4. Adding New Element to Beginning of List

The code for the actual program is:

```
void add_list(int item)
{
    /* pointer to the next item in the list */
    struct linked_list *new_ptr;

    new_ptr = (struct linked_list *)
              malloc(sizeof(struct linked_list));
    (void)strcpy((*new_ptr).data, item);
    (*new_ptr).next_ptr = first_ptr;
    first_ptr = new_ptr;
}
```

To see if the name is in the list, we must search each element of the list until we either find the item or run out of data. Program 16-2 contains the `find` program for searching through the items in the list.

Program 16-2.

```
/********************************************************
 * find -- look for a data item in the list             *
 *                                                      *
 * Parameters                                           *
 *      name -- name to look for in the list            *
 *                                                      *
 * Returns                                              *
 *      1 if name is found                              *
 *      0 if name is not found                          *
 ********************************************************/
int file(char *name)
{
    /* current structure we are looking at */
    struct linked_list *current_ptr;

    current_ptr = first_ptr;

    while ((strcmp(current_ptr->data, name) != 0) &&
           (current_ptr != NULL))
        current_ptr = current_ptr->next_ptr;

    /*
     * If current_ptr is null, we fell off the end of the list and
     * didn't find the name
     */
    return (current_ptr != NULL);
}
```

Question 16–1: Why does running this program sometimes result in a bus error? Other times it will report **FOUND** for an item that is not in the list.

Structure Pointer Operator

In our **find** program, we had to use the cumbersome notation **(*current_ptr).data** to access the data field of the structure. C provides a shorthand for this construct using the structure pointer (->) operator. The dot (**.**) operator indicates the field of a structure. The -> indicates the field of a structure pointer.

The following two expressions are equivalent:

```
(*current_ptr).data = value;
current_ptr->data = value;
```

Ordered Linked Lists

So far, we have only added new elements to the head of a linked list. Suppose we want to add elements in order. Figure 16-5 is an example of an ordered linked list.

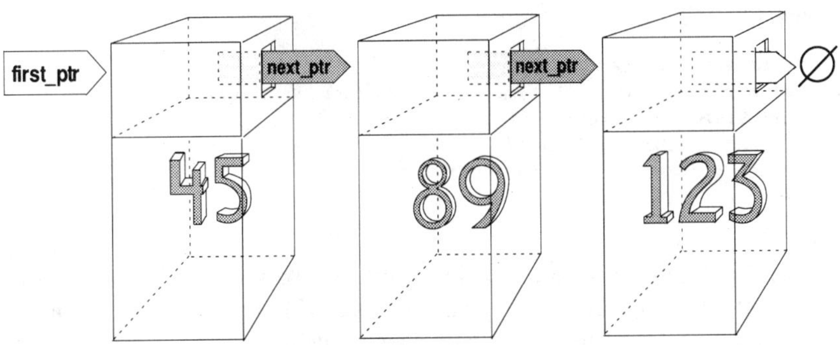

Figure 16-5. Ordered List

The following subroutine implements this function. The first step is to locate the insert point. **head_ptr** points to the first element of the list. The program moves the variable **before_ptr** along the list until it finds the proper place for the insert. The variable `after_ptr` is set to point to the element that follows the insertion. The new element will be inserted between these elements.

```
void enter(struct list *head_ptr, int item)
{
    struct list *before_ptr; /* insert before this element */
    struct list *after_ptr;  /* insert after this element */
    /*
     * Warning: This routine does not take
     *   care of the case where the element is
     *   inserted at the head of the list
     */
    before_ptr = head_ptr;
    while (1) {
        insert_ptr = before_ptr;
        insert_ptr = insert_ptr->next_ptr;
        /* did we hit the end of the list? */
        if (insert_ptr == NULL)
            break;
        /* did we find the place? */
        if (item >= insert_ptr->data)
            break;
    }
```

In Figure 16-6, we have positioned `before_ptr` so it points to the element before the insert point. The variable `after_ptr` points to the element after the insert. In other words, we are going to put our new element in between `before_ptr` and `after_ptr`.

Now that we have located the proper insert point, all we have to do is create the new element and link it in:

```
    /* create new item */
    new_ptr = (struct list *)malloc(sizeof(struct list));
    new_ptr->data = item;
    /* link in the new item */
    before_ptr->next_ptr = new_ptr;
    new_ptr->next_ptr = after_ptr;
}
```

Our new element must now be linked in. The first link we make is between the element pointed to by `before_ptr` (number 45) and our new element, `new_ptr` (number 53). This is done with the statement:

```
before_ptr->next_ptr = new_ptr;
```

(1) `before_ptr` points to the element before the insertion point, `after_ptr` to the element after the insertion point.

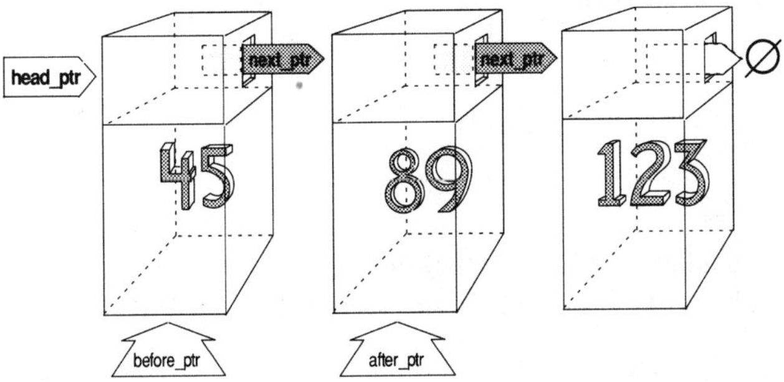

(2) Create new element.

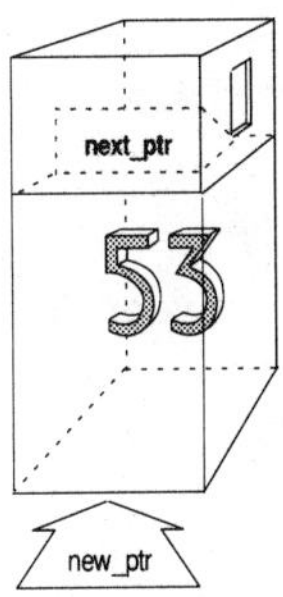

(3) Make the `next-ptr` of the new element point to the same element as `after_ptr`.

(4) Link the element pointed to by `before_ptr` to our new element by changing `before_ptr->next_ptr`.

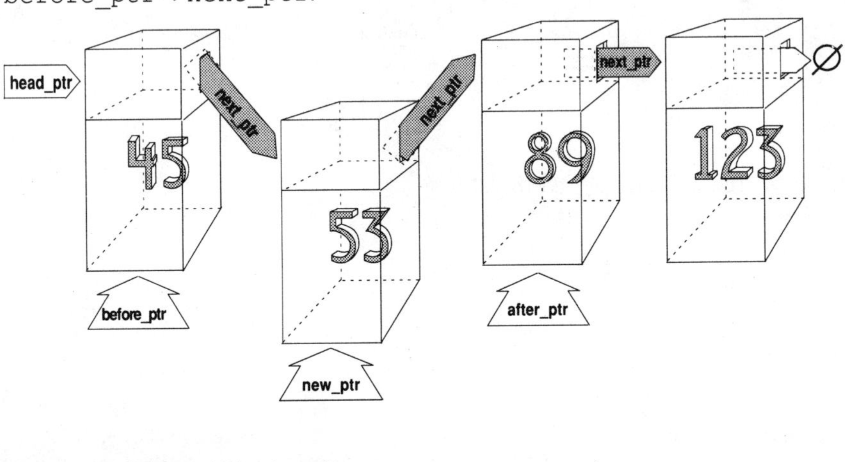

Figure 16-6. Ordered List Insert

Next we must link the new element, **new_ptr** (number 53), to the element pointed to by **after_ptr** (number 89). This is accomplished with the code:

```
new_ptr->next_ptr = after_ptr;
```

Double-linked List

A double-linked list contains two links. One link points forward to the next element; the other points backward to the previous element.

The structure for a double-linked list is:

```
struct double_list {
    int data;                        /* data item */
    struct  double_list *next_ptr;   /* forward link */
    struct  double_list *previous_ptr;/* backward link */
};
```

A double-linked list is illustrated in Figure 16-7. This is very similar to the single-linked list, except there are two links: one forward and one backward. The four steps required to insert a new element into the list are illustrated in Figures 16-8, 16-9, 16-10, and 16-11.

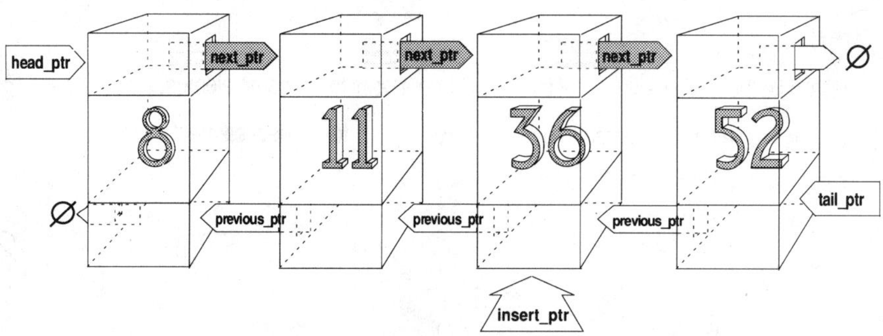

Figure 16-7. Double-linked List

The code to insert a new element in this list is:

```
void double_enter(struct double_list *head_ptr, int item)
{
    struct list *insert_ptr; /* insert before this element */
    /*
     * Warning: This routine does not take
     *   care of the case where the element is
     *   inserted at the head of the list
     *   or the end of the list
     */
    insert_ptr = head_ptr;
    while (1) {
        insert_ptr = insert_ptr->next;
        /* have we reached the end */
        if (insert_ptr == NULL)
            break;
        /* have we reached the right place */
        if (item >= insert_ptr->data)
            break;
    }
```

Let's examine this in detail. First we set up the forward link of our new element with the code:

```
new_ptr->next_ptr = insert_ptr;
```

This is illustrated in Figure 16-8.

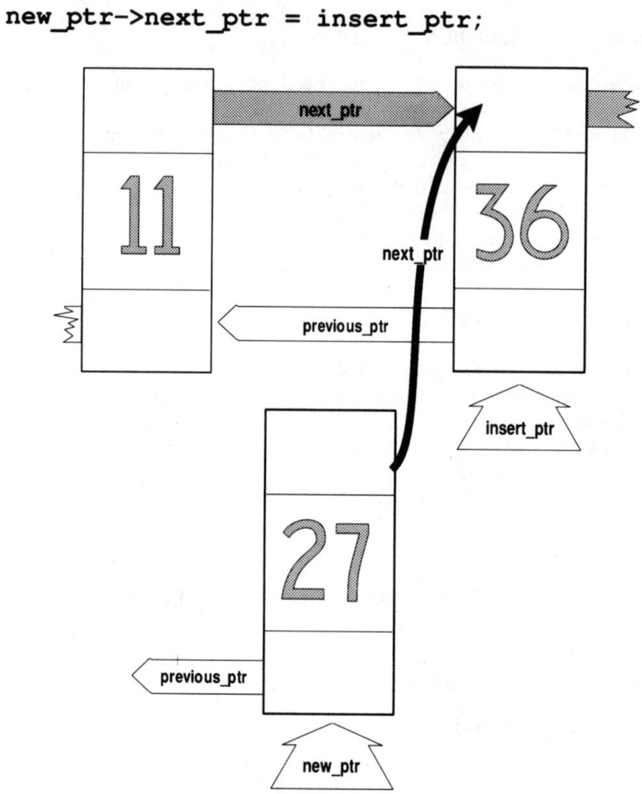

Figure 16-8. Double-linked List Insert, Part 1

Now we need to take off the backward pointer. This is accomplished with the statement:

```
new_ptr->previous_ptr = insert_ptr->previous_ptr;
```

Note that unlike the single-linked list, we have no **before_ptr** to point to the element in front of the insert point. Instead, we use the value of **insert_ptr->previous_ptr** to point to this element. Our linked list now looks like Figure 16-9.

```
new_ptr->previous_ptr = insert_ptr->previous_ptr;
```

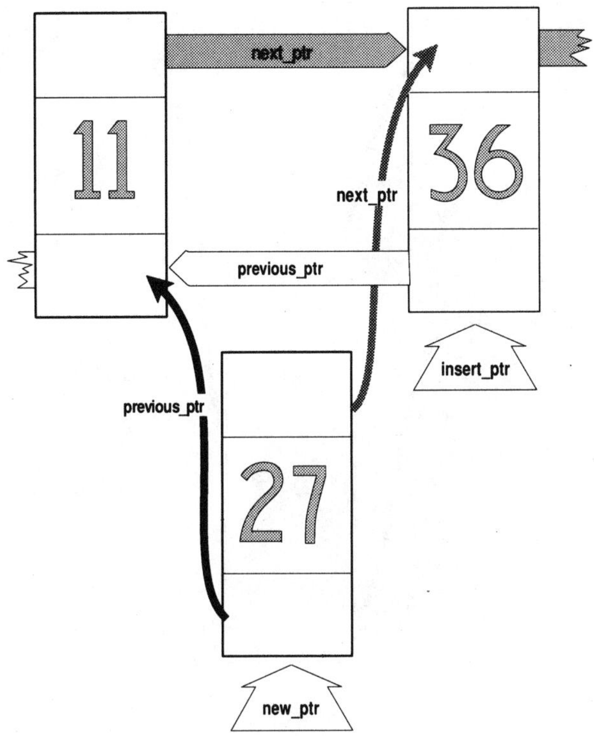

Figure 16-9. Double-linked List Insert, Part 2

We've set up the proper links in our new element; however, the links of the old elements (numbers 11 and 36) still need to be adjusted. We first adjust the field `next_ptr` in element 11. Getting to this element requires a little work. We start at `insert_ptr` (element 36) and follow the link `previous_ptr` to element 11. We want to change the field `next_ptr` in this element. The code for this is:

```
insert_ptr->previous_ptr->next_ptr = insert_ptr;
```

Our new link is illustrated in Figure 16-10.

```
insert_ptr->previous_ptr->next_ptr = new_ptr;
```

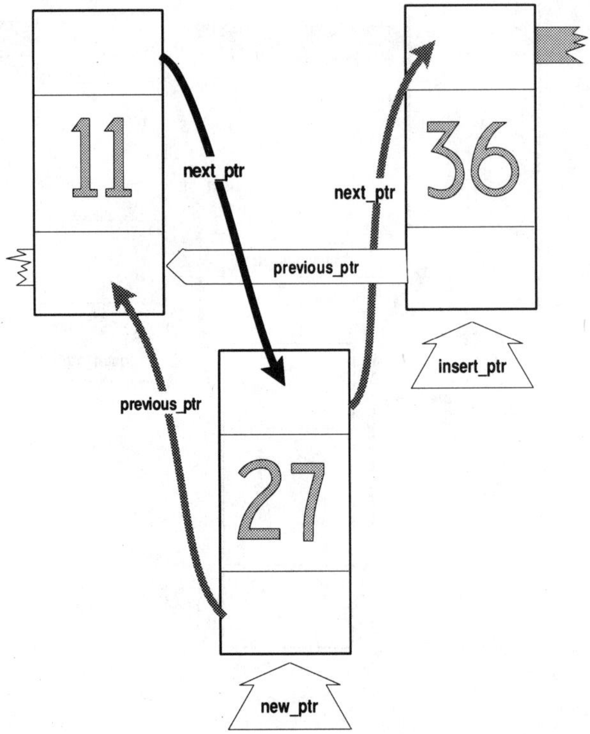

Figure 16-10. Double-linked List Insert, Part 3

We have three out of four links done. The final link is `previous_ptr` of element 36. This is set with code:

```
insert_ptr->previous_ptr = new_ptr;
```

The final version of our double link is illustrated in Figure 16-11.

```
insert_ptr->previous_ptr = new_ptr;
```

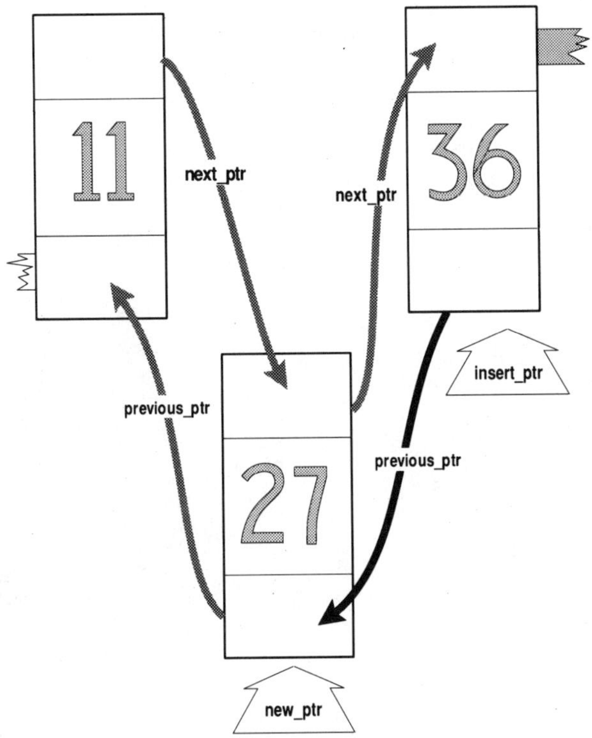

Figure 16-11. Double-linked List Insert, Part 4

Trees

Suppose we want to create an alphabetized list of the words that appear in a file. We could use a linked list; however, searching a linked list is slow because we must check each element until we find the correct insertion point. Using a data type called a *tree*, we can cut the number of compares down tremendously. A *binary tree structure* is shown in Figure 16-12.

Each box is called a *node* of the tree. The box at the top is the *root*, and the boxes at the bottom are the *leaves*. Each node contains two pointers, a left pointer and a right pointer, that point to the left and right subtrees.

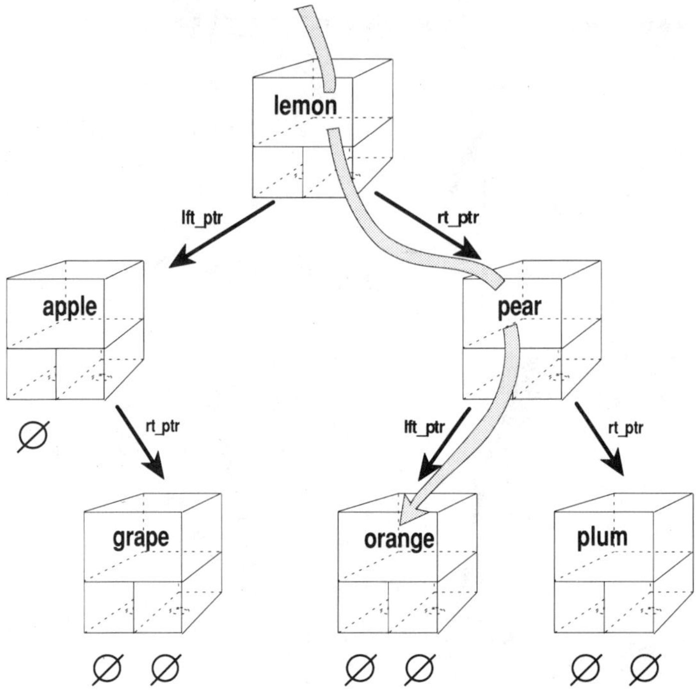

Figure 16-12. Tree

The structure for a tree is:

```
struct node {
    char    *data;              /* word for this tree */
    struct node *right;         /* tree to the right */
    struct node *left;          /* tree to the left */
};
```

Trees are often used for storing a *symbol table*, a list of variables used in a program. In this chapter we will use a tree to store a list of words and then print the list alphabetically. The advantage of a tree over a linked list is that searching a tree takes considerably less time.

In this example, each node stores a single word. The left subtree stores all words less than the current word, and the right subtree stores all the words greater than the current word.

For example, Figure 16-13 shows how we descend the tree to look for the word "orange." We would start at the root "lemon." Since "orange" > "lemon," we would descend to the right link and go to "pear." Because "orange" < "pear," we descend to the left link and we have "orange."

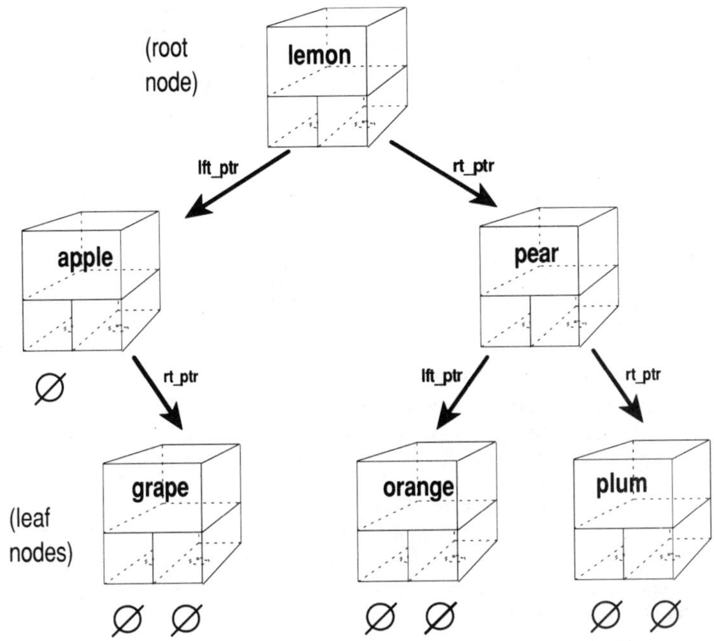

Figure 16-13. Tree Search

Recursion is extremely useful with trees. Our rules for recursion are:

1. The function must make things simpler.
2. There must be some endpoint.

The algorithm for inserting a word in a tree is:

1. If this is a null tree (or subtree), create a one-node tree with this word in it.
2. If this node contains the word, do nothing.
3. Otherwise, enter the word in the left or right subtree, depending on the value of the word.

Does this algorithm satisfy our recursion rules? The function has two definite endpoints:

1. A match is found.
2. We have a null node.

Otherwise we enter the word into a subtree (which is simpler than the whole tree).

To see how this works, consider what happens when we insert the word "fig" into the tree. First we check the word "fig" against "lemon." It's smaller so we go to "apple." Since "fig" is bigger, we go to "grape." Because "fig" is smaller than "grape," we try the left link. It is `NULL`, so we create a new node. The function to enter a value into a tree is:

```
void enter(struct node **node, char *word)
{
    int  result;                  /* result of strcmp */
    char *save_string();          /* save a string on the heap */
    void memory_error();          /* tell user no more room */
    /* see if we have reached the end */
    if ((*node) == NULL) {
        (*node) = (struct node *) malloc(sizeof(struct node));
        if ((*node) == NULL)
            memory_error();
        (*node)->left = NULL;
        (*node)->right = NULL;
        (*node)->word = save_string(word);
    }
    result = strcmp((*node)->word, word);
    if (result == 0)
        return;
    if (result < 0)
        enter(&(*node)->right, word);
    else
        enter(&(*node)->left, word);
}
```

This function is passed a pointer to the root of the tree. If the root is `NULL`, it will create the node. Because we are changing the value of a pointer, we must pass *a pointer to the pointer*. (We pass one level of pointer because that's the variable type outside the function; we pass the second level because we have to change it.)

Printing a Tree

Despite the complex nature of a tree structure, it is easy to print. Again, we use recursion. The printing algorithm is:

1. For the null tree, print nothing.

2. Print the data that comes before this node (left tree), then print this node and print the data that comes after this node (right tree).

The code for `print_tree` is:

```
void print_tree(struct node *top)
{
    if (top == NULL)
        return;                 /* short tree */
    print_tree(top->left);
    (void) printf("%s\n", top->word);
    print_tree(top->right);
}
```

The Rest of the Program

Now that we have the data structure defined, all we need to complete the program is a few more functions.

The `main` function checks for the correct number of arguments and then calls the scanner and the `print_tree` routine.

The `scan` function reads the file and breaks it into words. It uses the standard macro `isalpha`. The macro returns 1 if its argument is a letter and 0 otherwise. It is defined in the standard include file *ctype.h*. After a word is found, the function `enter` is called to put it in the tree.

`save_string` creates the space for a string on the heap, then returns the pointer to it.

`memory_error` is called if a `malloc` fails. This program handles the out-of-memory problem by writing an error message and quitting.

Program 16-3 is a listing of *words.c*.

Program 16-3.

```
/********************************************************
 * words -- scan a file and print out a list of words   *
 *              in ASCII order.                          *
 *                                                       *
 * Usage:                                                *
 *      words <file>                                     *
 ********************************************************/
#include <stdio.h>
#include <ctype.h>
#include <string.h>
#include <stdlib.h>     /* ANSI Standard only */
```

```
struct node {
    struct node    *right;      /* tree to the right */
    struct node    *left;       /* tree to the left */
    char           *word;       /* word for this tree */
};

/* the top of the tree */
static struct node *root = NULL;

main(int argc, char *argv[])
{
    void scan(char *);  /* scan the files for words */
    void print_tree(struct node *);/* print the words in the file */

    if (argc != 2) {
        (void) fprintf(stderr, "Error:Wrong number of parameters\n");
        (void) fprintf(stderr, "       on the command line\n");
        (void) fprintf(stderr, "Usage is:\n");
        (void) fprintf(stderr, "    words 'file'\n");
        exit(8);
    }
    scan(argv[1]);
    print_tree(root);
    return (0);
}
/********************************************************
 * scan -- scan the file for words                      *
 *                                                      *
 * Parameters                                           *
 *      name -- name of the file to scan                *
 ********************************************************/
void scan(char *name)
{
    char word[100];     /* word we are working on */
    int  index;         /* index into the word */
    int  ch;            /* current character */
    FILE *in_file;      /* input file */

    /* enter a word into the tree */
    void enter(struct node **, char *);

    in_file = fopen(name, "r");
    if (in_file == NULL) {
        (void) fprintf(stderr,
            "Error:Unable to open %s\n", name);
        exit(8);
    }
    while (1) {
        /* scan past the whitespace */
        while (1) {
            ch = fgetc(in_file);

            if (isalpha(ch) || (ch == EOF))
```

```
                break;
        }

        if (ch == EOF)
            break;

        word[0] = ch;
        for (index = 1; index < sizeof(word); index++) {
            ch = fgetc(in_file);
            if (!isalpha(ch))
                break;
            word[index] = ch;
        }
        /* put a null on the end */
        word[index] = '\0';

        enter(&root, word);
    }
    (void) fclose(in_file);
}
/********************************************************
 * enter -- enter a word into the tree                  *
 *                                                      *
 * Parameters                                           *
 *      node -- current node we are looking at          *
 *      word -- word to enter                           *
 ********************************************************/
void enter(struct node **node, char *word)
{
    int  result;        /* result of strcmp */

    char *save_string(char *);  /* save a string on the heap */
    void memory_error(void);    /* tell user no more room */

    /* see if we have reached the end */
    if ((*node) == NULL) {
        (*node) = (struct node *) malloc(sizeof(struct node));
        if ((*node) == NULL)
            memory_error();
        (*node)->left = NULL;
        (*node)->right = NULL;
        (*node)->word = save_string(word);
    }
    result = strcmp((*node)->word, word);
    if (result == 0)
        return;
    if (result < 0)
        enter(&(*node)->right, word);
    else
        enter(&(*node)->left, word);
}
```

```
/********************************************************
 * save_string -- save a string on the heap             *
 *                                                      *
 * Parameters                                           *
 *      string -- string to save                        *
 *                                                      *
 * Returns                                              *
 *      pointer to malloc-ed section of memory with     *
 *      the string copied into it.                      *
 ********************************************************/
char *save_string(char *string)
{
    char *new_string;   /* where we are going to put string */

    new_string = malloc((unsigned) (strlen(string) + 1));
    if (new_string == NULL)
        memory_error();
    (void) strcpy(new_string, string);
    return (new_string);
}
/********************************************************
 * memory_error -- write error and die                  *
 ********************************************************/
void memory_error(void)
{
    (void) fprintf(stderr, "Error:Out of memory\n");
    exit(8);
}
/********************************************************
 * print_tree -- print out the words in a tree          *
 *                                                      *
 * Parameters                                           *
 *      top -- the root of the tree to print            *
 ********************************************************/
void print_tree(struct node *top)
{
    if (top == NULL)
        return;                 /* short tree */

    print_tree(top->left);
    (void) printf("%s\n", top->word);
    print_tree(top->right);
}
```

Question 16–2: I once made a program that read the dictionary into memory using a tree structure, then used it in a program that searched for misspelled words. Although trees are supposed to be fast, this program was so slow you would think I used a linked list. Why?

Hint: Graphically construct a tree using the words "able," "baker," "cook," "delta," and "easy," and look at the result.

Data Structures for a Chess Program

One of the classic problems in artificial intelligence is the game of chess. In spite of all our advances in computer science, no one has ever been able to create a program that can play chess better than Grandmaster.

We are going to design a data structure for a chess-playing program. In chess you have several possible moves you can make. Your opponent has many responses to which you have many answers, and so on, back and forth, for several levels of moves.

Our data structure is beginning to look like a tree. This is not a binary tree since we have more than two branches for each node, as shown in Figure 16-14.

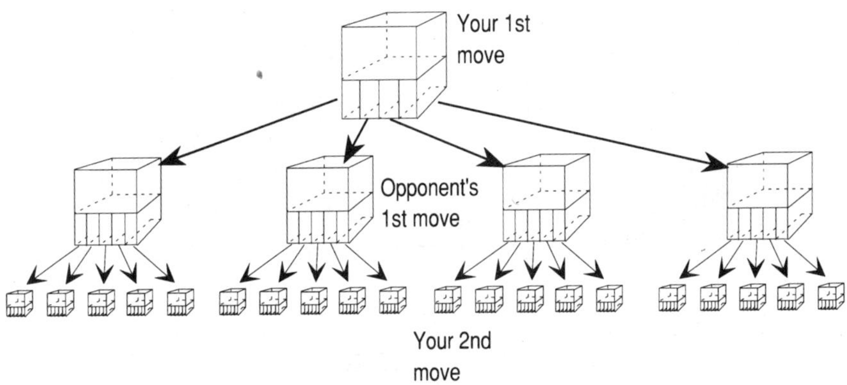

Figure 16-14. Chess Tree

We are tempted to use the following data structure:

```
struct chess {
    struct board board;     /* Current board position */
    struct next {
        struct move;        /* Our next move */
```

```
        struct *chess_ptr; /* Pointer to the resulting position */
    } next[MAX_MOVES];
};
```

The problem is that the number of moves from any given position can vary dramatically. For example, in the beginning you have lots of pieces running around.* Things like rooks, queens, and bishops can move any number of squares in a straight line. When you reach the end game (in an evenly matched game), each side probably has only a few pawns and one major piece. The number of possible moves has been greatly reduced.

We want to be as efficient in our storage as possible, since a chess program will stress the limits of our machine. We can reduce our storage requirements by changing the next-move array into a linked list. Our resulting structure is:

```
struct next {
    struct move;               /* Our next move */
    struct *chess_ptr;         /* Pointer to the resulting position */
};
struct chess {
    struct board board;        /* Current board position */
    struct next *list_ptr;     /* List of moves we can make from here */
    struct next this_move;     /* The move we are making */
};
```

This is shown graphically in Figure 16-15.

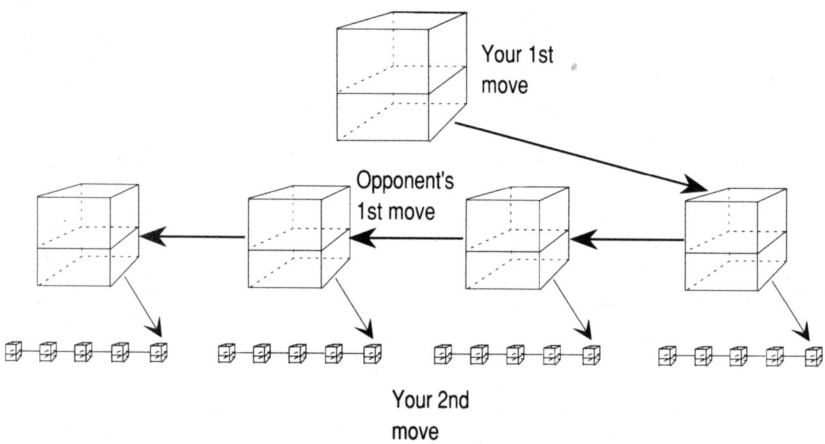

Figure 16-15. Revised Chess Structure

*Trivia question: What are the 21 moves you can make in chess from the starting position? (You can move each pawn up one (8 moves) or two (8 more), and the knights can move out to the left and right (4 more: 8+8+4=20.) What's the 21st move?

The new version adds a little complexity, but saves a great deal of storage. In the first version, we must allocate storage for pointers to all possible moves. If we have only a few possible moves, we waste a lot of storage for pointers to unused moves. Using a linked list, we allocate storage on an on-demand basis. So if there are 30 possible moves, our list is 30 long, but if there are only 3 possible moves, our list is 3 long. It grows only as needed, resulting in a more efficient use of storage.

Answers

Answer 16–1: The problem is with the statement:

```
while ((current_ptr->data != value) &&
        (current_ptr != NULL))
```

`current_ptr->data` is checked *before* we check to see if `current_ptr` is a valid pointer (!= **NULL**). If it is **NULL**, we can easily check a random memory location that could contain anything. The solution is to check `current_ptr` before checking what it is pointing to.

```
while (current_ptr != NULL) {
    if (current_ptr->data == value)
        break;
```

Answer 16–2: The problem was that because the first word in the dictionary was the smallest, every other word used the right-hand link. In fact, because the entire list was ordered, only the right-hand link was used. Although this was defined as a tree structure, the result was a linked list, as shown in Figure 16-16. Some of the more advanced books on data structures, like Donald Knuth's book *Algorithms + data structures = programs*, discuss ways of preventing this by balancing a binary tree.

Trivia Answer: You give up. That's right, the 21st move is to resign.

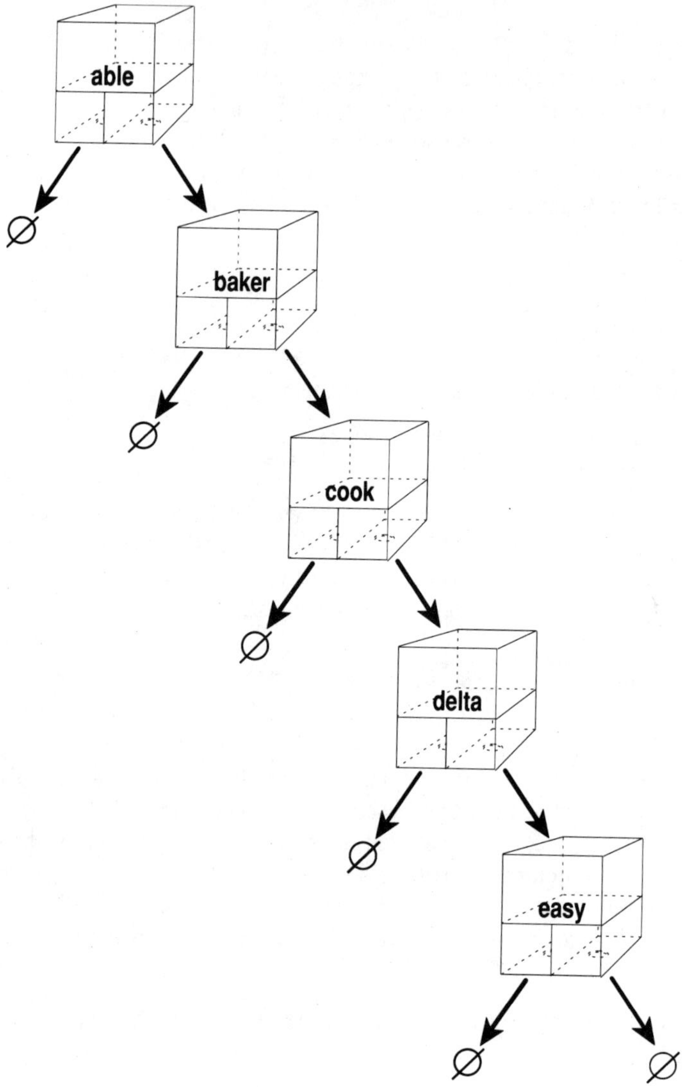

Figure 16-16. An Imbalanced Tree

Programming Problems

Exercise 1: Write a cross-reference program.

Exercise 2: Write a function to delete an element of a linked list.

Exercise 3: Write a function to delete an element of a double-linked list.

Exercise 4: Write a function to delete an element of a tree.

17

Modular Programming

Many hands make light work.
—John Heywood

All along we have been dealing with small programs. As programs grow larger and larger, it is more desirable to split them into sections or modules. C allows programs to be split into multiple files, compiled separately, and then combined (linked) to form a single program.

In this chapter, we will go through a programming example, discussing the C techniques needed to create good modules. You will be shown how to use `make` to put these modules together to form a program.

Modules

A module is a collection of functions that perform related tasks. For example, there could be a module to handle database functions such as `lookup`, `enter`, and `sort`. Another module could handle complex numbers, and so on.

Also as programming problems get bigger, more and more programmers are needed to finish them. An efficient way of splitting up a large project is to assign each programmer a different module. That way each programmer only worries about the internal details of a particular module.

In this chapter, we will discuss a module to handle *infinite arrays*. The functions in this package allow the user to store data into an array without worrying about its size. The infinite array grows as needed (limited only by the amount of memory in the computer). It will be used to store data for a histogram, but can be used to store things like line numbers from a cross-reference program or other types of data.

Public and Private

Modules are divided into two parts: *public* and *private*. The public part tells the user how to call the functions in the module. It contains the definition of data structures and functions that are to be used outside the module. These definitions are put in a header file, and it must be included in any program that depends on that module. In our infinite array example, we have put the public declarations in the file *ia.h*, which we will look at shortly.

Anything that is internal to the module is private. Everything that is not directly usable by the outside world should be kept private.

The extern Modifier

The **extern** modifier is used to indicate that a variable or function is defined outside the current file. For example, look at the contents of two files, *main.c* and *count.c*.

main.c

```
#include <stdio.h>
/* number of times through the loop */
extern int counter;

/* routine to increment the counter */
extern void inc_counter(void);

main()
{
    int   index; /* loop index */

    for (index = 0; index < 10; index++)
        inc_counter();
```

```
        (void) printf("Counter is %d\n", counter);
        return (0);
    }
```

count.c

```
    /* number of times through the loop */
    int     counter = 0;

    /* trivial example */
    void    inc_counter(void)
    {
        counter++;
    }
```

In this example, the function `main` uses the variable `counter`. The **extern** declaration is used by *main.c* to indicate that `counter` is declared outside it; in this case, it is defined in the file *counter.c*. The modifier **extern** is not used in *counter.c* because it contains the "real" declaration of the variable.

There are three modifiers that can be used to indicate where a variable is defined, as shown in Table 17-1.

Table 17-1. Modifiers

Modifier	Meaning
extern	Variable/function is defined in another file.
<blank>	Variable/function is defined in this file (public) and can be used in other files.
static	Variable/function is local to this file (private).

Notice that the word "static" has two meanings. For data defined globally, it means "private to this file." For data defined inside a function, it means "variable is allocated from static memory (instead of the temporary stack)."

C is very liberal in its use of the rules for the **static**, **extern**, and <blank> modifiers. It is possible to declare a variable **extern** at the beginning of a program and later define it as <blank>.

```
    extern sam;
    int sam = 1;      /* this is legal */
```

This is useful when you have all your external variables defined in a header file. The program includes the header file (and defines the variables as **extern**), then defines the variable for real.

Another problem concerns declaring a variable in two different files:

main.c

```
int     flag  = 0;       /* flag is off */
main()
{
    (void)printf("Flag is %d\n", flag);
}
```

sub.c

```
int     flag = 1;        /* flag is on */
```

What happens in this case?

- `flag` will be initialized to 0 because `main.c` is loaded first.
- `flag` will be initialized to 1 because the entry in *sub.c* will overwrite the one in *main.c*.
- The compiler will very carefully analyze both programs, then pick out the value that is most likely to be wrong.

There is only one global variable `flag`, and it will be initialized to either 1 or 0 depending on the whims of the compiler. Some of the more advanced compilers will issue an error message when a global is declared twice, but most compilers will silently ignore this error. It is entirely possible for the program `main` to print out:

```
flag is 1
```

even though we initialized it to 0 and did not change it before printing. To avoid the problem of hidden initializations, use the keyword **static** to limit the scope of variables to the file in which they are declared.

If we had written:

main.c

```
static int      flag  = 0;      /* flag is off */
main()
{
        (void)printf("Flag is %d\n", flag);
}
```

sub.c

```
static int      flag = 1;       /* flag is on */
```

then `flag` in *main.c* is an entirely different variable from `flag` in *sub.c*. However, it is still a good idea to give the variables different names to avoid confusion.

Headers

Information that is shared between modules should be put in a header file. By convention, all header filenames end with *.h*. In our infinite array example, we use the file *ia.h*.

The header should contain all the public information, such as:

- A comment section describing clearly what the module does and what is available to the user.
- Common constants.
- Common structures.
- Prototypes of all the public functions.
- **extern** declarations for public variables.

In our infinite array example, over half of the file *ia.h* is devoted to comments. This is not excessive; the real guts of the coding is hidden in the program file *ia.c*. The *ia.h* file serves both as a program file and as documentation to the outside world.

Notice there is no mention in the *ia.h* comments about how the infinite array is implemented. At this level we don't care how something is done, just what functions are available. Look through the file *ia.h*:

ia.h

```
/********************************************************
 * definitions for the infinite array (ia) package     *
 *                                                      *
 * An infinite array is an array whose size can grow   *
 * as needed.  Adding more elements to the array       *
 * will just cause it to grow.                          *
 *------------------------------------------------------*
 * struct infinite_array                                *
 *      used to hold the information on an infinite    *
 *      array                                           *
 *------------------------------------------------------*
 * Routines                                             *
 *                                                      *
 *      void ia_init(&array)                            *
 *      struct infinite_array array;                    *
 *                                                      *
```

```
*                                                    *
*       Initializes an infinite array (must be called *
*       before any other calls).                      *
*----------------------------------------------------*
*       ia_store(&array, index, data)                 *
*       struct infinite_array array;                  *
*       int index;                                    *
*       float data;                                   *
*                                                     *
* Stores the "data" into the infinite array "array"   *
*       in element "index."                           *
*                                                     *
*-----------------------------------------------------*
*                                                     *
*       float ia_get(&array, index)                   *
*       struct infinite_array array;                  *
*       int index;                                    *
*                                                     *
*       Returns the element in array "array" at index *
*       "index."                                      *
*******************************************************/

/* number of elements to store in each cell of the infinite array */
#define BLOCK_SIZE      100

struct infinite_array {
        /* the data for this block */
        float   data[BLOCK_SIZE];

        /* pointer to the next array */
        struct infinite_array *next;
};

#define ia_init(array_ptr)      {(array_ptr)->next = NULL;}

extern void ia_store(struct infinite_array*, int, float);
extern float ia_get(struct infinite_array*, int);
```

A few things should be noted about this file. Three functions are documented: `ia_get`, `ia_store`, and `ia_init`. `ia_init` isn't really a function but a macro. For the most part, people using this module do not need to know if a function is really a function or only a macro.

The macro is bracketed in curly braces ({}), so it will not cause syntax problems when used in something like an **if/else** sequence. The code:

```
if (flag)
  ia_init(array);
else
  (void)ia_store(&array, 0, 1.23);
```

will work as expected.

NOTE

The prototypes used in this header are in ANSI C format. These might not work with older UNIX compilers.

Everything in the file is a constant definition, a data structure definition, or an external definition. No code or storage is defined.

The Body of the Module

The body of the module contains all the functions and data for that module. Private functions that will not be called from outside the module should be declared **static**. Variables declared outside of a function that are not used outside the module are declared **static**.

A Program to Use Infinite Arrays

The program uses a simple linked list to store the elements of the array, as shown in Figure 17-1. A linked list can grow longer as needed (until we run out of room). Each list element or bucket can store 10 numbers. To find element 38, the program starts at the beginning, skips past the first three buckets, then extracts element 8 from the data in the current bucket.

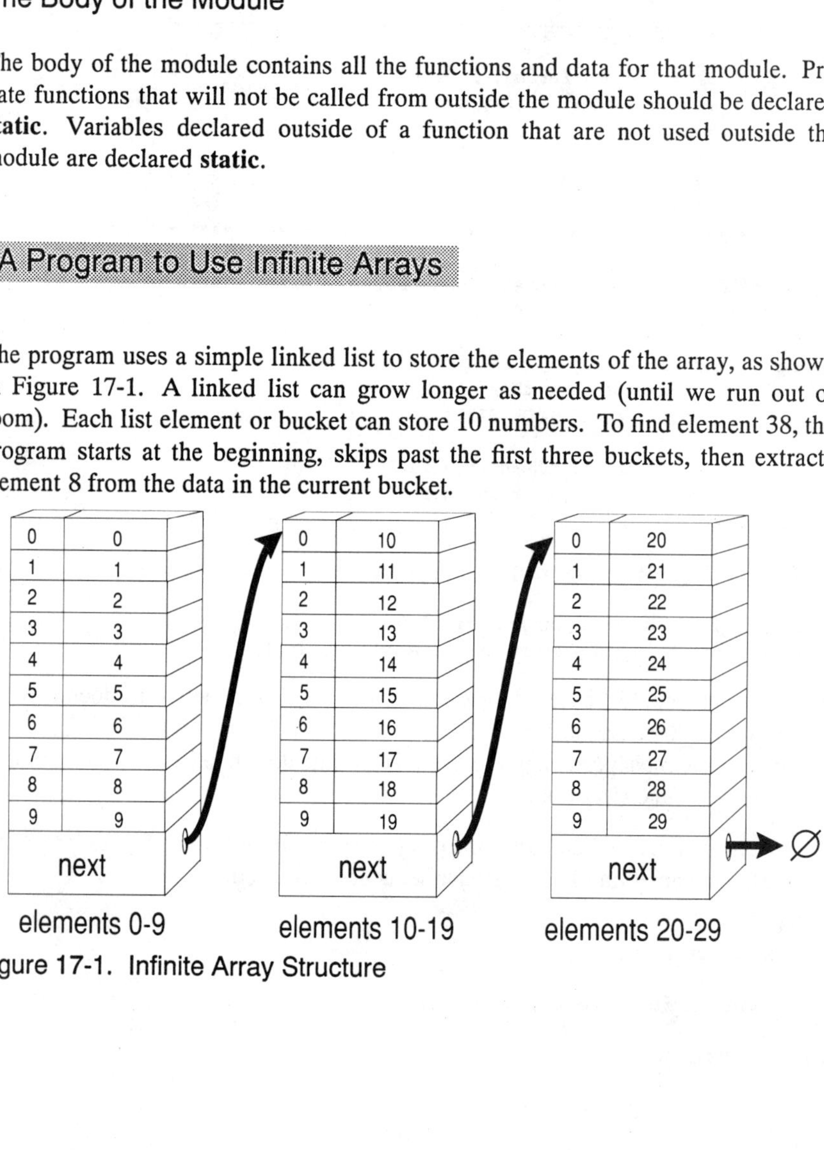

Figure 17-1. Infinite Array Structure

While writing this module, we noticed that most array accesses are sequential (1, 2, 3, ... etc.). If we just called to get element 5, the next call will probably be for element 6. A great deal of time is spent in this module going down the linked list chain searching for the proper bucket.

We can speed things up if we remember the last bucket we used and re-use it if possible. This is called a *cache* and is implemented with the three variables `cache_array_ptr`, `cache_bucket_ptr`, and `cache_index`.

The use of a cache is entirely hidden from the calling functions. There is no way (other than speed) they could know whether or not a cache is defined. It is an implementation detail that the caller does not need to know.

The code for the module *ia.c* is shown as Program 17-1.

Program 17-1.

```
/********************************************************
 * infinite-array -- routines to handle infinite arrays *
 *                                                      *
 * An infinite array is an array that grows as needed.  *
 * There is no index too large for an infinite array    *
 * (unless we run out of memory).                       *
 ********************************************************/
#include "ia.h"                 /* get common definitions */
#include <stdio.h>
#include <stdlib.h>     /* ANSI Standard only */

/*
 * the following three variables implement
 * a very simple pointer cache
 *
 * They store information on the last infinite array used,
 *       the last bucket we had and the last index used
 *
 * They are initialized to values we know will never
 * be used by any real array.
 */
static struct infinite_array *cache_array_ptr = NULL;
static struct infinite_array *cache_bucket_ptr = NULL;
static int cache_index = -1;
/********************************************************
 * ia_store -- store an element into an infinite array. *
 *                                                      *
 * Parameters                                           *
 *      array_ptr -- pointer to the array to use        *
 *      index     -- index into the array               *
 *      store_data -- data to store                     *
 ********************************************************/
void  ia_store(struct infinite_array * array_ptr,
    int index, float store_data)
```

```
{
    /* pointer to the current bucket */
    struct infinite_array *current_ptr;
    int   current_index;        /* index into the current bucket */

    /* get the location in an infinite array cell */
    struct infinite_array *ia_locate(
       struct infinite_array *, int, int *);

    current_ptr = ia_locate(array_ptr, index, &current_index);
    current_ptr->data[current_index] = store_data;
}
/********************************************************
 * ia_get -- get an element from an infinite array.     *
 *                                                      *
 * Parameters                                           *
 *      array_ptr -- pointer to the array to use        *
 *      index   -- index into the array                 *
 *                                                      *
 * Returns                                              *
 *      the value of the element                        *
 ********************************************************/
float ia_get(struct infinite_array *array_ptr, int index)
{
    /* pointer to the current bucket */
    struct infinite_array *current_ptr;
    int   current_index;        /* index into the current bucket */

    /* get the location an infinite array cell */
    struct infinite_array *ia_locate();

    current_ptr = ia_locate(array_ptr, index, &current_index);
    return (current_ptr->data[current_index]);
}
/********************************************************
 * ia_locate -- get the location of an infinite array   *
 *              element.                                *
 *                                                      *
 * Parameters                                           *
 *      array_ptr -- pointer to the array to use        *
 *      index   -- index into the array                 *
 *      current_index -- pointer to the index into this *
 *              bucket (returned)                       *
 *                                                      *
 * Returns                                              *
 *      pointer to the current bucket                   *
 ********************************************************/
static struct infinite_array ia_locate(
       struct infinite_array *array_ptr, int index
       int *current_index_ptr)
```

```
{
    /* pointer to the current bucket */
    struct infinite_array *current_ptr;

    /* see if the cache will do us any good */
    if ((cache_array_ptr == array_ptr) && (index >= cache_index)) {
        current_ptr = cache_bucket_ptr;
        *current_index_ptr = index - cache_index;
    } else {
        current_ptr = array_ptr;
        *current_index_ptr = index;
    }

    while (*current_index_ptr > BLOCK_SIZE) {
        if (current_ptr->next == NULL) {
            current_ptr->next =
                (struct infinite_array *)
                malloc(sizeof(struct infinite_array));
            if (current_ptr->next == NULL) {
                (void) fprintf(stderr, "Error:Out of memory\n");
                exit(8);
            }
        }
        current_ptr = current_ptr->next;
        *current_index_ptr -= BLOCK_SIZE;
    }

    cache_index = index - (index % BLOCK_SIZE);
    cache_array_ptr = array_ptr;
    cache_bucket_ptr = current_ptr;

    return (current_ptr);
}
```

This program uses an internal routine, `ia_locate`. Since this routine is not used outside the module, it is defined as **static**. It is also not put in the header *ia.h*.

The Makefile for Multiple Files

The program `make` is designed to aide the programmer in compiling and linking programs. Before `make`, the user had to explicitly type in compile commands for every change in the program, for example:

```
% cc -g -ohello hello.c
```

As programs grow, the number of commands needed to create them grows. Typing a series of 10 or 20 commands can be tiresome and error prone, so programmers started writing shell scripts (or *.BAT* files on MS-DOS.)

All the programmer had to type was **do-it**, and the computer would compile everything. This can be overkill, however, because all the files are recompiled whether or not they need to be.

As the number of files in a project grows, so does the time it takes to recompile. It can be frustrating to make a change in one small file, start the compilation, and then have to wait until the next day while the computer executes several hundred compile commands, especially when only one compile was really needed.

The program **make** was created to make compilation dependent upon whether a file has been updated since the last compilation. It allows you to specify the dependency of the program file and the source file, and the command that generates the program from its source.

The file *Makefile* (case sensitivity is important in UNIX) contains the rules used by **make** to decide how to build the program.

The *Makefile* contains the following sections:

- Comments
- Macros
- Explicit rules
- Default rules

Any line beginning with a hash mark (#) is a comment.

A macro has the format:

name = *data*

where *name* is any valid identifier and *data* is the text that will be substituted whenever **make** sees **$(***name***)**.

For example:

```
#
# Very simple Makefile
#
MACRO=Doing All
all:
        echo $(MACRO)
```

Explicit rules tell **make** what commands are needed to create the program. They can take several forms. The most common of these is:

> *target*: *source* [*source2*] [*source3*]
> *command*
> [*command*]
> [*command*]
> . . .

where *target* is the name of a file to create. It is "made" or created out of the source file *source*. If the *target* is created out of several files, they are all listed. The *command* that generates the target is specified on the next line. Sometimes it takes more than one command to create the target. Commands are listed one per line. Each is indented by a tab.

For example, the rule:

```
hello: hello.c
        cc -g -ohello hello.c
```

tells **make** to create the file *hello* from the file *hello.c* using the command:

```
cc -g -ohello hello.c
```

make will create *hello* only if necessary. The files used in the creation of *hello* arranged, in chronological order (by modification times), are:

UNIX:	MS-DOS:	
hello.c	*HELLO.C*	(oldest)
hello.o	*HELLO.OBJ*	(old)
hello	*HELLO.EXE*	(newest)

If the programmer changes the source file *hello.c*, its modification time will be out of date with respect to the other files. **make** will recognize that and recreate the other files.

Another form of the explicit rule is:

> *source*:
> *command*
> [*command*]

In this case, the commands are unconditionally executed each time **make** is run. If the commands are omitted from an explicit rule, **make** will use a set of built-in rules to determine what command to execute. For example, the rule:

```
hist.o: ia.h hist.c
```

tells **make** to create *hist.o* from *hist.c* and *ia.h*, using the standard suffix rule for making *file.o* from *file.c*. This rule is:

```
$(CC) $(CFLAGS) -c file.c
```

(**make** predefines the macros **$(CC)** and **$(CFLAGS)**.)

We are going to create a main program *hist.c* that calls the module *ia.c*. Both files include the header *ia.h*, so they depend on it. The UNIX *Makefile* which creates the program *hist* from *hist.c* and *ia.c* is:

```
CFLAGS = -g
SRC=ia.c hist.c
OBJ=ia.o hist.o

all: hist

hist: $(OBJ)
	$(CC) $(CFLAGS) -o hist $(OBJ)

lint:
	lint -x $(SRC)

hist.o:ia.h hist.c

ia.o:ia.h ia.c
```

The macro **SRC** is a list of all the C files. **OBJ** is a list of all the object (*.o*) files. The lines:

```
hist: $(OBJ)
	$(CC) $(CFLAGS) -o hist $(OBJ)
```

tell **make** to create *hist* from the object files. If any of the object files are out of date, **make** will recreate them.

The line:

```
hist.o:ia.h
```

tells **make** to create *hist.o* from *ia.h* and *hist.c* (the *hist.c* is implied). Since no command is specified, the default is used.

When the command **make lint** is executed, **make** will try to create the target **lint** as defined by:

```
lint:
	lint -x $(SRC)
```

Since there are no source files, this command will always be executed. So **make lint** will always cause **make** to run the files through **lint**.

The *Makefile* for DOS, using Turbo C, is:

```
#
SRCS=hist.c ia.c
OBJS=hist.obj ia.obj
CFLAGS=-ml -g -w -A
CC=tcc

ia: $(OBJS)
        $(CC) $(CFLAGS) -oia.exe $(OBJS)

hist.obj: hist.c ia.h
        $(CC) $(CFLAGS) -c hist.c

ia.obj: ia.c ia.h
        $(CC) $(CFLAGS) -c ia.c
```

This is similar to the UNIX *Makefile* except that Turbo C **make** does not provide any default rules.

There is one big drawback with **make**. It only checks to see if the files have changed, not the rules. If you have compiled all of your program with **CFLAGS=-g** for debugging and need to produce the production version (**CFLAGS=-O**), **make** will *not* recompile.

The command **touch** will change the modification date of a file. (It doesn't change the file, it just makes the operating system think it did.) If you **touch** a source file such as *hello.c* and then run **make**, the program will be recreated. This is useful if you have changed the compile-time flags and want to force a recompilation.

make provides you with a rich set of commands for creating programs. Only a few have been discussed here.*

Using the Infinite Array

The histogram program, **hist**, is designed to use the infinite array package. It takes one file as its argument. The file contains a list of numbers from 0 to 99. Any number of entries may be used. The program prints a histogram showing how many times each number appears. (A *histogram* is a graphic representation of the frequency of data.)

*If you are going to create programs that require more than 10 or 20 source files, read the Nutshell Handbook *Managing Projects with make,* by Steve Talbott.

A typical line of output from our program looks like:

```
16: 32- 33 (  50): **************
```

The first number (`16`) is the line index. This entry counts the numbers between `32` and `33`. In our sample data, there are 50 entries that fall in this range. The line of asterisks graphically represents our 50 entries.

Some data falls out of range and is not represented in our histogram. These are counted and listed at the end of the printout. Here is a sample printout:

```
 0:  0-  1 ( 100): **************
 1:  2-  3 ( 200): ****************************
 2:  4-  5 ( 100): **************
 3:  6-  7 ( 100): **************
 4:  8-  9 (   0):
 5: 10- 11 ( 100): **************
 6: 12- 13 (  50): *******
 7: 14- 15 ( 150): *********************
 8: 16- 17 (  50): *******
 9: 18- 19 (  50): *******
10: 20- 21 ( 100): **************
11: 22- 23 ( 100): **************
12: 24- 25 (  50): *******
13: 26- 27 ( 100): **************
14: 28- 29 (  50): *******
15: 30- 31 ( 100): **************
16: 32- 33 (  50): *******
17: 34- 35 (   0):
18: 36- 37 ( 100): **************
19: 38- 39 (   1):
20: 40- 41 ( 150): *********************
21: 42- 43 (  50): *******
22: 44- 45 ( 250): ***********************************
23: 46- 47 ( 100): **************
24: 48- 50 ( 150): *********************
25: 51- 52 ( 100): **************
26: 53- 54 (  50): *******
27: 55- 56 ( 200): ****************************
28: 57- 58 (  50): *******
29: 59- 60 (  50): *******
30: 61- 62 (  50): *******
31: 63- 64 ( 150): *********************
32: 65- 66 ( 100): *******************
33: 67- 68 (   0):
34: 69- 70 ( 199): ***************************
35: 71- 72 ( 200): ****************************
36: 73- 74 ( 100): **************
37: 75- 76 (  50): *******
38: 77- 78 ( 100): **************
39: 79- 80 ( 100): **************
40: 81- 82 ( 200): ****************************
41: 83- 84 ( 100): **************
```

```
42: 85- 86 (   0):
43: 87- 88 (   0):
44: 89- 90 (  50): *******
45: 91- 92 ( 150): *********************
46: 93- 94 ( 100): **************
47: 95- 96 (  50): *******
48: 97- 98 ( 100): **************
49: 99-100 (   0):
500 items out of range
```

This program contains a number of interesting programming techniques. The first one is: let the computer do the work whenever possible. Look at the following example, written by a C programmer doing the work himself:

```
#define LENGTH_X 300        /* width of the box in dots */
#define LENGTH_Y 400        /* height of the box in dots */
#define AREA 12000          /* total box area in dots */
```

The programmer has decided to multiply 300 × 400 to compute the area. It is far better to let the computer do the multiplying:

```
#define LENGTH_X 300        /* width of the box in dots */
#define LENGTH_Y 400        /* height of the box in dots */
/* total box area in dots */
#define AREA (LENGTH_X * LENGTH_Y)
```

That way, if either **LENGTH_X** or **LENGTH_Y** is changed, the **AREA** changes automatically. Also, the computer is more accurate in its computations. (Notice that the programmer made an error—the area is a factor of 10 too small.)

In the histogram program, the number of data points in each output line is computed by the definition:

```
#define FACTOR ((HIGH_BOUND - LOW_BOUND) / \
    ((float) (NUMBER_OF_LINES-1)))
```

The user should be helped whenever possible. In the **hist** program, if the user does not type the correct number of parameters on the command line, a message appears telling him what the error was and how to correct it.

The program uses the library routine **memset** to initialize the **counters** array. This routine is highly efficient for setting all values of an array to 0. The line:

```
(void)memset((char *)counters, ' ', sizeof(counters));
```

zeros the entire array **counters**.

The cast **(char *)** is needed because **memset** expects to work on character arrays. The **sizeof(counters)** makes sure that all of the array is zeroed. Program 17-2 contains the full listing of *hist.c*.

Program 17-2.

```
/********************************************************
 * hist -- generate a histogram of an array of numbers  *
 *                                                      *
 * Usage                                                *
 *      hist <file>                                     *
 *                                                      *
 * Where                                                *
 *      file is the name of the file to work on         *
 ********************************************************/
#include "ia.h"
#include <stdio.h>
#include <stdlib.h>     /* ANSI Standard only */
#include <mem.h>
/*
 * the following definitions define the histogram
 */
#define NUMBER_OF_LINES 50
#define LOW_BOUND 0.0
#define HIGH_BOUND 99.0
/*
 * if we have NUMBER_OF_LINES data to
 * output then each item must use
 * the following factor
 */
#define FACTOR \
  ((HIGH_BOUND - LOW_BOUND) / ((float) (NUMBER_OF_LINES-1)))

/* number of characters wide to make the histogram */
#define WIDTH 60

static struct infinite_array data_array;
static int data_items;

main(int argc, char *argv[])
{
    void  read_data(char *);     /* get the data into the array */
    void  print_histogram(void);/* print the data */

    if (argc != 2) {
        (void) fprintf(stderr,
               "Error:Wrong number of arguments\n");
        (void) fprintf(stderr,
               "Usage is:\n");
        (void) fprintf(stderr,
               "  hist <data-file>\n");
        exit(8);
    }
    ia_init(&data_array);
    data_items = 0;
```

```
    read_data(argv[1]);
    print_histogram();
    return (0);
}
/********************************************************
 * read_data -- read data from the input file into      *
 *              the data_array.                         *
 *                                                      *
 * Parameters                                           *
 *      name -- the name of the file to read            *
 ********************************************************/
void read_data(char *name)
{
    char  line[100];     /* line from input file */
    FILE *in_file; /* input file */
    float data;     /* data from input */

    in_file = fopen(name, "r");
    if (in_file == NULL) {
        (void) fprintf(stderr,
               "Error:Unable to open %s\n", name);
        exit(8);
    }
    while (1) {
        if (fgets(line, sizeof(line), in_file) == NULL)
            break;

        if (sscanf(line, "%f", &data) != 1) {
            (void) fprintf(stderr,
              "Error: Input data not floating point number\n");
            (void) fprintf(stderr, "Line:%s", line);
        }
        ia_store(&data_array, data_items, data);
        data_items++;
    }
    fclose(in_file);
}
/********************************************************
 * print_histogram -- print the histogram output.       *
 ********************************************************/
void  print_histogram(void)
{
    /* upper bound for printout */
    int   counters[NUMBER_OF_LINES];
    float low;           /* lower bound for printout */
    int   out_of_range = 0;/* number of items out of bounds */
    int   max_count = 0;/* biggest counter */
    float scale;         /* scale for outputting dots */
    int   index;         /* index into the data */

    (void) memset((char *) counters, '\0', sizeof(counters));
```

```
    for (index = 0; index < data_items; index++) {
        float data;/* data for this point */

        data = ia_get(&data_array, index);

        if ((data < LOW_BOUND) || (data > HIGH_BOUND))
            out_of_range++;
        else {
            /* index into counters array */
            int   count_index;

            count_index = (data - LOW_BOUND) / FACTOR;

            counters[count_index]++;
            if (counters[count_index] > max_count)
                max_count = counters[count_index];
        }
    }

    scale = ((float) max_count) / ((float) WIDTH);

    low = LOW_BOUND;
    for (index = 0; index < NUMBER_OF_LINES; index++) {
        /* index for outputting the dots */
        int   char_index;
        int   number_of_dots;   /* number of * to output */

        (void) printf("%2d:%3.0f-%3.0f (%4d): ",
                      index, low, low + FACTOR -1,
                      counters[index]);

        number_of_dots = (int) (((float) counters[index]) / scale);
        for (char_index = 0; char_index < number_of_dots;
             char_index++)
            (void) printf("*");
        (void) printf("\n");
        low += FACTOR;
    }
    (void) printf("%d items out of range\n", out_of_range);
}
```

Dividing a Task Up into Modules

Unfortunately, computer programming is more of an art than a science. There are no hard and fast rules that tell you how to divide up a task into modules. Knowing what makes a good module and what doesn't comes with experience and practice.

This section describes some general rules for module division and how they can be applied to real-world programs. The techniques described here have worked well for me. You should use whatever works for you.

Information is a key part of any program. The key to any program is deciding on what information is being used and what processing you want to perform on it. Information flow should be analyzed before the design begins.

Modules should be designed to minimize the amount of information that has to pass between them. If you look at the organization of an army, you'll see that it is divided up into modules. There is the infantry, artillery, tank corps, and so on. The amount of information that passes between these modules is minimized. For example, an infantry sergeant who wants the artillery to bombard an enemy position calls up the artillery command and says, "There's a pillbox at location Y-94. Get rid of it."

The artillery commander handles all the details of deciding which battery is to be used, how much fire power to allocate based on the requirements of other fire missions, keeping the guns supplied, and many more details.*

Programs should be organized the same way. Information that can be kept in a module should be. Minimizing the amount of intermodule communication cuts down on communication errors as well as limiting maintenance problems that occur when a module is upgraded.

Module Division Example: Text Editor

You are already familiar with using a *text editor*. It is a program that allows the user to display and change text files. Most editors are display-oriented and continually display about 24 lines of the current file on the screen. The text editor must also interpret commands that are typed in by the user. This information must be parsed so that the computer can understand it and act accordingly. The individual commands are small and perform similar functions ("delete line" is very much like "delete character"). Imposing a standard structure on the command execution modules improves readability and reliability.

The different modules that form a text editor are illustrated in Figure 17-2.

*This is a very general diagram of the chain of command for an ideal army. The system used by the United States Army is more complex and so highly classified that even the Army commanders don't know how it works.

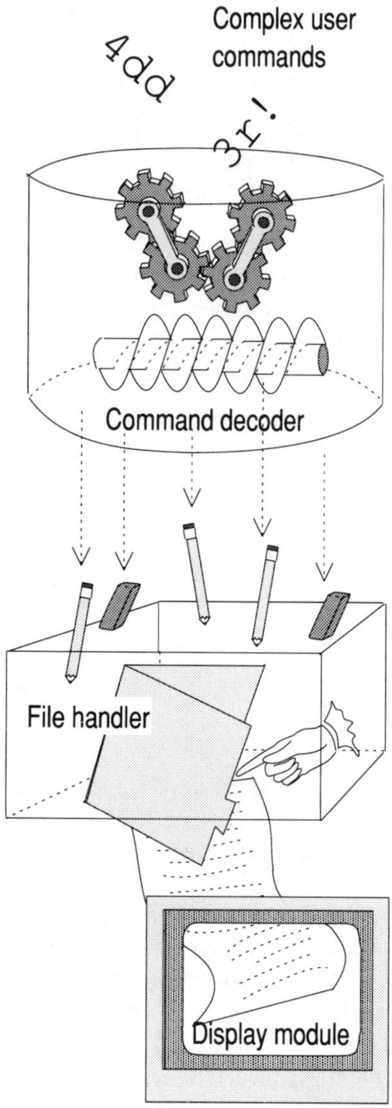

Figure 17-2. Text Editor Modules

There is minimal communication between the modules. The display manager needs to know only two things: where the cursor is and what the file currently looks like. All the file handler needs to do is read the file, write the file, and keep track of changes. Even the work involved in making changes can be minimized. All editing commands, no matter how complex, can be broken down into a series of inserts and deletes. It is the responsibility of the command module to take complex user commands and turn them into simple inserts and deletes that the file handler can process.

The information passing between the modules is minimal. In fact, no information passes between the command decoder and the display manager.

A word processor is just a fancy text editor. Where a simple editor only has to worry about ASCII characters (one font, one size), a word processor must be able to handle many different sizes and shapes.

Compiler

In a compiler, the information being processed is C code. The job of the compiler is to transform that information from C source to machine-dependent object code. There are several stages in this process. First, the code is run through the preprocessor to expand macros, take care of conditional compilation, and read in include files. Next the processed file is passed to the first stage of the compiler, the lexical analyzer.

The lexical analyzer takes as its input a stream of characters and returns a series of *tokens*. A token is a computer-science term meaning word or operator. For example, let's look at the English command:

```
Open the door.
```

There are 14 characters in this command. Lexical analysis would recognize three words and a period. These tokens are then passed to the parser, where they are assembled into sentences. At this stage, a symbol table is generated so that the parser can have some idea what variables are being used by the program.

Now the compiler knows what the program is supposed to do. The optimizer looks at the instructions and tries to figure out how to make them more efficient. This step is optional and is omitted unless the **–O** flag is specified on the command line.

The code generator turns the high-level statements into machine-specific assembly code. In assembly language, each assembly language statement corresponds to one machine instruction. The assembler turns assembly language into binary code that can be executed by the machine.

The general information flow of a compiler is shown in Figure 17-3.

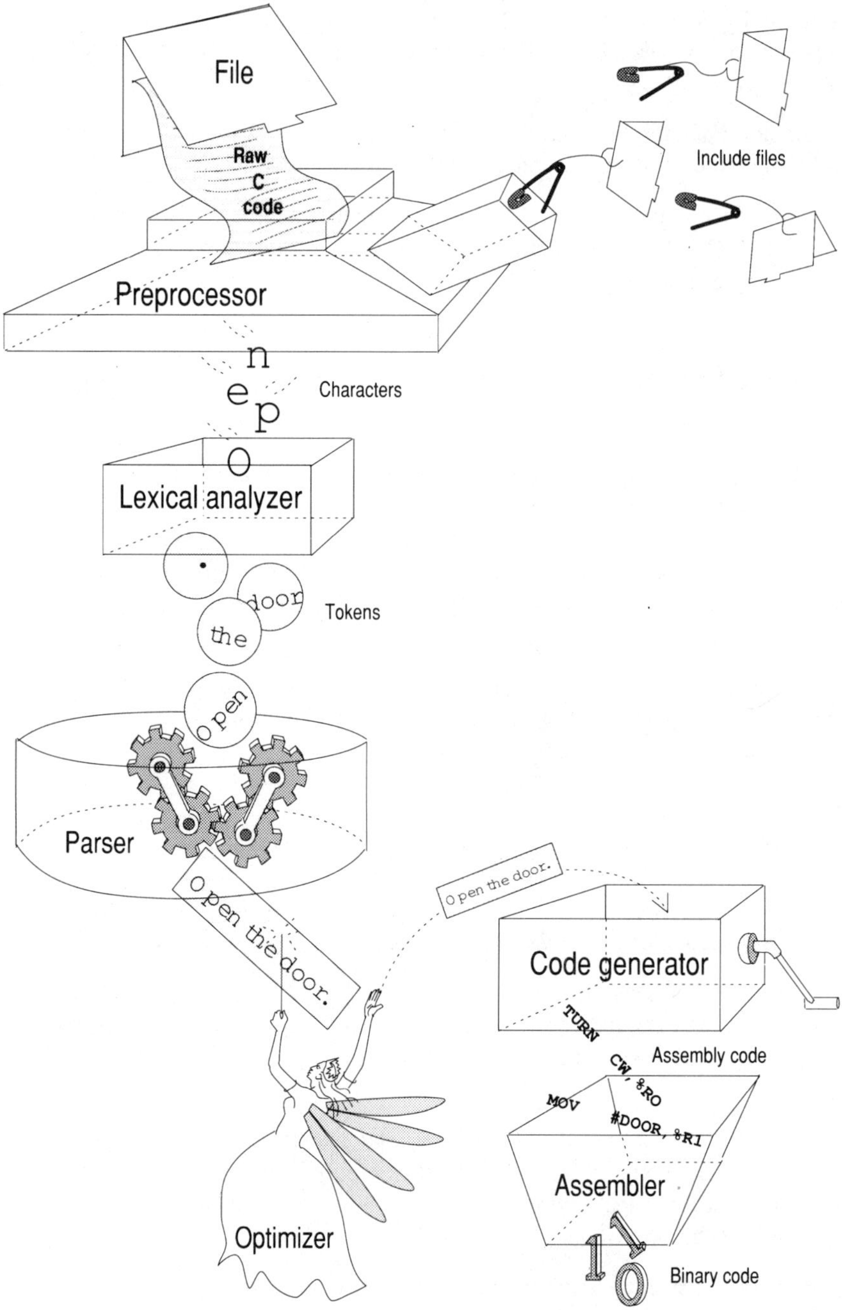

Figure 17-3. Compiler Modules

One of the contributing factors to C popularity is the ease with which a C compiler can be created for a new machine. AT&T distributes the source to the portable C compiler (PCC). Because it is written in modular fashion, you can port it to a new machine by changing the code generator and writing a new assembler. Both of these are relatively simple tasks (see the quote at the beginning of Chapter 6, *The Programming Process*).

Lexical analysis and parsing are very common and used in a wide variety of programs. The utility **`lex`** will generate the lexical analyzer module for a program, given a description of the tokens used by the program. Another utility, **`yacc`**, can be used to generate the parser module.*

Spreadsheet

A simple spreadsheet takes a matrix of numbers and equations and displays the results on the screen. This program manages equations and data.

The core of a spreadsheet are the equations. To change the equations into numbers, we need to go through lexical analyses and parsing, just like a compiler. But unlike a compiler, we don't generate machine code, instead we interpret the equations and compute the results.

These are passed off to the display manager, which puts them on the screen. Add to this an input module that allows the user to edit and change the equations and you have a spreadsheet, as shown in Figure 17-4.

*For descriptions of these programs, see the Nutshell Handbook *lex & yacc*, by Tony Mason and Doug Brown.

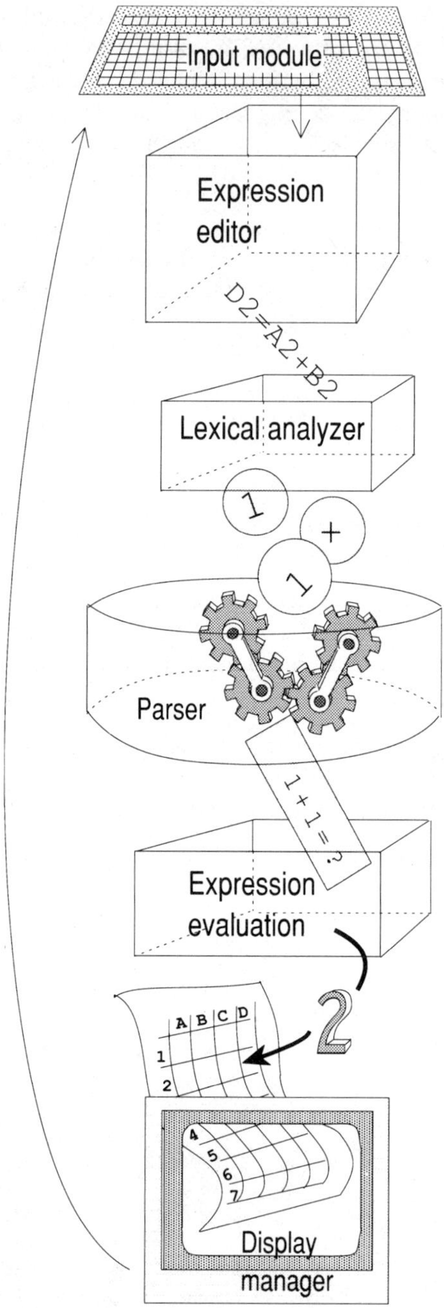

Figure 17-4. Spreadsheet Modules

Module Design Guidelines

There are no hard and fast rules when it comes to laying out the modules for a program. Some general guidelines are:

- The number of public functions in a module should be small.
- The information passed between modules should be limited.
- All the functions in a module should perform related jobs.

Programming Problems

Exercise 1: Write a module that will handle page formatting. It should contain the following functions:

`open_file(char *name)`	*Open the print file.*
`define_header(char *heading)`	*Define heading text.*
`print_line(char *line)`	*Send a line to the file.*
`page(void)`	*Start a new page.*
`close_file(void)`	*Close the printer file.*

Exercise 2: Write a module called `search_open` that is given an array of filenames, searches until it finds one that exists, and then opens it.

Exercise 3: Write a symbol table program consisting of the following functions:

`void enter(char *name)`	*Enter a name into the symbol table.*
`int lookup(char *name)`	*Returns 1 if name is in the table; returns 0 otherwise.*
`void delete(char *name)`	*Removes a name from the symbol table.*

Exercise 4: Take the `words` program from Chapter 16, *Advanced Pointers*, and combine it with the infinite array module to create a cross-reference program. (As an added bonus, teach it about C comments and strings to create a C cross-referencer.)

18

Portability Problems

Wherein I spake of most disastrous changes,
Of moving accidents by flood and field,
Of hair-breath 'scapes i' the imminent deadly breath...
—Shakespeare, on program porting (Othello, Act I, Scene III)

You've just completed work on your great masterpiece, a ray tracing program that renders complex three-dimensional shaded graphics on a Cray supercomputer using 30MB of memory and 500MB of disk space. What do you do when someone comes in and asks you to port this program to an IBM PC with 640K of memory and 10MB of disk space? Killing him is out; not only is it illegal, but it is considered unprofessional. Your only choice is to whimper and start the port. It is during this process that you will find that your nice, working program exhibits all sorts of strange and mysterious problems.

C programs are supposed to be portable; however, C contains many machine-dependent features. Also, because of the vast difference between UNIX and DOS, system deficiencies can frequently be found in many programs.

This chapter discusses some of the problems associated with writing truly portable programs as well as some of the traps you might encounter.

Modularity

One of the tricks to writing portablc programs is to put all the nonportable code into a separate module. For example, screen handling differs greatly on DOS and UNIX. To design a portable program, you'd have to write machine-specific modules that update the screen.

For example, the HP-98752A terminal has a set of function keys labeled F1 to F8. The PC terminal also has a function key set. The problem is that they don't send out the same set of codes. The HP terminal sends "<esc>p<return>" for F1 and the PC sends "<null>;". In this case, you would want to write a `get_code` routine that gets a character (or function key string) from the keyboard and translates function keys. Since the translation is different for both machines, a machine-dependent module would be needed for each one. For the HP machine, you would put together the program with *main.c* and *hp-tty.c*, while for the PC you would use *main.c* and *pc-tty.c*.

Word Size

A **long int** is 32 bits, a **short int** is 16 bits, and a normal **int** can be 16 or 32 bits depending on the machine. This can lead to some unexpected problems. For example, the following code works on a 32-bit UNIX system, but fails when ported to DOS:

```
int zip;
zip = 92126;
printf("Zip code %d\n", zip);
```

The problem is that on DOS, `zip` is only 16 bits—too small for 92126. To fix the problem, we declare `zip` as a 32-bit integer:

```
long int zip;
zip = 92126;
printf("Zip code %d\n", zip);
```

Now `zip` is 32 bits and can hold 92126.

Question 18–1: Why do we still have a problem? `zip` does not print correctly on a PC.

Byte Order Problem

A **short int** consists of 2 bytes. Consider the number 0x1234. The 2 bytes have the value 0x12 and 0x34. Which value is stored in the first byte? The answer is machine-dependent.

This can cause considerable trouble when trying to write portable binary files. The Motorola 68000-series machines use one type of byte order (ABCD), while Intel and Digital Equipment Corporation machines use another (BADC).

One solution to the problem of portable binary files is to avoid them. Put an option in your program to read and write ASCII files. ASCII offers the twin advantages of being far more portable as well as human readable.

The disadvantage is that text files are larger. Some files may be too big for ASCII. In that case, the magic number at the beginning of a file may be useful. Suppose the magic number is 0x11223344 (a bad magic number, but a good example). When the program reads the magic number, it can check against the correct number as well as the byte-swapped version (0x22114433). The program can automatically fix the file problem:

```
#define MAGIC 0x11223344      /* file identification number */
#define SWAP_MAGIC 0x22114433 /* magic number byte swapped */
FILE *in_file;                /* file containing binary data */
long int magic;               /* magic number from file */
in_file = fopen("data", "rb");
(void)fread((char *)&magic, 1, sizeof(magic), in_file);
switch (magic) {
    case MAGIC:
        /* No problem */
        break;
    case SWAP_MAGIC:
        (void)printf("Converting file, please wait\n");
        convert_file(in_file);
        break;
    default:
        (void)fprintf(stderr,"Error:Bad magic number %lx\n", magic);
        exit (8);
}
```

Alignment Problem

Some computers limit the address that can be used for integers and other types of data. For example, the 68000-series requires that all integers start on a 2-byte boundary. If you attempt to access an integer using an odd address, you will generate an error. Some processors have no alignment rules, while some are even more restrictive—requiring integers to be aligned on a 4-byte boundary.

Alignment restrictions are not limited to integers. Floating-point numbers and pointers must also be aligned correctly.

C hides the alignment restrictions from you. For example, if you declare the following structure on a 68000:

```
struct funny {
    char    flag;    /* type of data following */
    long int value; /* value of the parameter*/
};
```

C will allocate storage for this structure as shown on the left in Figure 18-1.

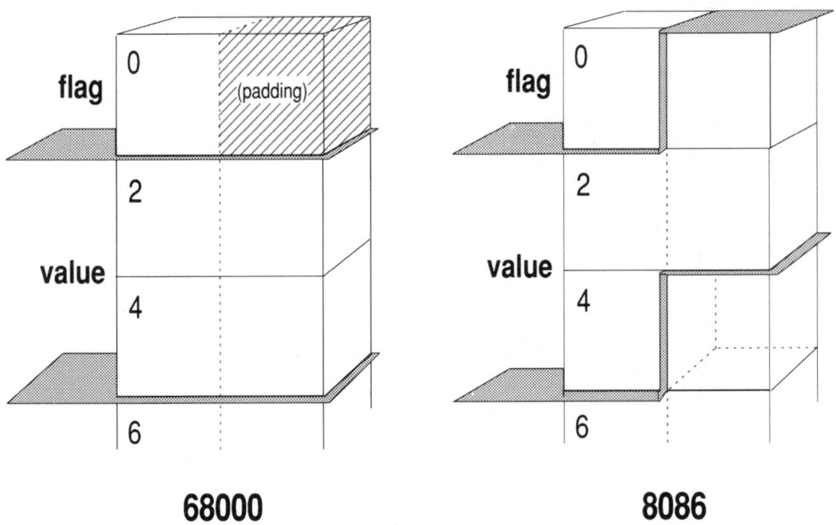

Figure 18-1. Structure on 68000 and 8086 Architectures

On an 8086-class machine with no alignment restrictions, this will be allocated as shown on the right in Figure 18-1. The problem is that the size of the structure changes from machine to machine. On a 68000 the structure size is 6 bytes, and on the 8086 it is 5 bytes. So if you write a binary file containing 100 records on a 68000, it will be 600 bytes long, while on an 8086, it will be only 500 bytes long. Obviously, the file is not written the same way on both machines.

One way around this problem is to use ASCII files. As we have said before, there are many problems with binary files. Another solution is to explicitly declare a pad byte:

```
struct new_funny {
        char    flag;   /* type of data following */
        char    pad;    /* not used */
        long int value; /* value of the parameter*/
};
```

The pad character makes the field value align correctly on a 68000 machine while making the structure the correct size on an 8086-class machine.

Using pad characters is difficult and error prone. For example, although `new_funny` is portable between machines with 1- and 2-byte alignment for 32-bit integers, it is not portable to any machine with a 4-byte integer alignment.

NULL Pointer Problem

Many programs and utilities were written using UNIX on VAX computers. On this computer the first byte of any program is 0. Many programs written on this computer contain a bug—they use the null pointer as a string.

For example:

```
#ifndef NULL
#define NULL 0
#endif NULL

char *string;

string = NULL;
(void)printf("String is '%s'\n", string);
```

This is actually an illegal use of `string`. Null pointers should never be dereferenced. On the VAX this error causes no problems. Since byte 0 of the program is 0, `string` points to a null string. This is due to luck, not design.

On a VAX, the following result is produced:

```
String is ''
```

On a Celerity computer, the first byte of the program is a `'Q'`. When this program is run on a C1200, it produces:

```
String is 'Q'
```

On other computers, this type of code can generate unexpected results. Many of the utilities ported from a VAX to a Celerity exhibited the `'Q'` bug.

Filename Problems

UNIX specifies files as */root/sub/file*, while DOS specifies files as *\root\sub\file*. When porting from UNIX to DOS, filenames must be changed. For example:

```
#ifndef __MSDOS__
#include <sys/stat.h> /* UNIX version of the file */
#else __MSDOS__
#include <sys\stat.h> /* DOS version of the file */
#endif __MSDOS__
```

Question 18–2: The following program works on UNIX, but when we run it on DOS, we get the following message:

```
oot
ew      able:   file not found.
```

```
FILE *in_file;

#ifndef __MSDOS__
#define NAME "/root/new/table"
#else __MSDOS__
#define NAME "\root\new\table"
#endif __MSDOS__

in_file = fopen(NAME, "r");
if (in_file == NULL) {
    (void)fprintf(stderr,"%s: file not found\n", NAME);
    exit(8);
}
```

File Types

In UNIX there is only one file type. In DOS there are two: text and binary. The flags `O_BINARY` and `O_TEXT` are used in DOS to indicate file type. No such flags are defined in UNIX.

One way of handling this problem is to write different open calls for each system:

```
#ifndef __MSDOS__
file_descriptor = open("file", O_RDONLY);
#else __MSDOS__
file_descriptor = open("file", O_RDONLY|O_BINARY);
#endif __MSDOS__
```

This is messy. A far better way is to define dummy `O_BINARY` and `O_TEXT` flags:

```
#ifndef O_BINARY  /* Do we have an O_BINARY? */
#define O_BINARY 0  /* If not define one  (BINARY and TEXT)*/
#define O_TEXT 0    /*  so they don't get in the way */
#endif O_BINARY
. . .

file_descriptor = open("file", O_RDONLY|O_BINARY);
```

Summary

It is possible to write portable programs in C. Because C runs on many different types of machines that use different operating systems, it is not easy. However, if you keep portability in mind when creating the code, you can minimize the problems.

Answers

Answer 18–1: The variable `zip` is a **long int**. The `printf` specification `%d` is for a normal **int**, not a **long int**. The correct specification is `%ld` to indicate a **long**:

```
printf("Zip code %ld\n", zip);
```

Answer 18–2: The problem is that C uses the backslash (\) as an escape character. The character `\r` is a carriage return, `\n` is newline, and `\t` is a tab. What we really have for a name is:

```
<return>oot<newline>ew<tab>able
```

The name should be specified as:

```
#define NAME "\\root\\new\\table"
```

NOTE

The **#include** uses a filename, not a C string. While you must use double backslashes (\\) in a C string, in an **#include** file, you use single backslashes (\). The following two lines are both correct:

```
#define NAME "\\root\\new\\table"
#include "\root\new\defs.h"
```

19

C's Dustier Corners

do/while
goto
The ?: Construct
The , Operator

There be of them that have left a name behind them.
—Ecclesiasticus 44:8

This chapter describes the few remaining features of C that have not been described in any of the previous chapters. It is titled *C's Dustier Corners* because these statements are hardly ever used in real programming.

do/while

The **do/while** statement has the following syntax:

```
do {
    statement
    statement
} while (expression);
```

The program will loop, test the expression, and stop if the expression is false (0).

NOTE

This construct will always execute at least once.

do/while is not frequently used in C, as most programmers prefer to use a **while/break** combination.

goto

All of the sample programs in this book were coded without using a single **goto**. In actual practice, I find a **goto** statement useful about once every other year. For those rare times that a **goto** is necessary, its syntax is:

goto *label* **;**

where *label* is a statement label. Statement labels follow the same naming convention as variable-names. Labeling a statement is done as follows:

label **:** *statement*

For example:

```
        for (x = 0; x < X_LIMIT; x++) {
            for (y = 0; y < Y_LIMIT; y++) {
                if (data[x][y] == 0)
                    goto found;
            }
        }
        (void) printf("Not found\n");
        exit(8);
    found:
        (void) printf("Found at (%d,%d)\n", x, y);
```

Question 19–1: Why does the following program *not* print an error message when an incorrect command is entered?

Hint: There is a reason we put this in the **goto** section.

```
#include <stdio.h>
#include <stdlib.h>                /* ANSI C only */

main()
{
    char  line[10];

    while (1) {
        (void) printf("Enter add(a), delete(d), quit(q): ");
        (void) fgets(line, sizeof(line), stdin);
```

```
            switch (line[0]) {
            case 'a':
                (void) printf("Add\n");
                break;
            case 'd':
                (void) printf("Delete\n");
                break;
            case 'q':
                (void) printf("Quit\n");
                exit(0);
            defualt:
                (void) printf("Error:Bad command %c\n", line[0]);
                break;
            }
        }
    }
```

The ?: Construct

The question mark (**?**) and colon (**:**) operators work much the same as **if/then/else**. Unlike **if/then/else**, the **?:** construct can be used inside of an expression. The general form of **?:** is:

(*expression*) **?** *value1* **:** *value2*

For example, the following assigns to **amount_owed** the value of the balance or zero, depending on the amount of the balance:

```
amount_owed = (balance < 0) ? 0 : balance;
```

The following macro returns the minimum of its two arguments:

```
#define min(x,y) ((x) < (y) ? (x) : (y))
```

The , Operator

The comma (**,**) operator can be used to group statements. For example:

```
if (total < 0) {
    (void)printf("You owe nothing\n");
    total = 0;
}
```

can be written as:

```
if (total < 0)
    (void)printf("You owe nothing\n"),total = 0;
```

In most cases curly braces ({}) should be used instead of a comma. About the only place the comma operator is useful is in a **for** statement. The following **for** loop increments two counters, `two` and `three`, by 2 and 3:

```
for (two = 0, three = 0;
     two < 10;
     two += 2, three += 2)
        (void)printf("%d %d\n", two, three);
```

Answers

Answer 19–1: The compiler didn't see our default line because we misspelled "default" as "defualt." This was not flagged as an error because "defualt:" is a valid **goto** label. Running this program through `lint` gives us the warning:

```
def.c(26): warning: defualt unused in function main
```

which means we defined a label for a **goto**, but never used it.

20

Putting It All Together

For there isn't a job on the top of the earth the beggar don't know, nor do.
—Kipling

In the preceding chapters, we have learned all about C. Now we use that knowledge to put together a well-crafted, well-designed program. We follow the rules we have learned: start with a specification, design the data structures, craft the code, and test the result.

We will use the modular design guidelines discussed in Chapter 17, *Modular Programming*, to create three well-defined modules: a main program, a macro checker, and a symbol table.

Assignment

Our assignment is to write a program to check `troff` files for syntax errors. Actually, since `troff` syntax is very complex and obscure, we are only going to check a small subset of the full language.

Specification

The program `tlint` will check `troff` files for syntax errors. `troff` input consists of text lines (for typesetting) and macro lines (typesetting commands). Macro lines begin with a dot (.) or single quote ('). The macro name itself is onc or two characters.

Macros can take up to nine arguments. Types of arguments are listed in Table 20-1.

Table 20-1. troff Arguments

Type	Description
Vertical bar	Begins absolute position command.
String	Single word or a series of words enclosed in double quotes (").
Number	Numeric expression.
Character	Single character.
Font	One- or two-character font name or font number.
Three-part title	Title of the form *'left'middle'right'*.

`troff` has a long list of macros. There is a problem with long lists: they change. Frequently, such lists are refined or tweaked.

A good rule of thumb is: if you have a long list of data, expect it to change and put it in an external configuration file. For our `tlint` program, the list of macros will be read in from a file.

I was once told to design a program for a special keyboard the company was creating for an automated cutting machine. We were taking a standard typewriter keyboard and putting special keycaps on it with names like "CUT," "ALIGN," "RESET," and so on. My job was to write the program that translated keycodes "A," "B," "C," into commands "CUT," "ALIGN," and "RESET." Management told me, "Keyboard layout is going to be frozen and never will change throughout the lifetime of the product. However, the final layout won't be decided until next week."

Specification for the Program
tlint
Check troff files for errors
Preliminary Specification
Feb 10, 1990
Steve Oualline

`tlint` is a program that checks `troff` files for errors. The program checks for too many arguments, illegal fonts, and arguments of the wrong type. The command line for the program is:

tlint [–m*file*] [–f*file*] [*file1*] [*file2*]

where:

–m*file* specifies a macro definition file (see format below). The file *standard.mac* is automatically read in. If you are using a macro package, you should include the syntax tables for it by using the **–m** option. Multiple **–m** options can appear on the command line.

–f*file* specifies a font file to be loaded. The standard font file, *standard.fonts*, loads automatically. The format of a font file is simple: each font is listed, while spaces or tabs may be used to separate fonts. Lines beginning with a hash mark (#) are comments.

file1, *file2* are a list of files. If no files are specified, the standard input is used.

The format of a macro definition file is as follows: comments begin with a hash mark and continue to the end of line. Each line consists of a macro name (one or two characters) followed by a series of argument description characters. The characters are:

Character	Description
|	Optional vertical bar
`s`	String
`n`	Numeric expression
`c`	Single character
`f`	Font specification
`t`	Three-part title

The last argument of some macros can be repeated many times. An asterisk (`*`) following the argument indicates that this argument can appear zero or more times. See the file *standard.mac* for examples.

Restriction: this tests a subset of `troff`. Expressions are limited to numeric expressions only. Characters are single characters only (character registers are not allowed). Fancier features of `troff` are not allowed.

I was told this for three weeks running. Finally, I gave up and designed my program so it read in a keyboard configuration file at startup. I figured that when they finally decided on the keyboard layout, I would just change my configuration file and everything would be ok.

It turned out that management found a flat keyboard that could take overlays. Soon they had a different keyboard layout for each major job to be done by the machine.

My program required little alteration. All I had to do was read a different configuration file for each mile instead of one at startup.

In addition to the built-in macros, **troff** comes with a set of standard macros. Also, the user can define his own set of macros. These can be used separately or combined. In order to handle this situation, we will design our program so it can read multiple macro configuration files.

troff uses four standard fonts: Roman, Italic, Bold, and Symbol. Each font is specified by a single-character name: R, I, B, and S. An updated version of **troff**, *d*evice-*i*ndependent **troff** (**ditroff**), allows the use of additional fonts. Each font is specified by a one- or two-character name.

The **troff** command:

```
.ft font
```

is used to change fonts. Our program should make sure that the font specified is a legal one. Again we will use an external configuration file for flexibility.

Code Design

This code breaks down naturally into three modules: a main driver program, a macro handler, and a font handler. Further examination of the program may result in additional modules being defined, but for now we are going to look only at these three.

Main Module

The purpose of the *main module* (**tlint.c**) is to handle all the bookkeeping associated with starting and stopping the program. It will also handle processing each file in the file list.

The program will read the file and check for a macro line. When it finds one, it will hand it off to the macro module for checking.

Macro Module

The *macro module* will read in the macro definition file. These macros will be stored in a symbol table so they may be used later to check each macro line for correct syntax. There are two public functions defined in this module: **load_macros** and **macro_check**. Their definitions and prototypes are placed in the header file *macro.h*.

Font Module

The *font module* will read in a list of fonts. The fonts are stored in a symbol table for later use. At this point we notice that we need two symbol tables, one for macros and one for fonts. Rather than invent the same thing twice, we decide we could use a fourth module containing common symbol table code. The public definitions for our font module are in the file *font.h*.

Symbol Table Module

The *symbol table module* consists of two functions: **enter**, for adding symbols to the table, and **lookup**, for finding symbols in the table.

There is a problem, though. The macro module must store an argument list with each symbol, while the font module has nothing to store. We need a different structure for each type of symbol.

We solve this problem by defining a generic structure that can be used by both modules:

```
/* For UNIX C use "#define generic char" */
#define generic void
/*
 * Defined for each node in the tree
 */
struct symbol {
    char name[3];          /* Name of the symbol */
    generic *data;         /* Pointer to data for the symbol */
    /* Left and right nodes of symbol tree */
    struct symbol *left_ptr, *right_ptr;
};
```

The symbol table module knows that each symbol has some data associated with it; however, exactly what type of data is left up to the calling modules. This technique is known as *information hiding*. The information associated with each kind of symbol is hidden from the symbol table module. The module doesn't care what type of information is used; all it knows is that whenever `enter` is called, it stores the information and, when `lookup` is called, it retrieves the information.

NOTE

> We use the `#define generic void` to emphasize that the field `data` in the structure `symbol` points to any type of data. When running on UNIX, you should `#define generic char`. Also, `lint` will complain of "possible pointer alignment errors." These may be safely ignored.

Coding

The coding is pretty straightforward. As I was typing in the code, I noticed I was frequently skipping past spaces and tabs with the lines:

```
while ((*(cur_char) <= ' ') && (*(cur_char) != ' '))
    (cur_char)++;
```

Rather than keep repeating this (or using cut and paste from the editor), I turned this into a macro, `SKIP_WHITESPACE`, which I placed in a general purpose header file *gen.h*.

Functional Description

This section describes the major functions in the program and what they do. For a complete and more detailed description, you should study the program listing at the end of the chapter.

tlint.c

main first loads the standard macro and font files. It next decodes the command-line arguments, looking for any additional files specified by the user. Finally, it loops through the files (or uses just standard if none are specified), opening them and passing them off to **do_file** for processing.

do_file is called once per file. It loops through each line in the file looking for macros. When it finds one, it calls **macro_check**, which scans for errors.

The rest of the module consists of two utility routines. The **usage** routine is called if the command line contains garbage. It prints out a short help message and dies. The **error** routine is called when a problem is detected in the file. It is responsible for printing an error message.

macros.c

This module contains the function **load_macros**, which reads the macro file and builds the macro symbol table. The table stores the macro's name as well as a pointer to the argument list.

The other function, **macro_check**, is called from the main module whenever a line containing a macro is detected. Its purpose is to check to make sure that the macro exists and the parameters are correct.

The function first calls **lookup** to check the macro and get the argument list. It then loops through the list performing a type check on each argument.

A **switch** statement is used to perform the actual type checking. If you look at this statement, you might detect a similarity between each of the cases. They almost all look something like this:

```
/* s -- a string */
case 's':
    cur_char = check_string(cur_char);
break;
```

The repetition is deliberate. The consistency makes the function easier to understand and helps limit the potential for error. Also, this code was easy to create; all it required was a little cut and paste in the editor, and I turned one case into six.

At this point the flow and function of the program is clear. There are differences between checking a font versus checking a string; however, these details are hidden in the individual functions.

The check functions themselves have the same parameter list and return value. Since they are all cousins, they all begin with the name **check_**. If we decided to write another routine, for example, **check_size**, you already have a good idea what the parameters and return value of the function would be.

The check functions were also created with a lot of cut and paste. A prototype function (with no body) was created and then pasted in six times. Next the body was filled in.

Repetition and consistency are very valuable in a program. Not only do they add clarity, but also they can make coding quicker.

font.c

This module consists of a single function, **load_fonts**, that reads a font file and builds a symbol table.

When entering a font name into the symbol table, we need to supply the **enter** function with a pointer to the data for the symbol. Fonts have no extra data associated with them. If they are in the symbol table, they are a legal font. If not, they are illegal.

But **enter** needs something. We could give it **NULL**, but that's the error return from **enter**. So we define a variable to point to (**an_object**). Note: in this context it doesn't matter what we point to, just so long as it's not **NULL**.

symbol.c

This module implements two symbol table functions: **enter** and **lookup**. **enter** puts a symbol in the table, and **lookup** finds it. The symbol table is stored as an unbalanced binary tree (see Chapter 16, *Advanced Pointers*). This is the classic way of implementing a simple, yet fairly efficient symbol table.

The only thing tricky about this code is that a pointer to extra data is associated with each symbol. Exactly what the extra data is (or its structure) is defined outside this module, so a generic pointer is used. This is an example of information hiding.

Testing

The test plan consisted of a shell script and a series of test files. The Sun UNIX utility `tcov` was used to check that every line in the code was executed at least once. (`tcov` is a utility supplied with Sun systems that counts the number of times each line in your code is executed.) An example of `tcov` output is:

```
            /********************************************************
             * error -- tell the user that there is an error        *
             *                                                      *
             * Parameters                                           *
             *   message -- error message                           *
             ********************************************************/
            void error(char *message)
   12 ->    {
                if (line_out == 0) {
   11 ->          (void)fprintf(stderr,"%s", line);
                  line_out = 1;
                }
   12 ->         (void)fprintf(stderr,"Error %s in file %s Line %d0,
                      message, file_name, line_number);
            }
```

The test script exercised all normal functions and produced all the error messages. The full test script is listed at the end of this chapter.

Testing is still more of an art than a science. Although the test procedure we used here exercises all the program, it may not detect all errors. It has been pointed out that testing can only discover the presence of errors, not the absence of them. In other words, you can never test every problem in a program.

The amount of testing you do depends on your application. For example, a program that is going to be used only once may receive very little testing. You run it for real, and if it works, you throw it away. On the other hand, a program that controls the flow rate of an I.V. drug dispenser used at a hospital will receive a tremendous amount of testing. This is a life-critical application where programming errors can have disastrous consequences.

Revisions

This program tests only a simple subset of the `troff` commands. `troff` is much more complex, and much more needs to be added to this program to make it useful to a `troff` programmer, such as full expression handling, string and number register checking, and checking escape sequences on text lines.

However, this program does serve as an example of good programming practices. It is well structured and uses modular programming techniques as well as information hiding to create a program that is simple to understand, debug, and enhance.

Program Files

The gen.h File

Program 20-1.

```
/********************************************************
 * gen.h -- general purpose macros.                     *
 ********************************************************/

/*
 * Define a boolean type
 */
#ifndef TRUE
typedef int boolean;
#define TRUE 1
#define FALSE 0
#endif /* TRUE */

/********************************************************
 * SKIP_WHITESPACE -- move a character pointer          *
 *      past whitespace                                 *
 *                                                      *
 * Parameters                                           *
 *      cur_char -- pointer to current character        *
 *              (will be moved)                         *
 ********************************************************/
/* Move past whitespace */
#define SKIP_WHITESPACE(cur_char) \
    while ((*(cur_char) <= ' ') && (*(cur_char) != '\0')) \
        (cur_char)++;
```

The font.h File

```
/********************************************************
 * font.h -- Definitions for the font package          *
 *              package.                                *
 *                                                      *
 * Procedures                                           *
 *      load_fonts -- load a font file onto the symbol  *
 *                              table                   *
 ********************************************************/

extern struct symbol *font_symbol_ptr;  /* A list of
                                legal fonts */
/********************************************************
 * load_fonts -- load fonts into symbol table           *
 *                                                      *
 * Parameters                                           *
 *      file_name -- filename of file to load           *
 *                                                      *
 * Aborts on error                                      *
 ********************************************************/
void load_fonts(char *name);
```

The macro.h File

```
/********************************************************
 * macros.h -- Definitions for the macro lookup         *
 *              package.                                *
 *                                                      *
 * Procedures                                           *
 *      load_macros -- load a macro onto the symbol tbl *
 *                                                      *
 *      macro_check -- check a macro line for           *
 *                      correctness                     *
 ********************************************************/
/********************************************************
 * load_macros -- load macros into symbol table         *
 *                                                      *
 * Parameters                                           *
 *      name -- filename of file to load                *
 ********************************************************/
void load_macros(char *name);

/********************************************************
 * macro_check -- check a macro line for correctness    *
 *                                                      *
 * Parameters                                           *
 *      line -- line to check                           *
 ********************************************************/
void macro_check(char *name);
```

The tlint.c File

```
/********************************************************
 * tlint -- check troff files for problems              *
 *                                                      *
 * Usage:                                               *
 *      tlint [options] [files]                         *
 *                                                      *
 * Options                                              *
 *      -m<file>        Add the data from <file>        *
 *                      to the tables used for syntax   *
 *                      checking.                       *
 *      -f<file>        Add font data from <file>       *
 *                      to list of legal fonts.         *
 *                                                      *
 *      [files] is a list of files to check.            *
 *              (none=check standard in.)               *
 *                                                      *
 ********************************************************/
#include <stdio.h>
#include "gen.h"
#include "macro.h"
#include "font.h"
#include <stdlib.h>

#define MAX_LINE 100            /* longest line we can expect */

#define MACRO_START_1   '.'     /* Macros can begin with a dot */
#define MACRO_START_2   '\''    /* or an apostrophe */

main(int argc, char *argv[])
{
    void usage(void);   /* Tell the user what to do */
    void do_file(char *, FILE *); /* Process a file */

    load_macros("standard.mac");
    load_fonts("standard.fonts");

    while ((argc > 1) && (argv[1][0] == '-')) {
        switch (argv[1][1]) {
            case 'm':
                load_macros(&argv[1][2]);
                break;
            case 'f':
                load_fonts(&argv[1][2]);
                break;
            default:
                usage();
        }
        argc--;
        argv++;
```

```
    }
    if (argc == 1) {
        do_file("standard-in", stdin);
    } else {
        while (argc > 1) {
            FILE *in_file;   /* File for reading data */

            in_file = fopen(argv[1], "r");
            if (in_file == NULL) {
                (void)fprintf(stderr,"Unable to open %s\n", argv[1]);
            } else {
                do_file(argv[1], in_file);
                (void)fclose(in_file);
            }
            argc--;
            argv++;
        }
    }
    return (0);
}
/********************************************************
 * usage -- tell the user what to do                    *
 ********************************************************/
static void usage(void)
{
    (void)printf("Usage is:\n");
    (void)printf("    tlint [options] [file1] [file2] ...\n");
    (void)printf("Options:\n");
    (void)printf("       -m<file> -- add <file> to list\n");
    (void)printf("                   of macro files\n");
    (void)printf("       -f<file> -- specify additional font file\n");
    exit (8);
}
static char *file_name; /* Name of the file we are processing */
static int line_number; /* Current line number */
static char line[MAX_LINE];     /* A line from the input file */
static int line_out;    /* True if a line has been output */
/********************************************************
 * do_file -- process a single file                     *
 *                                                      *
 * Parameters                                           *
 *      name -- name of the file to use                 *
 *      in_file -- file to check                        *
 ********************************************************/
static void do_file(char *name, FILE *in_file)
{

    file_name = name;
    line_number = 0;
    while (1) {
        if (fgets(line, sizeof(line), in_file) == NULL)
            break;
        line_out = 0;   /* We have not written the line */
```

```
        line_number++;

        if ((line[0] == MACRO_START_1) || (line[0] == MACRO_START_2))
            macro_check(line);
    }
}
/********************************************************
 * error -- tell the user that there is an error        *
 *                                                      *
 * Parameters                                           *
 *      message -- error message                        *
 ********************************************************/
void error(char *message)
{
    if (line_out == 0) {
        (void)fprintf(stderr,"%s", line);
        line_out = 1;
    }
    (void)fprintf(stderr,"Error %s in file %s Line %d\n",
        message, file_name, line_number);
}
```

The macros.c File

```
/********************************************************
 *  macros -- Handle macro related data structure.      *
 *                                                      *
 * Functions                                            *
 *      load_macros -- load a macro file into the macro *
 *                          symbol table                *
 *      macro_check -- check macro line                 *
 ********************************************************/
#include <stdio.h>
#include "gen.h"
#include "symbol.h"
#include "macro.h"
#include "font.h"
#include <string.h>
#include <ctype.h>
#include <stdlib.h>
extern void error(char *);      /* Write error message */

/*
 * Each argument to a macro has the following structure
 */
struct arg {
    char type;          /* Type of argument */
    boolean many;       /* True if we can repeat this argument */
};
```

```
#define MAX_ARGS 10      /* Max arguments for each macro */

struct arg_list {
    int num_args;        /* Number of arguments */
    struct arg args[MAX_ARGS];  /* The arguments */
};

/* the top of the symbol table */
static struct symbol *macro_symbol_ptr = NULL;

/*
 * Skip past remaining argument
 */
#define SKIP_ARG(cur_char) \
    while (*(cur_char) > ' ') \
        (cur_char)++;

/*******************************************************
 * load_macros -- load macros into symbol table        *
 *                                                     *
 * Parameters                                          *
 *      name -- filename of file to load               *
 *                                                     *
 * Aborts on error.                                    *
 *-----------------------------------------------------*
 * Input file format:                                  *
 *      # line -- comment                              *
 *      mac arg arg # comment                          *
 *                                                     *
 *      mac -- one or two-character macro name         *
 *      arg -- argument type letter                    *
 *              | -- vertical bar                      *
 *              s -- string                            *
 *              n -- number                            *
 *              c -- single character                  *
 *              f -- font specification                *
 *              t -- three-part title                  *
 *                                                     *
 *      If followed by a star, set the many flag.      *
 *******************************************************/
void  load_macros(char *name)
{
    FILE *in_file; /* Input file */
    int   line_number;  /* Line number of the input file */
    char *type_list = "|sncft"; /* Characters for argument type */
    int   num_args;/* Number of arguments we've seen */
    char  macro_name[3];        /* Name of the current macro */

    /* The macro we are working on */
    struct arg_list *arg_list_ptr;

    in_file = fopen(name, "r");
    if (in_file == NULL) {
```

```
        (void) fprintf(stderr, "Error:Can't open %s for reading\n", name);
        exit(8);
    }
    line_number = 0;

    while (1) {
        char  line[80]; /* Input line from data file */
        char *cur_char; /* Pointer to current input character */

        if (fgets(line, sizeof(line), in_file) == NULL) {
            (void) fclose(in_file);
            return;
        }
        line_number++;

        cur_char = line;
        /* Trim off leading whitespace */
        SKIP_WHITESPACE(cur_char);

        /* Continue on comment or blank line */
        if ((*cur_char == '#') || (cur_char == '\0'))
            continue;

        /* Copy two-character macro name */
        macro_name[0] = *cur_char;
        cur_char++;
        if (*cur_char > ' ') {
            macro_name[1] = *cur_char;
            cur_char++;
            macro_name[2] = '\0';
        } else
            macro_name[1] = '\0';

        /*
         * create new argument list
         */
        arg_list_ptr = (struct arg_list *) malloc(sizeof(struct arg_list));

        for (num_args = 0; num_args < MAX_ARGS; num_args++) {

            /* Move past whitespace */
            SKIP_WHITESPACE(cur_char);

            /* End of list? */
            if ((*cur_char == '#') || (cur_char == '\0'))
                break;

            /* Check for legal character */
            if (strchr(type_list, *cur_char) == NULL) {
                (void) fprintf(stderr,
                     "Error on line %d:Bad argument character %c\n",
                             line_number, *cur_char);
            }
```

```
            arg_list_ptr->args[num_args].type = *cur_char;
            cur_char++;

            if (*cur_char == '*') {
                arg_list_ptr->args[num_args].many = TRUE;
                cur_char++;
            } else
                arg_list_ptr->args[num_args].many = FALSE;

        }
        arg_list_ptr->num_args = num_args;
        enter(&macro_symbol_ptr, macro_name, (generic *) arg_list_ptr);
    }
}
/**********************************************************
 * macro_check -- check a macro line for correctness     *
 *                                                        *
 * Parameters                                             *
 *      line -- line to check                             *
 **********************************************************/
void  macro_check(char *line)
{
    char *cur_char = &line[1];  /* Pointer to current character */
    char  name[3]; /* Macro name */
    struct arg_list *arg_list_ptr;      /* The argument list */
    int   arg_index;    /* Index into argument list */

    extern char *check_string(char *);  /* String? */
    extern char *check_number(char *);  /* Number? */
    extern char *check_char(char *);    /* Character? */
    extern char *check_font(char *);    /* Font specification? */
    extern char *check_title(char *);   /* Three-part title? */

    SKIP_WHITESPACE(cur_char);

    /* Copy two-character macro name */
    name[0] = *cur_char;
    cur_char++;
    if (*cur_char > ' ') {
        name[1] = *cur_char;
        cur_char++;
        name[2] = '\0';
    } else
        name[1] = '\0';

    arg_list_ptr = (struct arg_list *) lookup(macro_symbol_ptr, name);

    if (arg_list_ptr == NULL) {
        char  error_msg[30];
        (void) sprintf(error_msg, "No such macro %s", name);
        error(error_msg);
        return;
    }
```

```
arg_index = 0;
while (1) {
    if (arg_index >= arg_list_ptr->num_args)
        break;

    /* Start at beginning of next macro */
    SKIP_WHITESPACE(cur_char);

    /* Check for end of string */
    if (*cur_char == '\0')
        break;

    switch (arg_list_ptr->args[arg_index].type) {
        /* Vertical Bar (optional) */
    case '|':
        if (*cur_char == '|')
            cur_char++;
        break;

        /* s -- a string */
    case 's':
        cur_char = check_string(cur_char);
        break;

        /* n -- number */
    case 'n':
        cur_char = check_number(cur_char);
        break;

        /* c -- character */
    case 'c':
        cur_char = check_char(cur_char);
        break;

        /* f -- font specification */
    case 'f':
        cur_char = check_font(cur_char);
        break;

        /* t -- three-part title */
    case 't':
        cur_char = check_title(cur_char);
        break;

    default:
        (void) printf("Internal error, bad type %c\n",
                    arg_list_ptr->args[arg_index].type);
        break;
    }

    if (arg_list_ptr->args[arg_index].many == FALSE)
        arg_index++;
```

```
    }
    SKIP_WHITESPACE(cur_char);
    if (*cur_char != '\0')
        error("Too many arguments");
}
/********************************************************
 * check_string -- check argument to make sure it's     *
 *              pointing to a string                    *
 *                                                      *
 * A string is a word or a set of words enclosed in     *
 *      double quotes.                                  *
 *                                                      *
 * I.E.   sam    "This is a test"                       *
 *                                                      *
 * Parameters                                           *
 *      cur_char -- pointer to the string               *
 *                                                      *
 * Returns                                              *
 *      pointer to character after the string           *
 ********************************************************/
char *check_string(char *cur_char)
{
    /* What type of string is it? */

    /* Quoted string? */
    if (*cur_char == '"') {
        cur_char++;

        /* Move to end of string */
        while ((*cur_char != '"') && (*cur_char != '\0'))
            cur_char++;

        /* Check for proper termination */
        if (*cur_char == '\0')
            error("Missing closing \" on string parameter");
        else
            cur_char++;         /* Move past closing quote */

    } else {
        /* Simple word string */
        while (!isspace(*cur_char))
            cur_char++;
    }
    return (cur_char);
}
/********************************************************
 * check_number -- check argument to make sure it's     *
 *              pointing to a expression                *
 *                                                      *
 * Parameters                                           *
 *      cur_char -- pointer to the integer expression   *
 *                                                      *
```

```
 *                                                      *
 * Returns                                              *
 *      pointer to character after the integer exp      *
 ********************************************************/
char *check_number(char *cur_char)
{
    /* Characters allowed in expressions */
    static char *number_chars = "0123456789+-*/%.";

    if (strchr(number_chars, *cur_char) == NULL) {
        error("Expression expected");
        SKIP_ARG(cur_char);
        return (cur_char);
    }
    while (strchr(number_chars, *cur_char) != NULL)
        cur_char++;

    if (!(isspace(*cur_char) || (*cur_char == '\0'))) {
        SKIP_ARG(cur_char);
        error("Illegal expression");
    }

    return (cur_char);
}
/********************************************************
 * check_char -- check argument to make sure it's       *
 *              pointing to a char                      *
 *                                                      *
 * Parameters                                           *
 *      cur_char -- pointer to the char                 *
 *                                                      *
 * Returns                                              *
 *      pointer to character after the char             *
 *                                                      *
 * Note: This is a simple character check and does not  *
 *       try to figure out all of the crazy \          *
 *       characters that can be used in troff.          *
 ********************************************************/
char *check_char(char *cur_char)
{
    cur_char++;

    if (!(isspace(*cur_char) || (*cur_char == '\0')))
        error("Expected single character");

    return (cur_char);
}
/********************************************************
 * check_font -- check argument to make sure it's       *
 *              pointing to a legal font                *
 *                                                      *
 * Parameters                                           *
 *      cur_char -- pointer to the font                 *
```

```
 *                                                     *
 * Returns                                             *
 *      pointer to character after the font            *
 *******************************************************/
char *check_font(char *cur_char)
{
    char  name[3]; /* Font name */

    name[0] = *cur_char;
    cur_char++;

    if (isalnum(*cur_char)) {
        name[1] = *cur_char;
        cur_char++;
        name[2] = '\0';
    } else
        name[1] = '\0';

    if (lookup(font_symbol_ptr, name) == NULL)
        error("Expected font");

    return (cur_char);
}

/*******************************************************
 * check_title -- check argument to make sure it's     *
 *                pointing to a three-part title       *
 *                of the form:  'xxxx'yyyy'zzz'.       *
 *                                                     *
 * Parameters                                          *
 *      cur_char -- pointer to the title               *
 *                                                     *
 * Returns                                             *
 *      pointer to character after the title           *
 *******************************************************/
char *check_title(char *cur_char)
{
    if (*cur_char != '\'') {
        error("Expected beginning of three-part title");
        SKIP_ARG(cur_char);
        return (cur_char);
    }
    cur_char++;

    while ((*cur_char != '\'') && (*cur_char != '\0'))
        cur_char++;

    if (*cur_char != '\'') {
        error("Expected middle part of three-part title");
        SKIP_ARG(cur_char);
        return (cur_char);
    }
    cur_char++;
```

```
    while ((*cur_char != '\'') && (*cur_char != '\0'))
        cur_char++;

    if (*cur_char != '\'') {
        error("Expected third part of three-part title");
        SKIP_ARG(cur_char);
        return (cur_char);
    }
    cur_char++;

    while ((*cur_char != '\'') && (*cur_char != '\0'))
        cur_char++;

    if (*cur_char != '\'') {
        error("Expected end of three-part title");
        SKIP_ARG(cur_char);
        return (cur_char);
    }
    cur_char++;
    return (cur_char);
}
```

The fonts.c File

```
/********************************************************
 *  fonts -- handle font-related data structures        *
 *                                                      *
 * Functions                                            *
 *      load_fonts -- load a font file                  *
 ********************************************************/
#include <stdio.h>
#include "gen.h"
#include "symbol.h"
#include <string.h>
#include <stdlib.h>

/* the top of the symbol table */
struct symbol *font_symbol_ptr = NULL;
/********************************************************
 * load_fonts -- load fonts into symbol table           *
 *                                                      *
 * Parameters                                           *
 *      file_name -- filename of file to load           *
 *                                                      *
 * Aborts on error.                                     *
 ********************************************************/
void load_fonts(char *file_name)
{
    FILE *in_file; /* Input file */
    char  name[3]; /* Name of the current font */
```

```
    /* We have to point to something for our data */
    static char *an_object = "an object";

    in_file = fopen(file_name, "r");
    if (in_file == NULL) {
        (void) fprintf(stderr, "Error:Can't open %s for reading\n", file_name);
        exit(8);
    }

    while (1) {
        char  line[80]; /* Input line from data file */
        char *cur_char; /* Pointer to current input character */

        if (fgets(line, sizeof(line), in_file) == NULL) {
            (void) fclose(in_file);
            return;
        }
        cur_char = line;

        while (*cur_char != '\0') {
            SKIP_WHITESPACE(cur_char);

            if (*cur_char == '\0')
                break;

            /* Copy two-character macro name */
            name[0] = *cur_char;
            cur_char++;
            if (*cur_char > ' ') {
                name[1] = *cur_char;
                cur_char++;
                name[2] = '\0';
            } else
                name[1] = '\0';

            enter(&font_symbol_ptr, name, (generic *) an_object);
        }
    }
}
```

The symbol.c File

```
/********************************************************
 *  symbol -- handle the symbol table                   *
 *                                                      *
 * Functions                                            *
 *      enter  -- put a symbol in a symbol table        *
 *      lookup -- get the data associated with a symbol *
 ********************************************************/
```

```
#include <stdio.h>
#include "symbol.h"
#include <string.h>
#include <stdlib.h>

/********************************************************
 * enter -- enter a word into the symbol table          *
 *                                                      *
 * Parameters                                           *
 *      node -- top node of the symbol table for add    *
 *      symbol -- symbol name to add (1 or 2 chars)     *
 *      data -- data associated with the symbol         *
 ********************************************************/
void enter(struct symbol **node_ptr, char *symbol, generic *data)
{
    int  result;        /* result of strcmp */
    /* New node that we are creating */
    struct symbol *new_node_ptr;

    /* see if we have reached the end */
    if ((*node_ptr) == NULL) {
        new_node_ptr = (struct symbol *) malloc(sizeof(struct symbol));
        (void)strcpy(new_node_ptr->name, symbol);
        new_node_ptr->data = data;
        new_node_ptr->left_ptr = NULL;
        new_node_ptr->right_ptr = NULL;
        *node_ptr = new_node_ptr;
        return;
    }
    /*
     * Need to sub-divide the symbol table and try again
     */
    result = strcmp((*node_ptr)->name, symbol);

    if (result == 0)
        return;

    if (result > 0)
        enter(&(*node_ptr)->left_ptr, symbol, data);
    else
        enter(&(*node_ptr)->right_ptr, symbol, data);
}
```

```
/********************************************************
 * lookup -- lookup a symbol in a table                 *
 *                                                      *
 * Parameters                                           *
 *      root -- root of the symbol table to search      *
 *      name -- name to lookup.                         *
 *                                                      *
 * Returns                                              *
 *      Pointer to the data or NULL if not found.       *
 ********************************************************/
generic *lookup(struct symbol *root_ptr, char *name)
{
    int result; /* Result of string compare */

    if (root_ptr == NULL)
        return (NULL);

    result = strcmp(root_ptr->name, name);

    if (result == 0) {
        return (root_ptr->data);
    }

    if (result > 0)
        return (lookup(root_ptr->left_ptr, name));
    else
        return (lookup(root_ptr->right_ptr, name));
}
```

UNIX Makefile

```
SRCS=tlint.c macros.c symbol.c fonts.c
OBJS=tlint.o macros.o symbol.o fonts.o

tlint:$(OBJS)
	cc $(CFLAGS) -o tlint $(OBJS)

lint:
	lint -xh $(SRCS)

fonts.o: fonts.c gen.h symbol.h

macros.o: font.h gen.h macro.h macros.c symbol.h

symbol.o: symbol.c symbol.h

tlint.o: font.h gen.h macro.h tlint.c
```

Turbo C Makefile

```
CC=tcc
CFLAGS=-ml -g -w -A
SRCS=tlint.c  macros.c  symbol.c  fonts.c
OBJS=tlint.obj macros.obj symbol.obj fonts.obj

tlint: $(OBJS)
	$(CC) $(CFLAGS) -etlint $(OBJS)

fonts.obj: fonts.c gen.h symbol.h
	$(CC) $(CFLAGS) -c fonts.c

macros.obj: font.h gen.h macro.h macros.c symbol.h
	$(CC) $(CFLAGS) -c macros.c

symbol.obj: symbol.c symbol.h
	$(CC) $(CFLAGS) -c symbol.c

tlint.obj: font.h gen.h macro.h tlint.c
	$(CC) $(CFLAGS) -c tlint.c
```

The standard.mac File

```
#
# This file contains the definitions for the built-in
# macros used by troff
#
# The format of the file is
#    macro <argument-list>
#
#    Arguments are:
#        |        Vertical bar
#        s        String
#        n        Numeric expression
#        c        Single character
#        f        Font specification
#        t        Three-part title
#
#        If followed by a * they can be repeated 0 or more
#        times
#
# Anything past a # is considered a comment
br             # Break
ad s           # Adjust margins
na             # No adjust
nf             # No fill
fi             # Fill
nh             # No hyphen
hy n           # Set hyphenation mode
```

```
hw s*          # Specify how to hyphenate words
hc c           # Hyphenation character
ce n           # Center lines
ul n           # Underline
cu n           # Continuous underline
uf f           # Select font for underline
po | n         # Page offset
ll n           # Line length
in | n         # Indent
ti | n         # Temporary indent
pl | n         # Page length
bp n           # Begin page
pn n           # Page number
ne n           # Specify need space
mk s           # Mark current location
sp | n         # Vertical space
ps n           # Point size
vs | n         # Vertical space
ls n           # Line spacing
sv n           # Save space
os             # Output saved space
ns             # Set no-space mode
rs             # Set restore-space mode
ss n           # Set character space size
cs s n n       # Constant space mode
ft f           # Specify font
fp f n         # Set font position
fz f n         # Font size request
bd f n         # Specify how to bold a font
lg n           # Select ligatures
ta n*          # Specify tabs
tc c           # Tab character
lc c           # Leader character
fc c s         # Field character
lt | n         # Title length
pc c           # Page character
tl t           # Title
so s           # Source another file
nx s           # Change to another file
pi s           # Pipe output to a program
rd s           # Read data from keyboard
ex s           # Exit
tm s*          # Send message to standard output
ds s s         # Define string
as s s         # Append string
de s s         # Define macro
rm s           # Remove macro
rn s s         # Rename macro
am s s         # Append to macro
di s           # Divert to macro
da s           # Append to diversion
wh n s         # Set place to execute macro
ch s n         # Change place macro executes
```

```
dt n s          # Set diversion trap
it n s          # Set input trap
em s            # Set macro for end of input
nr s n n        # Define number register
af s c          # Assign format
rr s            # Remove register
mc c            # Margin character
ec c            # Set escape character
eo              # Turn off escape
cc c            # Set control character
c2              # Set second control character
tr s            # Translate characters
nm n n n n      # Line number
nn n            # No numbering
ig s            # Ignore input
pm s            # Print macros
fl              # Flush output
ab s            # Abort
ev n            # Set environment
```

The standard.fonts File

```
R I B S
```

Test Script

```
#!/bin/csh
#
# Test file for the program tlint
#
#-----------------------------------------
# Print commands as they are executed
#
set echo
#-----------------------------------------
# Try something normal
#
tlint troff.test
#-----------------------------------------
# Try non-existent macro and font file
tlint -mno-name
tlint -fno-name
#-----------------------------------------
# Try a bad macro file
tlint -mbad.mac </dev/null
#-----------------------------------------
# Try font file with two-character name
```

```
tlint -ftwo.font </dev/null
#---------------------------------------
# Try a single-character macro
tlint -msingle.mac bold.test
#---------------------------------------
# Try an illegal option
tlint -qdummy
#---------------------------------------
# Try non-existent file
tlint  dummy
```

The troff.test File

```
Test file for the troff line program
.tm this is a test
    .tm test is more test
.tm test once again
.xx this is an error
Test of macro that has no arguments
.br
Put an argument where there should be none
.br
Expect string argument
.tm string
Two strings
.tm string string
Integer
.br
12+34
String where number expected
.br
test
Vertical bar
.lt |0
No vertical bar
.lt 0
Font check
Bad font check
Character
'left'middle'right'
bad
'bad
'bad'bad
'bad'bad'
"quoted string"
"almost quoted string
.sp 12.0
Cause an expression error
.sp 12.0_12.0
```

The Bad.mac File

```
#
# This contains a bad macro definition
#
ba q    # Q is not a legal name
```

The Two.font File

```
CW
```

Programming Problems

Exercise 1: Combine the **words** program from Chapter 16, *Advanced Pointers*, with the infinite array program from Chapter 17, *Modular Programming*, to create a cross-reference utility.

Exercise 2: Write a program that reads a file and checks for doubled words and also checks each word against a list of commonly misspelled words.

Exercise 3: Write a mailing list program. The program should be able to add, delete, change, and sort names in a file.

Exercise 4: Write a program that takes a file and splits up the long lines for readability on nice boundaries such as sentence endings, word boundaries, etc.

Exercise 5: Write a program that determines the ratio of comment lines to code lines in a C program. (Be careful about how you treat mixed lines.)

Exercise 6: Write a program to clean up the language used in a text file. This program will scan the file looking for four-letter words, replacing them with less emotional equivalents.

21

Programming Adages

Second thoughts are ever wiser.
—Euripides

General

- Comment, comment, comment. Put a lot of comments in your program. They tell other programmers what you did. They also tell you what you did.
- Use the "KISS" principal. (Keep it Simple, Stupid.) Clear and simple is better than complex and wonderful.
- Avoid side effects. Use ++ and -- on lines by themselves.
- Never put an assignment inside a conditional. Never put an assignment inside any other statement.
- Know the difference between = and ==. Using = for == is a very common mistake and is difficult to find.

- Never do "nothing" silently.

```
/* Don't program like this */
for (index = 0; data[index] < key; index++);
/* Did you see the semicolon at the end of the last line? */
```

- Always put in a comment.

```
for (index = 0; data[index] < key; index++)
        /* do nothing */;
```

Design

- When designing your program, keep in mind "The Law of Least Astonishment," which states that your program should behave in a way that least astonishes the user.
- Make the user interface as simple and consistent as possible.
- Give the user as much help as you can.
- Clearly identify all error messages with the word "error," and try to give the user some idea of how to correct his problem.

Declarations

- Put variable declarations one per line and comment them.
- Make variable-names long enough to be easily understood, but not so long that they are difficult to type in. Two or three words is usually enough.
- Never use default declarations. If a function returns an integer, declare it as type **int**.
- Never use default declarations. All parameters to a function should be declared and commented.

switch Statement

- Always put a default case in a **switch** statement. Even if it does nothing, put it in.

```
switch (expression) {
        default:
                /* do nothing */
}
```

- Every case in a switch should end with a **break** or `/* Fall through */` statement.

Preprocessor

- Always put parentheses, (), around each constant expression defined by a preprocessor **#define** directive.

```
#define BOX_SIZE (3*10) /* size of the box in pixels */
```

- Put () around each argument of a parameterized macro.

```
#define SQUARE(x) ((x) * (x))
```

- Surround macros that contain complete statements with curly braces ({}).

```
/* A fatal error has occurred.  Tell user and abort */
#define DIE(msg) {(void)printf(msg);exit(8);}
```

- When using the **#ifdef/#endif** construct for conditional compilation, put the **#define** and **#undef** statements near the top of the program and comment them.

Style

- A single block of code enclosed in {} should not span more than a couple of pages. Anything much bigger than that should probably be split up into several smaller, simpler procedures.
- When your code starts to run into the right margin, it is about time to split the procedure into several smaller, simpler procedures.

Compiling

- Always create a *Makefile* so others will know how to compile your program.
- On UNIX, use the utility `lint` to make your programs "lint free."
- When using Turbo C, turn on all the warning flags. You never know what the compiler will find.

Final Note

Just when you think you've discovered all the things that C can do to you—think again. There are still more surprises in store for you.

Question 21–1: Why does the following program think everything is two? (This inspired the last adage.)

```
#include <stdio.h>
main()
{
    char line[80];
    int number;

    (void)printf("Enter a number: ");

    (void)fgets(line, sizeof(line), stdin);
    (void)sscanf(line, "%d", &number);

    if (number =! 2)
        (void)printf("Number is not two\n");
```

```
        else
            (void)printf("Number is two\n");

        return (0);
    }
```

Answers

Answer 21–1: The statement `(number =! 2)` is not a relational equation, but an assignment statement. It is equivalent to:

```
number = (!2);
```

Since `2` is nonzero, `!2` is zero.

The programmer accidentally reversed the not equals, `!=`, so it became `=!`. The statement should read:

```
if (number != 2)
```

A

ASCII Chart

Table A-1. ASCII Character Chart

Dec	Oct	Hex	Char	Dec	Oct	Hex	Char
0	000	00	NUL	12	014	0C	NP
1	001	01	SOH	13	015	0D	CR
2	002	02	STX	14	016	0E	SO
3	003	03	ETX	15	017	0F	SI
4	004	04	EOT	16	020	10	DLE
5	005	05	ENQ	17	021	11	DC1
6	006	06	ACK	18	022	12	DC2
7	007	07	BEL	19	023	13	DC3
8	010	08	BS	20	024	14	DC4
9	011	09	HT	21	025	15	NAK
10	012	0A	NL	22	026	16	SYN
11	013	0B	VT	23	027	17	ETB

Dec	Oct	Hex	Char	Dec	Oct	Hex	Char
24	030	18	CAN	64	100	40	@
25	031	19	EM	65	101	41	A
26	032	1A	SUB	66	102	42	B
27	033	1B	ESC	67	103	43	C
28	034	1C	FS	68	104	44	D
29	035	1D	GS	69	105	45	E
30	036	1E	RS	70	106	46	F
31	037	1F	US	71	107	47	G
32	040	20	SP	72	110	48	H
33	041	21	!	73	111	49	I
34	042	22	"	74	112	4A	J
35	043	23	#	75	113	4B	K
36	044	24	$	76	114	4C	L
37	045	25	%	77	115	4D	M
38	046	26	&	78	116	4E	N
39	047	27	’	79	117	4F	O
40	050	28	(	80	120	50	P
41	051	29	)	81	121	51	Q
42	052	2A	*	82	122	52	R
43	053	2B	+	83	123	53	S
44	054	2C	,	84	124	54	T
45	055	2D	-	85	125	55	U
46	056	2E	.	86	126	56	V
47	057	2F	/	87	127	57	W
48	060	30	0	88	130	58	X
49	061	31	1	89	131	59	Y
50	062	32	2	90	132	5A	Z
51	063	33	3	91	133	5B	[
52	064	34	4	92	134	5C	\
53	065	35	5	93	135	5D	]
54	066	36	6	94	136	5E	^
55	067	37	7	95	137	5F	_
56	070	38	8	96	140	60	‘
57	071	39	9	97	141	61	a
58	072	3A	:	98	142	62	b
59	073	3B	;	99	143	63	c
60	074	3C	<	100	144	64	d
61	075	3D	=	101	145	65	e
62	076	3E	>	102	146	66	f
63	077	3F	?	103	147	67	g

Dec	Oct	Hex	Char	Dec	Oct	Hex	Char
104	150	68	h	116	164	74	t
105	151	69	i	117	165	75	u
106	152	6A	j	118	166	76	v
107	153	6B	k	119	167	77	w
108	154	6C	l	120	170	78	x
109	155	6D	m	121	171	79	y
110	156	6E	n	122	172	7A	z
111	157	6F	o	123	173	7B	{
112	160	70	p	124	174	7C	|
113	161	71	q	125	175	7D	}
114	162	72	r	126	176	7E	~
115	163	73	s	127	177	7F	DEL

B

Numeric Limits

Ranges

Ranges

Table B-1 and Table B-2 give the range of various declarations.

Table B-1. 32-bit UNIX Machine

Name	Bits	Low Value	High Value	Accuracy
int	32	–2147483648	2147483647	
short int	16	–32768	32767	
long int	32	–2147483648	2147483647	
unsigned int 32	0	4294967295		
unsigned short int	16	0	65535	
unsigned long int	32	0	4294967295	

Table B-1 32-bit UNIX Machine (continued)

Name	Bits	Low Value	High Value	Accuracy
char	8	System-dependent	System-dependent	System-dependent
unsigned char	8	0	255	
float	32	–3.4E+38	3.4E+38	6 digits
double	64	–1.7E+308	1.7E+308	15 digits
long double	64	–1.7E+308	1.7E+308	15 digits

Table B-2. Turbo C and Most 16-bit UNIX Systems

Name	Bits	Low Value	High Value	Accuracy
int	16	–32768	32767	
short int	16	–32768	32767	
long int	32	–2147483648	2147483647	
unsigned int	16	0	65535	
unsigned short int	16	0	65535	
unsigned long	int	32	0	4294967295
char	8	–128	127	
unsigned char	8	0	255	
float	32	–3.4E+38	3.4E+38	6 digits
double	64	–1.7E+308	1.7E+308	15 digits
long double	80	–3.4E+4932	3.4E+4932	17 digits

C

Operator Precedence Rules

ANSI Standard Rules
Practical Subset

ANSI Standard Rules

Precedence	Operators				
1	()	[]	->	.	
2	!	~	++	--	(type)
	- (unary)	* (dereference)			
	& (address of)	sizeof			
3	* (multiply)	/	%		
4	+	-			
5	<<	>>			
6	<	<=	>	>=	
7	==	!=			
8	& (bitwise and)				
9	^				

Precedence	Operators				
10	|				
11	&&				
12	||				
13	?:				
14	=	+=	-=	etc.	
15	,				

Practical Subset

Precedence	Operators		
1	* (multiply)	/	%
2	+	-	

Put parentheses, ( ), around everything else.

D

Program to Compute sine Using a Power Series

This program is designed to compute the *sine* function using a power series. A very limited floating-point format is used to demonstrate some of the problems that can occur when using floating point.

The program is invoked by:

> sine *value*

where *value* is an angle in radians.

The program will compute each term in the power series and display the result. It will continue computing terms until the last term is so small that it doesn't contribute to the final result.

For comparison purposes, the result of the library function `sin` is displayed as well as the computed sine.

Makefile

Makefile for UNIX:

```
sine: sine.c
        cc -g -o sine sine.c -lm

lint:
        lint sine.c -lm
```

Makefile for Turbo C:

```
#
SRCS=sine.c
OBJS=sine.obj
CFLAGS=-g -w -A
CC=tcc

sine: $(OBJS)
        $(CC) $(CFLAGS) -osine.exe $(OBJS)

sine.obj: sine.c
        $(CC) $(CFLAGS) -c sine.c
```

The sine.c Program

```
/********************************************************
 * sine -- compute sine using very simple floating      *
 *      arithmetic                                      *
 *                                                      *
 * Usage:                                               *
 *      sine <value>                                    *
 *                                                      *
 *      <value> is an angle in radians                  *
 *                                                      *
 * Format used in f.fffe+X                              *
 *                                                      *
 * f.fff is a 4 digit fraction                          *
 *      + is a sign (+ or -)                            *
 *      X is a single digit exponent                    *
```

```
 *                                                    *
 * sin(x) = x  - x**3 + x**5 - x**7                   *
 *              -----   ----   ---- . . . .           *
 *                3!     5!     7!                    *
 *                                                    *
 * Warning: This program is intended to show some of  *
 *      problems with floating point.  It not intended *
 *      to be used to produce exact values for the    *
 *      sin function.                                 *
 *                                                    *
 * Note: Even though we specify only one digit for the *
 *       exponent, two are used for some calculations. *
 *       This is due to the fact that printf has no   *
 *       format for a single-digit exponent.          *
 ******************************************************/
#include <stdlib.h>     /* ANSI Standard only */
#include <math.h>

#include <stdio.h>

main(int argc, char *argv[])
{
        float   total;          /* total of series so far */
        float   new_total;      /* newer version of total */
        float   term_top;       /* top part of term */
        float   term_bottom;    /* bottom of current term */
        float   term;           /* current term */
        float   exp;            /* exponent of current term */
        float   sign;           /* +1 or -1 (changes on each term) */
        float   value;          /* value of the argument to sin */
        int     index;          /* index for counting terms */

        char    *float_2_ascii(float);  /* turn floating point to ascii */
        float   fix_float(float);       /* round to correct digits */
        float   factorial(float);       /* compute n! */

        if (argc != 2) {
                (void)fprintf(stderr,"Usage is:\n");
                (void)fprintf(stderr,"  sine <value>\n");
                exit (8);
        }


        value = fix_float(atof(&argv[1][0]));

        total = 0.0;
        exp = 1.0;
        sign = 1.0;

        for (index = 0; /* take care of below */ ; index++) {
                term_top = fix_float(pow(value, exp));
```

```
                term_bottom = fix_float(factorial(exp));
                term = fix_float(term_top / term_bottom);
                (void)printf("x**%d     %s\n", (int)exp,
                                float_2_ascii(term_top));
                (void)printf("%d!       %s\n", (int)exp,
                                float_2_ascii(term_bottom));
                (void)printf("x**%d/%d! %s\n", (int)exp, (int)exp,
                        float_2_ascii(term));
                (void)printf("\n");
                new_total = fix_float(total + sign * term);
                if (new_total == total)
                        break;
                total = new_total;
                sign = -sign;
                exp = exp + 2.0;
                (void)printf("  total   %s\n", float_2_ascii(total));
                (void)printf("\n");
        }
        (void)printf("%d term computed\n", index+1);
        (void)printf("sin(%s)=\n", float_2_ascii(value));
        (void)printf("  %s\n", float_2_ascii(total));
        (void)printf("Actual sin(%g)=%g\n",
                atof(&argv[1][0]), sin(atof(&argv[1][0])));
        return (0);
}
/********************************************************
 * float_2_ascii -- turn a floating-point string        *
 *      into ascii                                      *
 *                                                      *
 * Parameters                                           *
 *      number -- number to turn into ascii             *
 *                                                      *
 * Returns                                              *
 *      Pointer to the string containing the number     *
 *                                                      *
 * Warning: Uses static storage, so later calls         *
 *              overwrite earlier entries               *
 ********************************************************/
char *float_2_ascii(float number)
{
        static char result[10]; /*place to put the number */

        (void)sprintf(result,"%8.3E", number);
        return (result);
}
/********************************************************
 * fix_float -- turn high-precision numbers into        *
 *              low-precision numbers to simulate a     *
 *              very dumb floating-point structure      *
 *                                                      *
 * Parameters                                           *
 *      number -- number to take care of                *
 *                                                      *
```

```
 * Returns                                              *
 *      number accurate to 5 places only                *
 *                                                      *
 * Note: This works by changing a number into ascii and *
 *       back.  Very slow, but it works.                *
 ********************************************************/
float fix_float(float number)
{
        float   result; /* result of the conversion */
        char    ascii[10];      /* ascii version of number */

        (void)sprintf(ascii,"%8.4e", number);
        (void)sscanf(ascii, "%e", &result);
        return (result);
}
/********************************************************
 * factorial -- compute the factorial of a number       *
 *                                                      *
 * Parameters                                           *
 *      number -- number to use for factorial           *
 *                                                      *
 * Returns                                              *
 *      factorial(number) or number!                    *
 *                                                      *
 * Note: Even though this is a floating-point routine,  *
 *       using numbers that are not whole numbers       *
 *       does not make sense.                           *
 ********************************************************/
float factorial(float number)
{
        if (number <= 1.0)
                return (number);
        else
                return (number *factorial(number - 1.0));
}
```

E

Automatic Type Conversion Used When Passing Parameters

In order to eliminate some of the problems that may occur when passing parameters to a function, C performs the following automatic conversions to function arguments as shown in Table E-1.

Table E-1. Automatic Conversions

Type	Converted To
char	**int**
short int	**int**
int	**int**
long int	**long int**
float	**double**
double	**double**
long double	**long double**
array	**pointer**

Glossary

! Symbol for the bitwise or operator.

!= Not equal relational operator.

" See **double quote**.

' See **single quote**.

`'\0'` End-of-string character (also called **`NUL`**).

% Symbol for the modulus operator.

& Symbol for the bitwise and operator.

`&` Symbol used to precede a variable name (as in `&`*x*). Means the address of the named variable (address of *x*). Used to assign a value to a pointer variable.

&& Symbol for the logical and operator (used in comparison operations).

* Symbol for the multiply operator.

* Symbol used to precede a pointer variable name that means get the value stored at the address pointed to by the pointer variable. (*x means get the value stored at x). Sometimes known as the dereferencing operator or indirect operator.

+ Symbol for the add operator.

++ Symbol for the incrementation operator.

- Symbol for the subtract operator.

-- Symbol for the decrementation operator.

== Equal relational operator.

/ Symbol for the divide operator.

< Less than relational operator.

<< Symbol for the left shift operator.

<= Less than or equal relational operator.

> Greater than relational operator.

>> Symbol for the right shift operator.

>= Greater than or equal relational operator.

^ Symbol for the bitwise exclusive or operator.

{} See **curly brace**.

| Symbol for the bitwise or operator.

|| Symbol for the logical or operator.

~ Symbol for bitwise complement operator. Inverts all bits.

#define
A C directive that defines a substitute text for a name.

#endif
The closing bracket to a preprocessor macro section that began with an **#ifdef** directive.

#ifdef
A preprocessor directive that checks to see if a macro name is defined. If defined, the code following is included in the source.

#ifndef
A preprocessor directive that checks to see if a macro name is undefined. If it is currently undefined, then the code following is included in the macro expansion.

#include
A preprocessor directive that causes the named file to be inserted in place of the **#include**.

#undef
A preprocessor directive that cancels a **#define**.

_ptr
A convention used in this book. All pointer variables end with the extension `_ptr`.

accuracy
A quantitative measurement of the error inherent in the representation of a real number.

address
A value that identifies a storage location in memory.

and
A Boolean operation that yields zero if either operation is zero and one if both operands are one.

ANSI C
Any version of C that conforms to the specifications of the *A*merican *N*ational *S*tandards *I*nstitute *C*ommittee X3J.

array

A collection of data elements arranged to be indexed in one or more dimensions. In C, arrays are stored in contiguous memory.

ASCII

*A*merican *S*tandard *C*ode for *I*nformation *I*nterchange. A code to represent characters.

assignment statement

An operation that stores a value in a variable.

auto

A C keyword used to create temporary variables.

automatic variable

See **temporary variable**.

bit

Binary digit; either of the digits zero or one.

bit field

A group of contiguous bits taken together as a unit. A C language feature that allows the access of individual bits.

bit flip

The inversion of all bits in an operand. See **complement**.

bit operator

See **bitwise operator**.

bitmapped graphics

Computer graphics where each pixel in the graphic output device is controlled by a single bit or a group of bits.

bitwise operator

An operator that performs Boolean operations on two operands, treating each bit in an operand as an individual bit and performing the operation bit by bit on corresponding bits.

block

A section of code enclosed in curly braces ({}).

boxing (a comment)

The technique of using a combination of asterisks, vertical and horizontal rules, and other typographic characters to draw a box around a comment in order to set if off from the code.

break
A statement that terminates the innermost execution of **for**, **while**, and **switch** statements.

breakpoint
A location in a program where normal execution is suspended and control is turned over to the debugger.

buffered I/O
Input/output where intermediate storage (a buffer) is used between the source and destination of an I/O stream.

byte
A group of 8 bits.

C
A general purpose computer programming language developed in 1974 at Bell Laboratories by Dennis Ritchie. C is considered to be a medium- to high-level language.

C code
A set of computer instructions written in the C language.

C compiler
Software that translates C source code into machine code.

C syntax
See **syntax**.

call by reference
A parameter-passing mechanism where the actual parameter is not passed to a function, but instead uses a pointer to point to it. C passes parameters using "call by value"; however, by explicit use of pointers, a programmer can use call by reference. (See **call by value**.)

call by value
A procedure call where the parameters are passed by passing the values of the parameters. This type of parameter passing is used by C. (See **call by reference**.)

case
Acts as a label for one of the alternatives in a **switch** statement.

cast
To convert a variable from one type to another type by explicitly indicating the type conversion.

CGA
*C*olor *g*raphics *a*daptor. A common color graphic card for the IBM PC.

char
A C keyword used to declare variables that represent characters or small integers.

class (of a variable)
See **storage class**.

clear a bit
The operation of setting an individual bit to zero. This is not a defined operation in C.

code design
A document that describes in general terms how the program is to perform its function.

coding
The act of writing a program in a computer language.

command-line option
An option to direct the course of a compilation that is entered from the computer console.

comment
Text included in a computer program for the sole purpose of providing information about the program. Comments are a programmer's personal notes and also notes for future programmers. The text is ignored by the compiler.

comment block
A group of related comments that convey general information about a program or a section of program.

compilation
The translation of source code into machine code.

compiler
A system program that does compilation.

compiling
See **compilation**.

complement
An arithmetic or logical operation. A logical complement is the same as an invert or not operation.

computer language
See **programming language**.

conditional compilation
The ability to selectively compile parts of a program based on the truth of conditions tested in conditional directives that surround the code.

continue
A flow control statement that causes the next execution of a loop to begin.

control statements
A statement that determines which statement is to be executed next based on a conditional test.

control variable
A variable that is systematically changed during the execution of the loop. When the variable reaches a predetermined value, the loop is terminated.

conversion specification
A C token that specifies how a variable will be printed.

curly brace
The characters { and }. Curly braces are used in C to delimit groups of elements that should be treated as a unit.

debugging
The process of finding and removing errors from a program.

decision statement
A statement that tests a condition created by a program and changes the flow of the program based on that decision.

declaration
A specification of the type and name of a variable to be used in a program.

default
Serves as a case label if no case value match is found within the scope of a **switch**.

define statement
See **#define**.

dereferencing operator
The operator that indicates access to the value pointed to by a pointer variable or an addressing expression. See also * operator.

directive

A command to the preprocessor (as opposed to a statement to produce machine code).

double

A C language keyword used to declare a variable that contains a real number. The number usually uses twice as much storage as type float.

double-linked list

A linked list with both forward and backward pointers. See also **linked list.**

double quote

The characters ", which is the ASCII character 34. Used in C to delimit character strings.

EGA

*E*nhanced *g*raphics *a*daptor. A common graphics card for the IBM PC.

else

A clause in an **if** statement specifying action to be taken in the event that the statement following the **if** conditional is false.

enum

A C keyword that is used to define an enumeration data type.

enumerated data type

A data type consisting of a named set of values. The C compiler assigns an integer to each member of the set.

EOF

*E*nd-*o*f-*f*ile value defined in *stdio.h.*

escape character

A special character used to change the meaning of the character(s) that follow. This is represented in C by the backslash character (\).

exclusive or

A Boolean operation that yields zero if both operands are the same and one if they are different.

executable file

A file containing machine code that has been linked and is ready to be run on a computer.

exponent
The component of a floating-point number that represents the integer power to which the number base is raised in order to determine the represented number.

exponent overflow
A condition resulting from a floating-point operation where the result is an exponent too large to fit within the bit field allotted to the exponent.

exponent underflow
A condition resulting from a floating-point operation where the result is an exponent too large in negative value to fit within the bit field allotted to the exponent.

extern
A C keyword used to indicate that a variable or function is defined outside the current file.

fast prototyping
A top-down programming technique that consists of writing the smallest portion of a specification that can be implemented that will still do something.

fclose
A function that closes a file.

fflush
A routine to force the flushing of a buffer.

fgetc
A function that reads a single character.

fgets
A stream input library function that reads a single line.

FILE
A macro definition in *stdio* used to declare a file variable.

file
A group of related records treated as a unit.

float
A C keyword used to declare a variable that can hold a real number.

floating point
A numbering system represented by a fraction and an exponent. The system will handle very large and very small numbers.

floating-point exception (core dumped)

An error caused by a divide by zero or other illegal arithmetic operation. It is a somewhat misleading error since it is caused by *integer* as well as floating-point errors.

floating-point hardware

Circuitry that can perform floating-point operations directly without resorting to software. In personal computers this is found in the math coprocessor.

fopen

A function that opens a file for stream I/O.

fprintf

A function to convert binary data to character data and write it to a file.

fputc

A function that writes a single character.

fputs

A function that writes a single line.

fread

A binary I/O input function.

free

A function that returns data to the memory pool. See **malloc**.

Free Software Foundation

A group of programmers who create and distribute high-quality software for free. They can be contacted at Free Software Foundation, Inc., 675 Massachusetts Avenue, Cambridge, MA 02139; (617) 876-3296.

fscanf

An input routine similar to **scanf**.

function

A procedure that returns a value.

fwrite

A binary I/O output function.

generic pointer

A pointer that can point to any variable without restriction as to type of variable. A pointer to storage without regard to the contents.

ghostscript
A PostScript-like interpreter that is freely available from the Free Software Foundation.

global variable
A variable that is known throughout an entire program.

guard digit
An extra digit of precision used in floating-point calculations to ensure against loss of accuracy.

header file
See **include file.**

heap
A portion of memory used by some compilers to store pointer variables during program execution.

hexadecimal number
A base 16 number.

high-level language
A level of computer language that is between machine language and natural (human) language.

IEEE floating-point standard
IEEE standard 754 which standardizes floating-point format, precision, and certain non-numerical values.

if
A statement that allows selective execution of parts of a program based on the truth of a condition.

implementation dependence
The situation where the result obtained from the operation of a computer or from software is not standardized because of variability among computer systems. A particular operation may yield different results when run on another system.

include file
A file that is merged with source code by invocation of the preprocessor directive **#include**. Also called a "header file."

inclusive or
See **or**.

index

A value, variable, or expression that selects a particular element of an array.

indirect operator

See **dereferencing operator**.

information hiding

A code design system that tries to minimize the amount of information that is passed between modules. The idea is to keep as much information as possible hidden inside the modules and only make information public if absolutely necessary.

instruction

A group of bits or characters that defines an operation to be performed by the computer.

int

A C keyword for declaring an integer.

integer

A whole number.

interactive debugger

A program that aids in the debugging of programs.

invert operator

A logical operator that performs a not.

left shift

The operation of moving the bits in a bit field left by a specified amount and filling the vacated positions with zeros.

library

A collection of files or a collection of functions combined in a single file, in a special manner, that allow the linker to extract individual functions as needed.

linked list

A collection of data nodes. Each node consists of a value and a pointer to the next item in the list.

lint

A strict syntax checker for UNIX programs. (It is designed to remove the fuzz from your programs, hence the name **lint.**)

local include file
A file from a private library that can be inserted with the preprocessor by the directive **#include** *filename*.

local variable
A variable whose scope is limited to the block in which it is declared.

logical and
A Boolean operation that returns true if its two arguments are both true. When used on integers, each bit is operated on separately.

logical operator
A C operator that performs a logical operation on its two operands and returns a true or a false value.

logical or
A Boolean operation that returns true if any one of its two arguments are true. When used on integers, each bit is operated on separately.

long
A qualifier to specify a data type with longer than normal accuracy.

machine code
Machine instructions in a binary format that can be recognized directly by the machine without further translation.

machine language
See **machine code**.

macro
A short piece of text, or text template, which can be expanded into a longer text.

macro processor
A program which generates code by replacement of values into positions in a defined template.

magnitude of the number
The value of a number without regard to sign.

maintenance (of a program)
Modification of a program because of changing conditions external to the computer system.

make
A utility of both UNIX and Turbo C that manages the compilation of programs.

Makefile
The file that contains the commands for the utility `make`.

malloc
A C procedure that manages a memory heap.

mask
A pattern of bits used to control the retention or elimination of another group of bits.

module
One logical part of a program.

MS-DOS
An operating system for IBM personal computers developed by Microsoft.

newline character
A character that causes an output device to go to the beginning of a new line.

nonsignificant digit
A leading digit that does not affect the value of a number (zeros for a positive number, ones for a negative number in complement form.)

normalization
The shifting of a floating-point fraction (and adjustment of the exponent) so there are no leading nonsignificant digits in the fraction.

not
A Boolean operation that yields the logical inverse of the operand—not one yields a zero, not zero yields a one.

not a number
A special value defined in IEEE 754 to signal an invalid result from a floating-point operation.

NULL
A constant of value zero, defined in the standard include file *stdio.h*.

null pointer
A pointer whose bit pattern is all zeros. This indicates the pointer does not point to valid data.

octal number
A base 8 number.

operator
A symbol that represents an action to be performed.

or
A Boolean operation that yields a one if either of the operands is a one or yields a zero if both of the operands are zero.

overflow error
An arithmetic error caused by the result of an arithmetic operation being greater than the space the computer provides to store the result.

packed structure
A data structure technique whereby bit fields are used that are only as large as needed, regardless of word boundaries.

pad byte
A byte added to a structure whose sole purpose is to insure memory alignment.

parameter
A data item to which a value may be assigned. Often used to mean the arguments that are passed between a caller and a called procedure.

parameterized macro
A macro consisting of a template with insertion points for the introduction of parameters.

parameters of a macro
The values to be inserted into the parameter positions in the definition of a macro. The insertion occurs during the expansion of the macro.

permanent variables
A variable that is created before the program starts and retains its memory during the entire execution of the program.

pixel
The smallest element of a display that can be individually assigned intensity and color. From *pic*ture *el*ement.

pointer
A data type that holds the address of a location in memory.

pointer arithmetic

C allows three arithmetic operations on pointers:

1. A numeric value can be added to a pointer.
2. A numeric value can be subtracted from a pointer.
3. One pointer can be subtracted from another pointer.

pointer variable

See **pointer**.

portable C compiler

A C compiler written by Stephen Johnson making it relatively easy to adapt the compiler to different computer architectures.

precision

A measure of the ability to distinguish between nearly equal values.

preprocessor

A program that performs preliminary processing with the purpose of expanding macro code templates to produce C code.

preprocessor directive

A command to the preprocessor.

printf

A C library routine that produces formatted output.

procedure

A program segment that can be invoked from different parts of a program or programs. It does not return a value (function of type **void**).

program

A group of instructions that cause a computer to perform a sequence of operations.

program header

The comment block at the beginning of the program.

program specification

A written document that states what a program will do.

programmer

An individual who writes programs for a computer.

programming (a computer)

The process of expressing the solution to a problem in a language that represents instructions for a computer.

programming language
A scheme of formal notation used to prepare computer programs.

pseudo-code
A coding technique where precise descriptions of procedures are written in easy-to-read language constructs without the bother of precise attention to syntax rules of a computer language.

qualifier
A word used to modify the meaning of a data declaration.

radix
The positive integer by which the weight of the digit place is multiplied to obtain the weight of the next higher digit in the base of the numbering system.

real numbers
A number that may be represented by a finite or infinite numeral in a fixed-radix numbering system.

recursion
Occurs when a function calls itself directly or indirectly. (For a recursive definition, see **recursion**.)

redirect
The command-line option >*file* allows the user to direct the output of a program into a file instead of the screen. A similar option, <*file*, exists for input, taking input from the file instead of the keyboard.

reduction in strength
The process of substituting cheap operations for expensive ones.

relational operator
An operator that compares two operands and reports either true or false based on whether the relationship is true or false.

release
The completion of a programming project to the point where it is ready for general use.

replay file
A file that is used instead of the standard input for keyboard data.

return statement
A statement that signals the completion of a function and causes control to return to the caller.

revision
The addition of significant changes to the program.

right shift
The operation of moving the bits in a bit field to the right by a specified amount and filling the vacated positions with zeros.

round
To delete or omit one or more of the least significant digits in a positional representation and adjust the part retained in accordance with some specific rule, e.g., minimize the error.

rounding error
An error due to truncation in rounding.

save file
A debugging tool where all the keystrokes typed by the user are saved in a file for future use. See also **replay file**.

scanf
A library input function which reads numbers directly from the keyboard. It's hard to use. In most cases a `gets/sscanf` combination is used.

scope
The scope of a variable is the portion of a program where the name of the variable is known.

segmentation violation
An error caused by a program trying to access memory outside its address space. Can be caused by dereferencing a bad pointer.

set a bit
The operation of setting a specified bit to one. This is not a defined operation in C.

shift
The operation of moving the bits in a bit field either left or right.

short
An arithmetic data type that is the same size or smaller than an integer.

side effect
An operation performed in addition to the main operation of a statement such as incrementing a variable in an assignment statement:

```
result = begin++ - end;
```

significand
The most significant digits of a floating-point number without regard to placement of the radix point.

significant digit
A digit that must be kept to preserve a given accuracy.

single quote
The character `'`, which is ASCII character 39. Used in C to delimit a single character.

sizeof
A C library function that returns the length of a string.

source code
A version of the program written in C and before translation into machine code.

source code
Symbolic coding in its original form before being translated by a computer.

source file
A file containing source code.

specification
A document that describes what the program does.

sprintf
Similar to **`fprintf`** except it uses a string input.

sscanf
A library input routine.

stack
An area of memory used to hold a list of data and instructions on a temporary basis.

stack overflow
An error caused by a program using too much temporary space (stack space) for its variables. Caused by a big program or by infinite recursion.

stack variable
See **temporary variable**.

static
A storage class attribute. Inside a set of curly braces ({}), this indicates a permanent variable. Outside a set of curly braces, this indicates a file-local variable.

stderr
The predefined standard error file.

stdin
The predefined input source.

stdio.h
A system include file that contains definitions of constants used to define the standard I/O package.

stdout
The predefined standard output.

storage class
An attribute of a variable definition that controls how the variable will be stored in memory.

string
A sequence of characters or an array of characters.

struct
A C keyword that identifies a structure data type.

structure
A hierarchical set of names that refers to an aggregate of data items that may have different attributes.

style sheet
A document that describes the style of programming used by a particular company or institution.

Sunview
A graphics and windowing system available on SUN workstations.

switch
A multi-way branch that transfers control to one of several **case** statements based on the value of an index expression.

syntax
Rules that govern the construction of statements.

syntax error
An error in the proper construction of a C expression.

temporary variable
A variable whose storage is allocated from the stack. It is initialized each time the block in which it is defined is entered. It exists only during the execution of that block.

test a bit
The operation of determining if a particular bit is set. This is not a defined operation in C.

test plan
A specification of the tests that a program must undergo.

text editor
Software used to create or alter text files.

translation
Creation of a new program in an alternate language, logically equivalent to an existing program in a source language.

tree
A hierarchical data structure.

truncation
An operation on a real number whereby any fractional part is discarded.

Turbo C
A version of the C language for personal computers developed by Borland.

typecast
See **cast**.

typedef
An operator used to create new types from existing types.

typing statement
A statement that establishes the characteristics of a variable.

unbuffered I/O
Each read or write results in a system call.

union
A data type that allows different data names and data types to be assigned to the same storage location.

UNIX
A popular multi-user operating system first developed by Ken Thompson and Dennis Ritchie of the Bell Telephone Laboratories.

unsigned
A qualifier used to specify **int** and **char** variables that do not contain negative numbers.

upgrading (of a program)

Modification of a program to provide improved performance or new features.

value

A quantity assigned to a constant.

variable

A name that refers to a value. The data represented by the variable name can, at different times during the execution of a program, assume different values.

variable-name

The symbolic name given to a section of memory used to store a variable.

version

A term used to identify a particular edition of software. A customary practice is to include a version number. Whole numbers indicate major rewrites. Fractions indicate minor rewrites or corrections of problems.

void

A data type in C. When used as a parameter in a function call, it indicates there is no return value. `void *` indicates that a generic pointer value is returned. When used in casts, it indicates that a given value is to be discarded.

while

An iterative statement that repeats a statement as long as a given condition is true.

X Windows

A graphics and windowing system available from MIT which is currently running on many computing systems.

zero-based counting

A system of counting where the first object is given the count 0 rather than 1.

Index

A

B

C

S

T

About the Author

Steve Oualline wrote his first program when he was eleven. It had a bug in it. Since that time he has studied practical ways of writing programs so that the risk of generating a bug is reduced. He has worked for Motorola, Celerity Computing and is currently a special consultant for Hewlett Packard working in the research department of their Ink-Jet division.

Colophon

Our look is the result of reader comments, our own experimentation, and distribution channels.

Distinctive covers complement our distinctive approach to technical topics, breathing personality and life into potentially dry subjects. UNIX and its attendant programs can be unruly beasts. Nutshell Handbooks help you tame them.

The animal featured on the cover of *Practical C Programming* is a Jersey cow. The Jersey, one of the many breeds of modern cows, originated from a now extinct stock of wild cattle that inhabited western Asia, North Africa, and continental Europe. Cows were first introduced into the western hemisphere by Christopher Columbus on his second voyage in 1493.

Jerseys, bred on the British isle of Jersey since 1789, were first introduced to America in the 1850s. Smallest of the modern dairy cows, this fawn-colored beast typically weighs between 1000 and 1500 pounds. As a milk producer, Jerseys are the least prolific of any American dairy cow. However, their milk is creamier than that of any other breed.

Edie Freedman designed this cover and the entire UNIX bestiary that appears on other Nutshell Handbooks. The beasts themselves are adapted from 19th-century engravings from the Dover Pictorial Archive.

The text of this book is set in Times Roman; headings are Helvetica; examples are Courier. Text was prepared using SortQuad's sqtroff text formatter. Figures are produced with a Macintosh. Printing is done on a Tegra Varityper 5000.

UNIX

From the best-selling The Whole Internet *to our Nutshell Handbooks, there's something here for everyone. Whether you're a novice or expert UNIX user, these books will give you just what you're looking for: user-friendly, definitive information on a range of UNIX topics.*

Using UNIX

Connecting to the Internet: An O'Reilly Buyer's Guide — NEW

By Susan Estrada
1st Edition August 1993
188 pages
ISBN 1-56592-061-9

More and more people are interested in exploring the Internet, and this book is the fastest way for you to learn how to get started. This book provides practical advice on how to determine the level of Internet service right for you, and how to find a local access provider and evaluate the services they offer.

!%@:: A Directory of Electronic Mail Addressing & Networks — NEW

By Donnalyn Frey & Rick Adams
3rd Edition August 1993
458 pages, ISBN 1-56592-031-7

The only up-to-date directory that charts the networks that make up the Internet, provides contact names and addresses, and describes the services each network provides. It includes all of the major Internet-based networks, as well as various commercial networks such as CompuServe, Delphi, and America Online that are "gatewayed" to the Internet for transfer of electronic mail and other services. If you are someone who wants to connect to the Internet, or someone who already is connected but wants concise, up-to-date information on many of the world's networks, check out this book.

Learning the UNIX Operating System — NEW

By Grace Todino, John Strang & Jerry Peek
3rd Edition August 1993
108 pages, ISBN 1-56592-060-0

If you are new to UNIX, this concise introduction will tell you just what you need to get started and no more. Why wade through a six-hundred-page book when you can begin working productively in a matter of minutes? This book is the most effective introduction to UNIX in print. This new edition has been updated and expanded to provide increased coverage of window systems and networking. It's a handy book for someone just starting with UNIX, as well as someone who encounters a UNIX system as a visitor via remote login over the Internet.

The Whole Internet User's Guide & Catalog

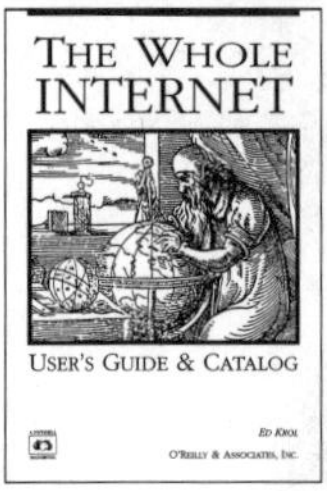

By Ed Krol
1st Edition September 1992
400 pages, ISBN 1-56592-025-2

A comprehensive—and best-selling—introduction to the Internet, the international network that includes virtually every major computer site in the world. The Internet is a resource of almost unimaginable wealth. In addition to electronic mail and news services, thousands of public archives, databases, and other special services are available: everything from space flight announcements to ski reports. This book is a comprehensive introduction to what's available and how to find it. In addition to electronic mail, file transfer, remote login, and network news, *The Whole Internet* pays special attention to some new tools for helping you find information. Whether you're a researcher, a student, or just someone who likes electronic mail, this book will help you to explore what's possible.

Smileys

By David W. Sanderson, 1st Edition March 1993
93 pages, ISBN 1-56592-041-4

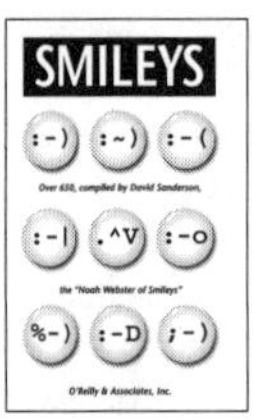

Originally used to convey some kind of emotion in an e-mail message, smileys are some combination of typographic characters that depict sideways a happy or sad face. Now there are hundreds of variations, including smileys that depict presidents, animals, and cartoon characters. Not everyone likes to read mail messages littered with smileys, but almost everyone finds them humorous. The smileys in this book have been collected by David Sanderson, whom the *Wall Street Journal* called the "Noah Webster of Smileys."

UNIX Power Tools

By Jerry Peek, Mike Loukides, Tim O'Reilly, et al.
1st Edition March 1993
1162 pages
(Bantam ISBN)
0-553-35402-7

Ideal for UNIX users who hunger for technical—yet accessible—information, *UNIX Power Tools* consists of tips, tricks, concepts, and freely-available software. Covers add-on utilities and how to take advantage of clever features in the most popular UNIX utilities. CD-ROM included.

Learning the Korn Shell **NEW**

By Bill Rosenblatt
1st Edition June 1993
363 pages, ISBN 1-56592-054-6

This new Nutshell Handbook is a thorough introduction to the Korn shell, both as a user interface and as a programming language. Provides a clear explanation of the Korn shell's features, including ***ksh*** string operations, co-processes, signals and signal handling, and command-line interpretation. Also includes real-life programming examples and a Korn shell debugger ***(kshdb)***.

Learning perl **NEW**

By Randal L. Schwartz, 1st Edition November 1993 (est.)
220 pages (est.), ISBN 1-56592-042-2

Perl is rapidly becoming the "universal scripting language". Combining capabilities of the UNIX shell, the C programming language, *sed*, ***awk***, and various other utilities, it has proved its use for tasks ranging from system administration to text processing and distributed computing. *Learning perl* is a step-by-step, hands-on tutorial designed to get you writing useful perl scripts as quickly as possible. In addition to countless code examples, there are numerous programming exercises, with full answers. For a comprehensive and detailed guide to programming with Perl, read O'Reilly's companion book *Programming perl.*

Programming perl

By Larry Wall & Randal L. Schwartz
1st Edition January 1991, 428 pages, ISBN 0-937175-64-1

Authoritative guide to the hottest new UNIX utility in years, co-authored by its creator. Perl is a language for easily manipulating text, files, and processes.

Learning GNU Emacs

By Deb Cameron & Bill Rosenblatt
1st Edition October 1991
442 pages, ISBN 0-937175-84-6

An introduction to the GNU Emacs editor, one of the most widely used and powerful editors available under UNIX. Provides a solid introduction to basic editing, a look at several important "editing modes" (special Emacs features for editing specific types of documents), and a brief introduction to customization and Emacs LISP programming. The book is aimed at new Emacs users, whether or not they are programmers.

sed & awk

By Dale Dougherty, 1st Edition November 1990
414 pages, ISBN 0-937175-59-5

For people who create and modify text files, *sed* and *awk* are power tools for editing. Most of the things that you can do with these programs can be done interactively with a text editor. However, using *sed* and *awk* can save many hours of repetitive work in achieving the same result.

MH & xmh: E-mail for Users & Programmers

By Jerry Peek, 2nd Edition September 1992
728 pages, ISBN 1-56592-027-9

Customize your e-mail environment to save time and make communicating more enjoyable. *MH & xmh: E-mail for Users & Programmers* explains how to use, customize, and program with the MH electronic mail commands available on virtually any UNIX system. The handbook also covers *xmh*, an X Window System client that runs MH programs. The new second edition has been updated for X Release 5 and MH 6.7.2. We've added a chapter on *mhook*, new sections explaining under-appreciated small commands and features, and more examples showing how to use MH to handle common situations.

Learning the vi Editor

By Linda Lamb, 5th Edition October 1990
192 pages, ISBN 0-937175-67-6

A complete guide to text editing with *vi*, the editor available on nearly every UNIX system. Early chapters cover the basics; later chapters explain more advanced editing tools, such as *ex* commands and global search and replacement.

UNIX in a Nutshell: For System V & Solaris 2.0

By Daniel Gilly and the staff of O'Reilly & Associates
2nd Edition June 1992, 444 pages, ISBN 1-56592-001-5

You may have seen UNIX quick reference guides, but you've never seen anything like *UNIX in a Nutshell*. Not a scaled-down quick-reference of common commands, *UNIX in a Nutshell* is a complete reference containing all commands and options, along with generous descriptions and examples that put the commands in context. For all but the thorniest UNIX problems this one reference should be all the documentation you need. Covers System V Releases 3 and 4 and Solaris 2.0.

An alternate version of this quick-reference is available for Berkeley UNIX.
Berkeley Edition, December 1986
(latest update October 1990)
272 pages, ISBN 0-937175-20-X

Using UUCP and Usenet

By Grace Todino & Dale Dougherty
1st Edition December 1986 (latest update October 1991)
210 pages, ISBN 0-937175-10-2

Shows users how to communicate with both UNIX and non-UNIX systems using UUCP and *cu* or *tip*, and how to read news and post articles. This handbook assumes that UUCP is already running at your site.

System Administration

Managing UUCP and Usenet

By Tim O'Reilly & Grace Todino
10th Edition January 1992
368 pages, ISBN 0-937175-93-5

For all its widespread use, UUCP is one of the most difficult UNIX utilities to master. This book is for system administrators who want to install and manage UUCP and Usenet software. "Don't even TRY to install UUCP without it!"—Usenet message 456@nitrex.UUCP

sendmail **NEW**

By Bryan Costales, with Eric Allman & Neil Rickert
1st Edition October 1993 (est.)
600 pages (est.), ISBN 0-937175-056-2

This new Nutshell Handbook is far and away the most comprehensive book ever written on *sendmail*, a program that acts like a traffic cop in routing and delivering mail on UNIX-based networks. Although *sendmail* is the most widespread of all mail programs, it's also one of the last great uncharted territories—and most difficult utilities to learn—in UNIX system administration. The book covers both major versions of *sendmail*: the standard version available on most systems, and IDA *sendmail*, a version from Europe.

termcap & terminfo

By John Strang, Linda Mui & Tim O'Reilly
3rd Edition July 1992
270 pages, ISBN 0-937175-22-6

For UNIX system administrators and programmers. This handbook provides information on writing and debugging terminal descriptions, as well as terminal initialization, for the two UNIX terminal databases.

DNS and BIND

By Cricket Liu & Paul Albitz, 1st Edition October 1992
418 pages, ISBN 1-56592-010-4

DNS and BIND contains all you need to know about the Domain Name System (DNS) and BIND, its UNIX implementation. The Domain Name System (DNS) is the Internet's "phone book"; it's a database that tracks important information (in particular, names and addresses) for every computer on the Internet. If you're a system administrator, this book will show you how to set up and maintain the DNS software on your network.

Essential System Administration

By Æleen Frisch, 1st Edition October 1991
466 pages, ISBN 0-937175-80-3

Provides a compact, manageable introduction to the tasks faced by everyone responsible for a UNIX system. This guide is for those who use a standalone UNIX system, those who routinely provide administrative support for a larger shared system, or those who want an understanding of basic administrative functions. Covers all major versions of UNIX.

X Window System Administrator's Guide

By Linda Mui & Eric Pearce
1st Edition October 1992
372 pages, With CD-ROM: ISBN 1-56592-052-X
Without CD-ROM: ISBN 0-937175-83-8

This book is the first and only book devoted to the issues of system administration for X and X-based networks, written not just for UNIX system administrators but for anyone faced with the job of administering X (including those running X on stand-alone workstations). The *X Window System Administrator's Guide* is available either alone or packaged with the XCD. The CD provides X source code and binaries to complement the book's instructions for installing the software. It contains over 600 megabytes of X11 source code and binaries stored in ISO9660 and RockRidge formats. This will allow several types of UNIX workstations to mount the CD-ROM as a filesystem, browse through the source code and install pre-built software.

Practical UNIX Security

By Simson Garfinkel & Gene Spafford
1st Edition June 1991
512 pages, ISBN 0-937175-72-2

Tells system administrators how to make their UNIX system—either System V or BSD—as secure as it possibly can be without going to trusted system technology. The book describes UNIX concepts and how they enforce security, tells how to defend against and handle security breaches, and explains network security (including UUCP, NFS, Kerberos, and firewall machines) in detail.

Managing NFS and NIS

By Hal Stern
1st Edition June 1991
436 pages, ISBN 0-937175-75-7

Managing NFS and NIS is for system administrators who need to set up or manage a network filesystem installation. NFS (Network Filesystem) is probably running at any site that has two or more UNIX systems. NIS (Network Information System) is a distributed database used to manage a network of computers. The only practical book devoted entirely to these subjects, this guide is a must-have for anyone interested in UNIX networking.

TCP/IP Network Administration

By Craig Hunt
1st Edition July 1992
502 pages, ISBN 0-937175-82-X

A complete guide to setting up and running a TCP/IP network for practicing system administrators. Covers how to set up your network, how to configure important network applications including *sendmail*, and discusses troubleshooting and security. Covers BSD and System V TCP/IP implementations.

System Performance Tuning

By Mike Loukides, 1st Edition November 1990
336 pages, ISBN 0-937175-60-9

System Performance Tuning answers the fundamental question, "How can I get my computer to do more work without buying more hardware?" Some performance problems do require you to buy a bigger or faster computer, but many can be solved simply by making better use of the resources you already have.

Computer Security Basics

By Deborah Russell & G.T. Gangemi Sr.
1st Edition July 1991
464 pages, ISBN 0-937175-71-4

Provides a broad introduction to the many areas of computer security and a detailed description of current security standards. This handbook describes complicated concepts like trusted systems, encryption, and mandatory access control in simple terms, and contains a thorough, readable introduction to the "Orange Book."

UNIX Programming

Understanding Japanese Information Processing **NEW**

By Ken Lunde
1st Edition September 1993 (est.)
450 pages (est.), ISBN 1-56592-043-0

Understanding Japanese Information Processing provides detailed information on all aspects of handling Japanese text on computer systems. It tries to bring all of the relevant information together in a single book. It covers everything from the origins of modern-day Japanese to the latest information on specific emerging computer encoding standards. There are over 15 appendices which provide additional reference material, such as a code conversion table, character set tables, mapping tables, an extensive list of software sources, a glossary, and much more.

lex & yacc

By John Levine, Tony Mason & Doug Brown
2nd Edition October 1992
366 pages, ISBN 1-56592-000-7

Shows programmers how to use two UNIX utilities, *lex* and *yacc*, in program development. The second edition of *lex & yacc* contains completely revised tutorial sections for novice users and reference sections for advanced users. The new edition is twice the size of the original book, has an expanded index, and now covers Bison and Flex.

High Performance Computing **NEW**

By Kevin Dowd, 1st Edition June 1993
398 pages, ISBN 1-56592-032-5

High Performance Computing makes sense of the newest generation of workstations for application programmers and purchasing managers. It covers everything, from the basics of modern workstation architecture, to structuring benchmarks, to squeezing more performance out of critical applications. It also explains what a good compiler can do—and what you have to do yourself. The book closes with a look at the high-performance future: parallel computers and the more "garden variety" shared memory processors that are appearing on people's desktops.

ORACLE Performance Tuning **NEW**

By Peter Corrigan & Mark Gurry
1st Edition September 1993 (est.)
650 pages (est.), ISBN 1-56592-048-1

The ORACLE relational database management system is the most popular database system in use today. With more organizations downsizing and adopting client/server and distributed database approaches, system performance tuning has become vital. This book shows you the many things you can do to dramatically increase the performance of your existing ORACLE system. You may find that this book can save you the cost of a new machine; at the very least, it will save you a lot of headaches.

POSIX Programmer's Guide

By Donald Lewine, 1st Edition April 1991
640 pages, ISBN 0-937175-73-0

Most UNIX systems today are POSIX-compliant because the Federal government requires it for its purchases. However, given the manufacturer's documentation, it can be difficult to distinguish system-specific features from those features defined by POSIX. The *POSIX Programmer's Guide*, intended as an explanation of the POSIX standard and as a reference for the POSIX.1 programming library, helps you write more portable programs.

Understanding DCE

By Ward Rosenberry, David Kenney & Gerry Fisher
1st Edition October 1992
266 pages, ISBN 1-56592-005-8

A technical and conceptual overview of OSF's Distributed Computing Environment (DCE) for programmers and technical managers, marketing and sales people. Unlike many O'Reilly & Associates books, *Understanding DCE* has no hands-on programming elements. Instead, the book focuses on how DCE can be used to accomplish typical programming tasks and provides explanations to help the reader understand all the parts of DCE.

Guide to Writing DCE Applications

By John Shirley
1st Edition July 1992
282 pages, ISBN 1-56592-004-X

A hands-on programming guide to OSF's Distributed Computing Environment (DCE) for first-time DCE application programmers. This book is designed to help new DCE users make the transition from conventional, nondistributed applications programming to distributed DCE programming. Covers the IDL and ACF files, essential RPC calls, binding methods and the name service, server initialization, memory management, and selected advanced topics. Includes practical programming examples.

Power Programming with RPC

By John Bloomer
1st Edition February 1992
522 pages, ISBN 0-937175-77-3

RPC, or remote procedure calling, is the ability to distribute the execution of functions on remote computers. Written from a programmer's perspective, this book shows what you can do with RPC's, like Sun RPC, the de facto standard on UNIX systems. It covers related programming topics for Sun and other UNIX systems and teaches through examples.

Managing Projects with make

By Andrew Oram & Steve Talbott
2nd Edition October 1991
152 pages, ISBN 0-937175-90-0

make is one of UNIX's greatest contributions to software development, and this book is the clearest description of ***make*** ever written. This revised second edition includes guidelines on meeting the needs of large projects.

Software Portability with imake **NEW**

By Paul DuBois
1st Edition July 1993
390 pages, 1-56592-055-4

imake is a utility that works with ***make*** to enable code to be complied and installed on different UNIX machines. This new Nutshell Handbook—the only book available on ***imake***—is ideal for X and UNIX programmers who want their software to be portable. It includes a general explanation of ***imake***, how to write and debug an ***Imakefile***, and how to write configuration files. Several sample sets of configuration files are described and are available free over the Net.

UNIX for FORTRAN Programmers

By Mike Loukides
1st Edition August 1990
264 pages, ISBN 0-937175-51-X

This book provides the serious scientific programmer with an introduction to the UNIX operating system and its tools. The intent of the book is to minimize the UNIX entry barrier and to familiarize readers with the most important tools so they can be productive as quickly as possible. *UNIX for FORTRAN Programmers* shows readers how to do things they're interested in: not just how to use a tool such as ***make*** or ***rcs***, but how to use it in program development and how it fits into the toolset as a whole. "An excellent book describing the features of the UNIX FORTRAN compiler *f77* and related software. This book is extremely well written." — American Mathematical Monthly, February 1991

Practical C Programming

By Steve Oualline
2nd Edition January 1993
396 pages, ISBN 1-56592-035-X

C programming is more than just getting the syntax right. Style and debugging also play a tremendous part in creating programs that run well. *Practical C Programming* teaches you not only the mechanics of programming, but also how to create programs that are easy to read, maintain, and debug. There are lots of introductory C books, but this is the Nutshell Handbook! In the second edition, programs now conform to ANSI C.

Checking C Programs with lint

By Ian F. Darwin
1st Edition October 1988
84 pages, ISBN 0-937175-30-7

The *lint* program is one of the best tools for finding portability problems and certain types of coding errors in C programs. This handbook introduces you to *lint*, guides you through running it on your programs, and helps you interpret *lint's* output.

Using C on the UNIX System

By Dave Curry
1st Edition January 1989
250 pages, ISBN 0-937175-23-4

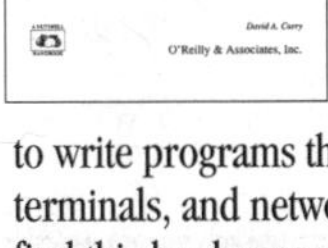

Using C on the UNIX System provides a thorough introduction to the UNIX system call libraries. It is aimed at programmers who already know C but who want to take full advantage of the UNIX programming environment. If you want to learn how to work with the operating system and to write programs that can interact with directories, terminals, and networks at the lowest level you will find this book essential. It is impossible to write UNIX utilities of any sophistication without understanding the material in this book. "A gem of a book. The author's aim is to provide a guide to system programming, and he succeeds admirably. His balance is steady between System V and BSD-based systems, so readers come away knowing both." — SUN Expert, November 1989

Guide to OSF/1

By the staff of O'Reilly & Associates
1st Edition June 1991
304 pages, ISBN 0-937175-78-1

This technically competent introduction to OSF/1 is based on OSF technical seminars. In addition to its description of OSF/1, it includes the differences between OSF/1 and System V Release 4 and a look ahead at DCE.

Understanding and Using COFF

By Gintaras R. Gircys
1st Edition November 1988
196 pages, ISBN 0-937175-31-5

COFF—Common Object File Format—is the formal definition for the structure of machine code files in the UNIX System V environment. All machine-code files are COFF files. This handbook explains COFF data structure and its manipulation.

Career

Love Your Job! **NEW**

By Dr. Paul Powers, with Deborah Russell
1st Edition August 1993
210 pages, ISBN 1-56592-036-8

Do you love your job? Too few people do. In fact, surveys show that 80 to 95 percent of Americans are dissatisfied with their jobs. Considering that most of us will work nearly 100,000 hours during our lifetimes (half the waking hours of our entire adult lives!), it's sad that our work doesn't bring us the rewards—both financial and emotional—that we deserve. *Love Your Job!* is an inspirational guide to loving your work. It consists of a series of one-page reflections, anecdotes, and exercises aimed at helping readers think more deeply about what they want out of their jobs. Each can be read individually (anyplace, anytime, whenever you need to lift your spirits), or the book can be read and treated as a whole. *Love Your Job!* informs you, inspires you, and challenges you, not only to look outside at the world of work, but also to look inside yourself at what work means to you.

O'Reilly Online Services

How to Get Information about O'Reilly & Associates

The online O'Reilly Information Resource is a Gopher server that provides you with information on our books, how to download code examples, and how to order from us. There is also a UNIX bibliography you can use to get information on current books by subject area.

Connecting to the O'Reilly Information Resource

Gopher is an interactive tool that organizes the resources found on the Internet as a sequence of menus. If you don't know how Gopher works, see the chapter "Tunneling through the Internet: Gopher" in *The Whole Internet User's Guide and Catalog* by Ed Krol.

An easy way to use Gopher is to download a Gopher client, either the tty Gopher that uses curses or the Xgopher.

Once you have a local Gopher client, you can launch Gopher with:

```
gopher gopher.ora.com
```

To use the Xgopher client, enter:

```
xgopher -xrm "xgopher.rootServer:
gopher.ora.com"
```

If you have no client, log in on our machine via telnet and run Gopher from there, with:

```
telnet gopher.ora.com
login: gopher  (no password)
```

Another option is to use a World Wide Web browser, and enter the http address:

```
gopher://gopher.ora.com
```

Once the connection is made, you should see a root menu similar to this:

```
  Internet Gopher Information Client v1.12
     Root gopher server: gopher.ora.com

-->1. News Flash! -- New Products and
      Projects of ORA/.
   2.About O'Reilly & Associates.
   3.Book Descriptions and Information/
   4.Complete Listing of Book Titles.
   5.FTP Archive and E-Mail Information/
   6.Ordering Information/
   7.UNIX Bibliography/

Press ? for Help, q to Quit, u to go up a
menu                               Page: 1/1
```

From the root menu you can begin exploring the information that we have available. If you don't know much about O'Reilly & Associates, choose `About O'Reilly & Associates` from the menu. You'll see an article by Tim O'Reilly that gives an overview of who we are—and a little background on the books we publish.

Getting Information About Our Books

The Gopher server makes available online the same information that we provide in our print catalog, often in more detail.

Choose `Complete Listing of Book Titles` from the root menu to view a list of all our titles. This is a useful summary to have when you want to place an order.

To find out more about a particular book, choose `Book Descriptions and Information`; you will see the screen below:

```
Internet Gopher Information Client v1.12
     Book Descriptions and Information

-->1.New Books and Editions/
   2.Computer Security/
   3.Distributed Computing Environment
     (DCE)/
   4.Non-Technical Books/
   5.System Administration/
   6.UNIX & C Programming/
   7.Using UNIX/
   8.X Resource/
   9.X Window System/
   10.CD-Rom Book Companions/
   11.Errata and Updates/
   12.Keyword Search on all Book
      Descriptions <?>
   13.Keyword Search on all Tables of
      Content <?>
```

All of our new books are listed in a single category. The rest of our books are grouped by subject. Select a subject to see a list of book titles in that category. When you select a specific book, you'll find a full description and table of contents.

For example, if you wanted to look at what books we had on administration, you would choose selection 5, `System Administration`, resulting in the following screen:

```
           System Administration

   1.DNS and BIND/
   2.Essential System Administration/
   3.Managing NFS and NIS/
   4.Managing UUCP and Usenet/
   5.sendmail/
   6.System Performance Tuning/
   7.TCP/IP Network Administration/
```

If you then choose `Essential System Administration`, you will be given the choice of looking at either the book description or the table of contents.

```
      Essential System Administration

->1.Book Description and Information.
  2.Book Table of Contents.
```

Selecting either of these options will display the contents of a file. Gopher then provides instructions for you to navigate elsewhere or quit the program.

Searching For the Book You Want

Gopher also allows you to locate book descriptions or tables of contents by using a word search. (We have compiled a full-text index WAIS.)

If you choose `Book Descriptions and Information` from the root menu, the last two selections on that menu allow you to do keyword searches.

Choose `Keyword Search on all Book Descriptions` and you will be prompted with:

```
Index word(s) to search for:
```

Once you enter a keyword, the server returns a list of the book descriptions that match the keyword. For example, if you enter the keyword `DCE`, you will see:

```
Keyword Search on all Book Descriptions:
                  DCE

-> 1.Understanding DCE.
   2.Guide to Writing DCE Applications.
   3.Distributed Applications Across DCE
     and Windows NT.
   4.DCE Administration Guide.
   5.Power Programming with RPC.
   6.Guide to OSF/1.
```

Choose one of these selections to view the book description.

Using the keyword search option can be a faster and less tedious way to locate a book than moving through a lot of menus.

You can also use a WAIS client to access the full-text index or book descriptions. The name of the database is

```
O'Reilly_Book_Descriptions.src
```

and you can find it in the WAIS directory of servers.

Note: We are always adding functions and listings to the O'Reilly Information Resource. By the time you read this article, the actual screens may very well have changed.

E-mail Accounts

E-mail ordering promises to be quick and easy, even faster than using our 800 number. Because we don't want you to send credit card information over a non-secure network, we ask that you set up an account with us in advance. To do so, either call us at 1-800-998-9938 or use the application provided in `Ordering Information` on the Gopher root menu. You will then be provided with a confidential account number.

Your account number allows us to retrieve your billing information when you place an order by e-mail, so you only need to send us your account number and what you want to order.

For your security, we use the credit card information and shipping address that we have on file. We also verify that the name of the person sending us the e-mail order matches the name on the account. If any of this information needs to change, we ask that you contact `order@ora.com` or call our Customer Service department.

Ordering by E-mail

Once you have an account with us, you can send us your orders by e-mail. Remember that you can use our online catalog to find out more about the books you want. Here's what we need when you send us an order:

1. Address your e-mail to: `order@ora.com`
2. Include in your message:
   - The title of each book you want to order (including ISBN number, if you know it)
   - The quantity of each book
   - Method of delivery: UPS Standard, Fed Ex Priority...
   - Your name and account number
   - Anything special you'd like to tell us about the order

When we receive your e-mail message, our Customer Service representative will verify your order before we ship it, and give you a total cost. If you would like to change your order after confirmation, or if there are ever any problems, please use the phone and give us a call—e-mail has its limitations.

This program is an experiment for us. We appreciate getting your feedback so we can continue improving our service.

How to Order by E-mail

E-mail ordering promises to be quick and easy. Because we don't want you sending credit card information over a non-secure network, we ask that you set up an account with us before ordering by e-mail.
To find out more about setting up an e-mail account, you can either call us at (800) 998-9938 or select `Ordering Information` from the Gopher root menu.

O'Reilly & Associates Inc.

103A Morris Street, Sebastopol, CA 95472

(800) 998-9938 • (707) 829-0515 • FAX (707) 829-0104 • `order@ora.com`

How to get information about O'Reilly books online

• If you have a local gopher client, then you can launch gopher and connect to our server:
`gopher gopher.ora.com`
• If you want to use the Xgopher client, then enter:
`xgopher -xrm "xgopher.rootServer: gopher.ora.com"`
• If you want to use telnet, then enter:
`telnet gopher.ora.com` login: `gopher` [no password]
• If you use a World Wide Web browser, you can access the gopher server by typing the following http address:
`gopher://gopher.ora.com`

WE'D LIKE TO HEAR FROM YOU

Company Name

Name

Address

City/State

Zip/Country

Telephone

FAX

Internet or *Uunet* e-mail address

Which O'Reilly book did this card come from? ______________________

Is your job: ❏ SysAdmin? ❏ Programmer?

❏ Other? What?______________________

Do you use other computer systems besides UNIX? If so, which one(s)?

____

Please send me the following:

❏ A free catalog of titles

❏ A list of bookstores in my area that carry O'Reilly books

❏ A list of distributors outside of the U.S. and Canada

❏ Information about bundling O'Reilly books with my product